COMPELLED TO EXCEL

Compelled to Excel

IMMIGRATION, EDUCATION,

AND OPPORTUNITY

AMONG CHINESE AMERICANS

Vivian S. Louie

Stanford University Press
Stanford, California 2004

Stanford University Press
Stanford, California

Printed in the United States of America
on acid-free, archival-quality paper.

Library of Congress Cataloging-in-Publication Data

Louie, Vivian S.
  Compelled to excel : immigration, education, and opportunity among
Chinese Americans / Vivian S. Louie.
    p. cm.
  Based on the author's thesis (Ph.D.—Yale University).
  Includes bibliographical references and index.
  ISBN 0-8047-4984-1 (acid-free paper)
  ISBN 0-8047-4985-X (pbk. : acid-free paper)—
    1. Chinese Americans—Social conditions. 2. Chinese Americans—
Economic conditions. 3. Children of immigrants—Education—United States.
4. Chinese Americans—Education. 5. United States—Race relations.
I. Title.
E184.C5L685 2004
305.895'1073—DC22
                                                        2004011167

Original Printing 2004

Last figure below indicates year of this printing:
13   12   11   10   09   08   07   06   05   04

For my mother

CONTENTS

There are many stages to researching, writing, and publishing a book, and at each one I drew on the intellectual and emotional support of mentors, colleagues, friends, and family. I began this journey at the Department of Sociology, Yale University, where I wrote the dissertation that eventually became this book. I owe special thanks to Kai Erikson, who provided my introduction to the field of sociology. Kai has been a source of invaluable mentorship and friendship. The opportunity to learn from someone so well-versed in capturing the complexities of human societies with insight, creativity, and grace has been a great gift. The fieldwork sequence that he and Joshua Gamson taught, and my participation in an international fieldwork project led by Deborah Davis, gave me a whole set of tools with which to pursue sociological inquiry. They were the sources of ample direction and encouragement throughout my graduate student career.

I was also fortunate to benefit from the guidance of mentors at institutions besides my own. I owe a special debt of gratitude to William Julius Wilson, whom I met during the earliest stages of thinking through my ideas for the dissertation. As an exchange scholar at Harvard, I gained admittance to Wilson's popular class on Sociological Perspectives on Racial Inequality. The course contributed immeasurably to my development as a scholar, opening up important ways for me to think rigorously about and study social life. Wilson's support of my work thereafter, in the midst of his many public and scholarly obligations, speaks to his generosity as a person and as a scholar. Later, after I had moved back to New York City to start my dissertation research, I was fortunate to work for the Second Generation Metropolitan New York Project at the CUNY Graduate Center, under the direction of John Mollenkopf, Mary Waters, and Philip Kasinitz, who provided wonderful research training, insightful career advice, and, always, a great sense of humor about life. Working with them was a deeply rewarding experience. The project and all the researchers involved, in particular Jennifer Holdaway and Nancy López, pointed me to new and exciting ways of thinking about and doing research on immigration.

It was Mary Waters's heartfelt encouragement and guidance, especially in that crucial year after finishing my doctorate, which led to a new and fruitful journey at Harvard University. This journey began as a lecturer in the Department of Sociology, where I benefited from the stimulating intellectual environment. Nearly a year later, I was quite fortunate to join the Harvard Graduate School of Education, first as a Harvard Postdoctoral Fellow and then as a faculty member.

The fellowship, and I mean this on many levels, that I found at the Harvard Graduate School of Education, a vibrant interdisciplinary community of thinkers, has been the key to the actual creation of this book. Sara Lawrence-Lightfoot, long familiar to me as a public intellectual but someone I never expected to meet, led an inspired writing and professional development seminar, where I first realized this could be a book. Sara was unflagging in her conviction that this was a book and that I could actually write it, offering encouragement and advice with her trademark combination of warmth and wisdom. I owe thanks to all my colleagues in the writing seminar, and to several colleagues for their support throughout the process and for suggestions of work that I found very helpful: Kurt Fischer, Howard Gardner, Wendy Luttrell, Kathy McCartney, Gary Orfield, Robert Selman, Judy Singer, and Catherine Snow. I owe special thanks to Marcelo Suárez-Orozco and Carola Suárez-Orozco, who served as my mentors during my postdoctoral fellowship. I am only one of many who can speak to their fullness of heart as individuals, their profound engagement with scholarly inquiry, and their support of scholars at the beginning of their careers.

As I was writing, it was useful to share my ideas, and several individuals were so helpful in this regard. I remember calling Joshua Gamson, who had just moved back to San Francisco, started a new job, and was still living amid boxes, but who somehow found time to listen patiently to the story I wanted to tell, and as always, provide insightful feedback. After assuring me that I was indeed making sense, he simply said, "Now, go write it." I did just that, and three months later Fabienne Doucet graciously read several chapters of this early draft and offered wonderful comments. Margaret Chin was kind enough to read this first version in its entirety and bring her discernment to bear. Patricia Katayama, then at Stanford University Press, was an early and kind supporter of this work, and Nazli Kibria and an anonymous reviewer offered very helpful comments. When Patricia left the Press, Alan Harvey and Muriel Bell did a terrific job of ensuring a smooth transition. Kate Wahl soon expertly took up the reins, and along with Tim Roberts, ably shepherded the book through production. I also owe thanks to Ruth Steinberg's copyediting and Carmen Borbon-Wu, for her careful management of the publication process.

I am especially grateful to my student respondents and their parents and siblings for all their time, patience, and good humor. Without their willingness to open up to me about their experiences, and to fit me into their already hectic lives, this work would truly not have been possible. Many students who did not fit the respondent criteria still gave generously of their time and insights. Among the many faculty members and administrators who assisted me with this research or with the mysteries of the publication process I wish to pay particular thanks to Shirley Hune, Philip Kasinitz, Peter Kwong, Roger Lehecka, John Lie, Gary Okihiro, Ruth Sidel, Chi-Ping Sobelman, and Min Zhou. Ann Fitzpatrick ably assisted me with the transcription of some interviews. Matthew Slayton provided wonderful support in preparing the manuscript for publication.

This work was supported by a Yale University Dissertation Fellowship, a dissertation grant from the National Science Foundation, a dissertation fellowship from the International Migration Section of the Social Science Research Council, which also provided a wonderful community of intellectual support, a China Times Cultural Foundation Scholarship, and the Harvard Fellowship on Race, Culture and Education.

Several other people enriched my journey: Arline McCord, who provided much advice; Joanna Erikson, who, along with Kai Erikson, opened their home and lives to me with their characteristic grace; Yun Fan, Annette Chin, and Jennifer Mathis, who all listened to me endlessly as I negotiated the processes that went into this book.

Mark J. Zimny deserves special mention. Mark and I began our journey at Yale at the same time, quite by chance, and I am honored to still be with him. Yale has given me so many gifts, and he is the best one. He has enormous reserves of patience and strength and never fails to brighten up my day with much-needed laughter. He is also a brilliant researcher and writer, whose words of advice were always on target—write from the heart as well as from the mind.

Finally, I wish to express my gratitude to my family, who has offered support in countless deeply felt ways. Chester Lee has been a staunch supporter of my work, and it was his extensive contacts at Columbia University that helped me actualize my research question into a viable research project. Daniel Yee has always been there to listen and offer guidance and wisdom. From Stephen Louie, who predicted I would be a writer, I learned to take chances in life. My brothers, Danny and David, did not enjoy the same opportunities that I did; nonetheless, they have achieved success in their own right against much higher odds. I have long relied on my sister-in-law Nancy's common sense, caring, and good humor to keep me grounded. I simply have no words that would adequately convey my thanks to my mother, who has persevered, working nearly forty years in Chinese garment factories until failing eyesight made this impossible, to provide for our family. My generation and the next owe everything to her. My only wish is that she knew enough English to read this book, or that I knew enough Chinese to translate it to her in its entirety.

The flows of immigration that have at once characterized and given shape to the previous American century have entered a unique period since the post-1960s. One legacy of the unprecedented era of the 1960s social movements that transformed America has been a dramatic shift in the national opportunity structure. In the wake of the civil rights and women's movements, the channels of upward mobility—access to higher education and employment in major corporations, the government, and the academy—have opened up to white ethnics, blacks, other ethnic and racial minorities, gays, and women of all groups (Farley 1996). Only forty years ago, someone's race, ethnicity, and/or gender would have been enough to bar that person from an elite school, a prestigious position, or a neighborhood. Today, equality of opportunity is not only mandated by law but also supported by strong public sentiment that lends validation to its existence as a cornerstone of our society. Consider the Immigration Act of 1965, itself born of ethnocentric aims and the point of departure for the new, large-scale immigration that continues today. Even when it became apparent that the arrivals were largely hailing from Latin America, the Caribbean, and Asia, rather than Europe, as lawmakers had originally envisioned, the United States allowed the new immigration to continue and, indeed, to expand (Alba and Nee 2003).

Yet, despite such remarkable strides, equality of condition has proven elusive. Racial inequality continues to exist, albeit in different forms, giving rise to new racial paradoxes. In the case of blacks, for example, there is cause for optimism. For the first time in American history, middle-class black families can pass on their advantages to their children with little difficulty (Hochschild 1995). There is also cause for pessimism, as blacks are still subject to residential segregation and suffer income disparities compared to whites, even when educational levels are taken into account (Massey and Denton 1993; Conley 1999). Race continues to matter in the daily life of middle-class blacks (Lawrence Lightfoot 1994; Hochschild 1995; Patillo-Mc-Coy 1999), and poor blacks have actually done worse over time, slipping further into poverty (Wilson 1987, 1997). Nor are the effects of the past so easily cast off, as historically derived inequalities in wealth along the lines of race continue to shape black–white differences in life outcomes among those born in the post–civil rights period (Conley 1999).

This context, of equality alongside persistent inequality, is what post-1960s immigrants have encountered. It is equality of opportunity, however, and notably the open opportunity structure available to immigrants, that mostly resonates in the national imagination. Hence the term "immigrant strivers" (used by at least one national newspaper—see *New York Times*, 2 August 2001, B2; and 7 October 2001, sec. 1A, p. 39),[1] which is sometimes utilized to distinguish immigrants from native-born minority groups who apparently are not striving enough themselves. This book focuses on Asian Americans, who, as a group, arguably hold a special place in the American collective consciousness as one of the quintessential immigrant strivers, especially in education. This popularly held belief has some basis in fact. In some Asian American families, children acquire higher education and enter elite educational, social, and institutional settings at an unprecedented pace for immigrant minorities (Takagi 1998). Asian Americans have been typified as a model minority, one that can supposedly offer lessons to everyone, but especially to other racial minorities, native and immigrant, on how to achieve upward mobility in today's America. To those who have argued that race no longer matters, or that class and culture (e.g., motivation) are more relevant today than race (Takagi 1998; Schuck 2003), the story of Asian Americans and education contradicts the very idea that race and class can influence educational opportunity and life outcomes.

This story also adheres to the popular cultural narrative about class and upward mobility, namely, that one can easily rise from humble origins to prominence through hard work (Newman 1999; *New York Times*, 12 January 2003, Arts and Leisure, 1). Before the civil rights movement, it was understood that one had to be white to qualify for such a meteoric rise, and for a long period, whiteness necessarily meant being Protestant and Anglo-Saxon.[2]

Post–civil rights, however, class mobility is thought to be fluid for all Americans, regardless of race and ethnicity. Seen from this perspective, Asian American educational success is all the more compelling because it appears to be both a middle- *and* working-class phenomenon. The working-class aspects are evident in the demanding academic preparatory weekend and after-school programs that have sprung up in the Chinese and Korean immigrant communities of Los Angeles (Zhou 2001b) and New York City. Parents who speak little English and who often have only gone as far as middle school themselves enroll children as young as ten in so-called cram schools, in the hope that the cram schools will set them on the path to a top-tier college (*New York Times*, 10 October 2001, D9). With each tale of an Asian American family transcending humble beginnings through education, the assumption that race and class do not matter in upward mobility is confirmed.

But does the story of Asian Americans and education really call to mind an American society where race and class are no longer relevant, as is frequently claimed? The goal of this book is to explore this question through looking at educational experiences among the children of Chinese immigrants. At its heart, the story of Asian Americans and education, both in the media and in scholarly work, is a story of the immigrant family.[3] Countless studies have shown that the Asian immigrant family plays an important role in shaping children's educational aspirations and achievement. It is how this happens that is a matter of debate. Some scholars emphasize the ethnic cultures of Asian immigrants, as transported from their homelands, and in particular, Confucian values. This ethnic cultures model, widely reported on in the popular press, draws on the idea that there is something distinctive about Asian cultures that leads to academic achievement among immigrant children. Other observers have looked to economic forces, specifically, how different immigrants are incorporated into the American labor market. Such structural explanations highlight the pull factors that attract certain types of immigrants and the various ways in which they are incorporated in the United States to explain why some Asian immigrant children do so well.

Noticeably absent from such accounts are matters related to race and comparisons across class. The goal of this book is to address this gap through examining how race and class matter in the educational messages that the children of Chinese immigrants hear from their parents and in the paths that the children take to college. Despite the attention paid to the Asian immigrant family, we know surprisingly little about how the children themselves situate the influence of the family in their schooling, and how it fits in with their own understandings of the social world they live in. I focused on the U.S.-born and/or U.S.-raised children of Chinese immigrants (what social scientists like to describe as the second and 1.5 generations, respectively[4]), as they are regarded as the best positioned to achieve, due to their native, or near-native, English facility and their parents' immigrant drive.[5]

To more fully explore the range of Chinese American experiences with higher education, I looked at students attending a non-elite college and how their perspectives and paths compared to those of students at an elite college. There are, in fact, many different Asian American student populations today. One would not know this, however, from looking at media and scholarly accounts, which have both tended to focus on students who are at the top of their class, have won prizes, and are bound for or are already enrolled at elite postsecondary institutions. The notable exception is the growing number of studies on the risk of school failure among Southeast Asians, who, generally speaking, have lower levels of educational attainment (Siu 1996). The attention being paid to Southeast Asians is highly necessary and long overdue. At the same time, there is a tendency to see other Asian groups, particularly East Asians like the Chinese, through the prism of high academic achievement and to overlook any lines of variation therein.

As a way of examining this variation, I drew my sample from two very different four-year institutions along the private/public and residential/commuter spectrum: Columbia University, an Ivy League school, and Hunter College of the City University of New York (CUNY), a public commuter school. The decision to draw respondents from these two schools also allowed me to tap into social-class background, which is often correlated with the type of postsecondary institution attended (Kwong 1987; Weinberg 1997). In short, I expected that my Hunter respondents would tend to come from working-class backgrounds and my Columbia students to come primarily from suburban, middle-class families, although I expected some from working-class backgrounds as well. Through interviews with sixty-eight students and fieldwork conducted during 1998–99,[6] I examined how respondents from such diverse class backgrounds understood the role of the family in their paths to such different colleges. As I argue in the pages to come, my respondents' understandings of education are indeed centered on the immigrant family, but they are in decided contrast to conventional wisdom; as it turned out, race, class, and gender do matter, and in particularly powerful ways.

Asian Americans and Race: Model Minorities and Honorary Whites?

That race is largely missing from previous discussions of Asian Americans and education is, on one level, surprising. I should say that race is defined here as a system of power structured by socially constructed labels in the interests of the dominant group. Along these lines, the very term "Asian American" (and "Oriental," its predecessor) identifies a racialized ethnicity and subsumes individual group differences under an externally imposed racial label. According to the U.S. Census Bureau, "Asian Americans" refers to people whose ancestral origins lie in such diverse and extensive geographic environs as the Far East, Southeast Asia, or the Indian subcontinent.[7] Yet, apart from the work of Tuan (1998) and Kibria (2002), we know little about how children interpret their parents' perceptions of racial hierarchy in the United States and the extent to which such parental understandings of race factor into their views about education.

The absence of race in previous discussions is even more telling, when we consider that race is strongly implicated in when and how the story of Asian Americans and education, as we know it, came into being. The model-minority myth was introduced in 1966 at the height of the civil rights movement, a time of great racial transformation. As with all transitions, there were those who did not welcome change, particularly the claims of injustice voiced by blacks and Latinos and their supporters. Seen from that light, the model-minority myth was an effective way of disciplining such claims of inequality without ever naming the dominant group's vested interest in the existing paradigm of race relations. The model-minority myth does this by brilliantly articulating the popular belief that ours is an open society where success is attainable by dint of hard work alone. The very success of Asians implicitly speaks to the question of why other minority groups are struggling and having a much harder time entering the ranks of higher education. If the model-minority hypothesis is to be believed, the relative lack of mobility of those other groups is due to individual or group-level cultural failings (e.g., an un-willingness to work hard and value education) rather than an opportunity structure blocked along the lines of race and class (Steinberg 1982; Osajima 1988; Nakayama 1988; Slaughter-Defoe et al. 1990; Glenn and Yap 1994; Lee 1996; Kim 2000). If Asians can make it, why can't everyone else?

The empirical origins of the model-minority hypothesis can be traced to the mobility experienced by the descendants of the first wave of Asian immigrants, largely Chinese and Japanese, who arrived in the United States during the late nineteenth and early twentieth centuries. Most of these immigrants and their children faced considerable discrimination that as late as the 1930s meant that more than four-fifths of all Chinese work-ers in the United States were relegated to manual labor as cooks, waiters, domestics, and laundrymen (Siu 1992a, 19). In 1940 Chinese Americans had a median of 5.5 years of schooling, as compared to 8.7 years for whites, and they were "only half as likely to complete high school or col-lege as whites" (Weinberg 1997, 23). After World War II, however, the op-portunity structure in the United States was opened to Asian Americans, and mobility patterns started to change; over the next two decades, Chi-nese and Japanese Americans started to move into more integrated neigh-borhoods and employment (Nee and Wong 1985; Kwong 1987; Siu 1992a; Chen 1996; Alba and Nee 2003). It was this mobility in the face of prior adversity that formed the initial empirical thread of the model-minority myth.

The years since the 1960s have brought a set of ironies with regard to the model-minority hypothesis: on the one hand, it has been actively challenged in some quarters,[8] while on the other, a confluence of factors has given rise to enough mobility among Asian immigrant families to reinforce and, in-deed, even enhance its claims. The key to understanding the latter trend is the post-1960s historical context, occasioned as it was by a dramatic lessening of formerly extreme levels of exclusion. Enrollments in postsecondary educa-tional institutions, for example, steadily grew, and there was a twofold increase in their number, fueled largely by the influx of women and racial and ethnic minorities (Lucas 1994, 227–29; Brubacher and Rudy 1996, 399).

It was also in 1965 that lawmakers reformed previously exclusionary im-migration policies (Farley 1996; Alba and Nee 2003),[9] setting into motion a new wave of large-scale immigration. As Asian Americans were gaining a reputation as academic exemplars, they were also becoming more visible nationally as one of the nation's fastest-growing ethnic groups, due to high levels of immigration. In 1960, there were only 877,934 Asian Americans in the general population; by 1990, after more than two decades of immigration, the number had increased almost tenfold, to 7.3 million, and included a far wider range of Asian ethnic groups (Hune and Chan 1997). In the 2000 census, approximately 11.9 million people, or 4.2 percent of the population, identified themselves as Asian, either solely or in combination with one or more other races.[10] Vis-à-vis Asians and education, this immigration has had two significant outcomes. First, it has brought substantial numbers of mobile Asian immigrants, who come to the United States for higher education or who already have postsecondary and/or advanced degrees. Second, less-educated Asian families benefit from the open and accessible K–12 educational system, which offers their children the possibility for some kind of mobility through education.

In other words, the fruits of the civil rights movement along with the class selectivity that has characterized aspects of Asian immigration, combined with the immigrants' own efforts and family resources, have created a unique experience. It is true that no other group has done as well as quickly as Asian Americans, at least in the aggregate. As I will soon discuss, the disaggregate picture is more complex. It is equally the case, and this is the part that often goes unsaid, that key institutional changes have made this possible. If we keep this in mind, we can better understand why, historically, Asians have achieved mobility at a faster rate than other immigrant groups. Consider American Jews—the immigrant success story of the first great wave of immigration that occurred in the late nineteenth and early twentieth centuries. It has been pointed out that Asian Americans today are assimilating even more quickly than Jewish immigrants of the previous century. And yet, should we be surprised, given the challenging circumstances confronted by American Jews until after World War II—namely, high levels of exclusion and a largely closed opportunity structure? A significant proportion of the contemporary Asian American population has benefited from the much more inclusive context of immigration that has characterized the period from the mid-1960s through to the present day.

The overall high levels of post-1960s immigration have inserted Asian

Americans into a debate about immigration that both draws from and ex-
pands the model-minority image, with important consequences for inter-
group relations. The immigrant-striver image, for example, has been accompanied by pointed comparisons between immigrants from Latin America and
Asia, the two largest sources of contemporary immigration. In public discourse, Asian immigrants are routinely portrayed as having "good culture," in
essence, they are seen as hard-working strivers who make good use of their
opportunities in the United States. Latino immigrants, on the other hand, are
routinely portrayed as having "bad culture," as likely to turn to crime, to have
too many kids, to seek out welfare, a group that is ultimately doomed to failure in the United States (Fukuyama 1994; Espenshade and Belanger 1997;
Rumbaut 1997).

We see this counterpoint in national opinion surveys that ask Americans
to rank their preferences for immigrant-sending countries; Europe consistently comes out on top, Asia in the middle, and Latin America at the very
bottom (Espenshade and Belanger 1997). Even Americans who believe the
nation is letting in too many immigrants generally view Latin Americans as
"less desirable" than Asians (Espenshade and Belanger 1997). Thus, whether
compared to native-born minority groups or to immigrant groups, Asian
Americans seem to arrive at the same outcome, honorary white status (Tuan
1998), and they function as a rebuke to those unable to do the same.

And yet, for all the claims of an honorary white status, Asian Americans
are still subject to racial discrimination and marginalization (Lowe 1996; Espiritu 1997). We know that Asian Americans are often seen as perpetually
foreign, with their loyalties constantly in question and thus inauthentically
American (Lowe 1996; Tuan 1998; Kim 2000). As Kibria notes, the cam-
paign-finance scandals of the late 1990s highlighting the involvements of
Asians are continuing evidence of the "challenges to the legitimacy of their
membership and belonging in dominant society" (2002, 13). Indeed, all the
public attention given to the supposed acceptance of Asian Americans over-
looks the fact that they continue to be the subjects of hate crimes (National
Asian Pacific American Legal Consortium 2002). In 1982 a Chinese American man, mistaken as a Japanese was beaten by two white, laid-off auto
workers in Detroit; they blamed Japanese corporations for the decline of the
American automobile industry.[11] It was the ensuing legal aftermath, when
the two men were convicted of manslaughter but were given a sentence of

only three years' probation, that in fact galvanized the Asian American activist community (Clemetson 2002).

Asian Americans and Class

Similar to race, socioeconomic status has been an underexamined facet of Asian Americans and education, despite its being a defining line of difference among Asian Americans themselves. Immigration patterns in the years after the 1960s have given rise to both an ethnically and economically heterogeneous Asian American population. Along with the arrival of Asian immigrants with enough educational credentials and financial resources to climb the mobility ladder, there have also been more disadvantaged immigrants (Espiritu 1997). Yet, we know little about how socioeconomic status matters in one's experience of schooling and educational attainment in this diverse population. Do children in working-class Asian immigrant families have the same attitudes toward education as children in families where the parents are highly educated professionals and belong to the middle class? My decision to focus on Chinese Americans is thus rooted not only in their sheer numbers (they are, in fact, the largest Asian ethnic group), but also in the class bifurcation within the population.

The Two Worlds of Chinese America

The class bifurcation in the Chinese American population has its roots in the Immigration Act of 1965, which took effect in 1968 (Hing 1993). As I mentioned earlier, the Act was a watershed event, opening immigration to people from all countries and discontinuing policies that had been based on national origin. These earlier policies had favored Northern and Western Europeans by restricting the immigration of Asians from the late nineteenth century onward, and of those from South-Central Eastern Europe starting in the early twentieth century.

Under the new system, the Eastern hemisphere was assigned 120,000 visas per year, with up to 20,000 entries per country per year. There were no limits set on the entry of spouses, children, and parents of U.S. citizens (Foner 1987). Preference was given to family reunification and occupational skills, which would shape the class character of overall immigration patterns (Wong 1988). The response was overwhelming, and today, more than two-thirds of the Chinese American population is foreign-born, while the remainder are the children of immigrants and persons whose families have been in the United States for as long as several generations (Hune and Chan 1997). Migrants who have come with different waves have brought with them varying resources and have encountered differing economic, political, and social contexts of reception (Portes and Rumbaut 1980, 2001a).

In the Chinese immigrant population, for example, an individual's social class background is often tied to her place of origin and date of entry (Nakanishi 1995; Rumbaut 1997, 22 n. 9). As an example, in the years prior to 1979, Taiwanese immigrants tended to be characterized by high levels of education and skills, with a significant percentage coming to the United States for advanced studies and choosing to stay (Pan 1990; Rumbaut 1997). According to Ling (1997, 96), in an eight-year span between 1979 and 1987, "approximately 186,000 students from Taiwan came to America to continue their education, with only 10,000 returning home." Family members sponsored by these migrants have generally not been as highly educated. And the decision of the Taiwanese government to lift restrictions on overseas travel for its citizens in 1979 brought a new wave of immigrants from more diverse educational backgrounds. These migrants entered the United States on tourist visas, and some chose to remain (Chen 1992, 6).

The years leading up to the 1997 reunification of the British colony of Hong Kong and the People's Republic of China saw the immigration of Hong Kong professionals and capitalists (Wong 1988, 201). At the other end of the spectrum, there has been a recent influx of poor, illegal immigrants mainly from Fujian Province in mainland China. The province came into sudden national view when the *Golden Venture*, a smuggling ship carrying Fukienese migrants, ran aground off the shores of Queens in 1993. The ship's grounding revealed a system of involuntary servitude, with migrants each paying as much as $30,000 to smugglers to ensure their entry into the United States, a sum that often took years to pay off while working at menial jobs in the ethnic economy (Kwong 1997; Sachs 2001).

These differences according to place of origin are reflected in census data. Nationally, about 31 percent of the immigrants from the People's Republic of China are college graduates, and they have a median income of $34,225. Immigrants from Taiwan and Hong Kong fare significantly better, with 62 percent of the Taiwanese and 47 percent of Hong Kongers having bachelor's degrees, and with median incomes of $45,325 for the Taiwanese and $49,618 for those from Hong Kong (Portes and Rumbaut 2001a, 50). Writers like Peter Kwong and Morrison Wong have typified the difference as being between "uptown Chinese," who work high-paid jobs as professionals in the mainstream economy and live in upscale suburban communities, and the "downtown Chinese," who have little formal schooling and live and work at low-paid jobs in garment factories and restaurants in the city, typically in an urban ethnic economic enclave such as a Chinatown (Kwong 1987; Wong 1995a).[12] Today, nearly as many Chinese Americans reside outside the central cities as in them (Alba and Nee 2003, 254).

My respondents come from families who inhabit these two very different worlds of Chinese immigrants in the United States: one that is part of middle-class, suburban America, the long-time mainstream ideal for immigrants to assimilate into; and the other, the working-class ethnic enclaves of urban America that replicate in some measure the cultural landscape of the immigrants' homelands. The project of this book is to illuminate the interpretive process through which children from such different worlds make sense of their parents' educational aspirations and to examine how they see family influence informing their own experiences with school and their respective paths to college. Central to these accounts are the respondents' points of view concerning their particular identities: as either second- or 1.5 generation Americans, straddling two worlds, the one that their parents left behind and the world in which they live in America; as residents of different neighborhoods and as hailing from different class cultures that have characterized much of the Chinese immigrant experience post-1965; and as children of the post-civil rights era, where the fruits of equality exist alongside the burdens of continuing inequity, and where a racial and ethnic landscape is being continuously transformed by the new immigration's diversity in color, class, and cultural origins (Rumbaut and Portes 2001). In short, this book will look at how the views and experiences of 1.5 and second-generation Chinese Americans, with respect to education and the family, have much to do with the challenges and contradictions that immigrants and their children confront in the United States.

Race and Class at the Level of Lived Experience

The way in which abstract concepts at the core of this book, matters such as immigration, race, and socioeconomic status, manifest themselves in lived experience is evident from the following accounts of two Chinese American college students. Diana Chin,[13] the daughter of Chinese immigrants, was a senior at Columbia University, the very kind of Ivy League institution that has been linked with Asian Americans in the public mind. Reflecting on her parents' views on education, she said:

> My parents always stressed education as the most important thing. I mean, I think that it's the way things are done in America, you know, it's a certain tracking, and I think they just want the best for me and that's what they view as the best thing.

Diana's parents were themselves very highly educated, and in fact, could be well-described as uptown Chinese. During the late 1960s, Diana's father was a Fulbright Scholar to the United States from Malaysia, and her mother was an international student from Hong Kong. The two met and married in Boston. After a brief stint in England, where Diana was born, they returned to Boston. The Chins, an attorney and an accountant, quickly purchased a condominium in Brookline, an affluent suburb known for its highly ranked and nationally recognized public school system. Diana's memories of the years from kindergarten through high school are overwhelmingly positive: she was placed in honors classes, came into contact with nurturing teachers, and along the way won a number of academic prizes. When I asked her what Brookline High was like, Diana lauded the school in the following terms: "Very liberal. Very upper-middle-class. Public but in an area where, I mean, we had the best public schools in the state. I was pretty much tracked into every AP class that you can handle. So I took the top whatever classes." As a college senior, Diana looked to the future with confidence. Although she had struggled with the decision to abandon her childhood dream of a career in medicine, she was applying for positions in financial consulting and figured she stood a good chance of landing one.

Paul Chen, also the child of Chinese immigrants, attended Hunter College of the City University of New York (CUNY). In the public imagination, urban commuter universities like Hunter are not associated with Asian

Americans, who nonetheless made up 17 percent of the student body when I was conducting this research. Similar to Diana, Paul spoke of his parents as a key force in his education:

> Education, it's like one of the most important things, my mother and father, they value it. They always push us to do this, do good in school, it doesn't always work, but they really value it. I think they look at education as a key to a better life.

This shared belief in education is one of the few things that the two families had in common, as Paul's parents followed a different path to the United States, one typical of the downtown Chinese. In 1971 his parents left their village in Southern China and came to the United States via Hong Kong. Given their lack of English-language facility, their grade school educations, and their limited skills, they doubted their abilities to land jobs in the American mainstream economy. And so they turned to the ethnic economy in New York City's Chinatown, where their new life was regulated by the rhythms of manual labor. Both parents worked long hours, and they raised their three American-born sons in a one-bedroom apartment off of a busy Chinatown thoroughfare. Paul went to his neighborhood public schools and then to a nearby public high school. Paul's dominant memory of school is one of disengagement, which is reflected in his characterization of Humanities High School as a "waste of time." His high school career was hardly illustrious, as he was the first to admit:

> The high school I went to, no one really cared. Just no one cared. It has a 60 percent, 70 percent drop-out rate. It was such a waste of time in that school, if I would have just dropped out, got my GED, gone to a community college, and transferred [here], I would be in the same position as I am now. So I think it was one big waste of time, and half of the time you know, I cut a lot. I wasn't really there. . . . I had a 60–something average, very low.

Although he was also a college senior, Paul was unsure about his future. His interactions with the Hunter faculty in his major, economics, had been mostly with adjuncts, who were enthusiastic but who rarely stayed very long. Although Paul knew he wanted some kind of an office job, he was uncertain of his chances of landing one.

Diana's and Paul's shared frame on parental educational messages is one part of the story that I tell in this book, namely, of how Chinese American students, both women and men, from diverse class and educational backgrounds constructed a similar narrative of Asian American parents as paramount in their children's educational lives. The similarities lie in the language they use to speak of this role and in the particulars they saw in the role itself, like hard work, strict monitoring of children, the prestige of the college one attended, and the career aspirations held by parents. It is, I argue, a powerfully shared common cultural ground that my respondents see as not only specific to Chinese, but to Asians in general, who come from a diverse range of countries where the native peoples see themselves as having very little in common with one another.

Although the way they spoke about achievement hearkened to the cultural norms of their parents' countries of origin, my respondents believed such attitudes to be rooted in the experiences of Asian immigrant families in the United States. The basis for such attitudes were social contexts such as the openness of the American educational system and the payoff to higher education that gave rise to an immigrant optimism about the outcomes of the second generation. This is consistent with the immigrant-optimism hypothesis, namely that across race and ethnicity immigrant parents have high educational aspirations for their children and expect them to achieve mobility (Kao and Tienda 1995). Immigrant optimism, however, only explains part of the story here. The emphasis on education was also rooted in parental perceptions of a society closed along the lines of race that shaped a profound immigrant pessimism.

Diana's and Paul's varying levels of engagement with schooling en route to college speak to the other part of the story I tell here. If the prevailing idea among my respondents was that Asian parents play such an important role in their children's educational outcomes, then how did my Hunter students understand their own path to college? Hunter is a good school, to be sure, one with an illustrious past, but it is a city college nonetheless, and one with an embattled present over funding cutbacks and academic standards. And how did the children who attended Columbia make sense of their own trajectories? Such themes speak to the puzzle posed by today's Asian Americans in education, and the nexus of immigration, ethnicity, and class within which it has been situated.

The Puzzle of Asian Americans and Education

The challenge for researchers studying Asian Americans and education starts with uncovering the lines of commonality and difference in such a heterogeneous population. As with all discussion of Asian Americans, it is important to distinguish between aggregate data that lumps together subgroups and disaggregated data that parses them out. Certainly, in the aggregate, the academic achievement of Asian Americans is remarkable: they have a higher likelihood than whites, Hispanics, and blacks of entering and staying in school, they outrank all other groups in GPA and math SAT scores, they surpass the national average in college graduation rates, and they are more likely to pursue further education (Hsia 1988; Sue and Okazaki 1990; Espiritu 1997; Kao and Tienda 1998; *New York Times*, 1 September 1999, B9).

At the same time, the various ethnic groups that make up the Asian American population have distinct histories, socioeconomic backgrounds, and cultures, and they fare quite differently in education. In standardized tests and other measures of academic achievement, for instance, Asian Indians and Japanese students perform the best, on average, followed by Chinese, Koreans, Filipinos, and Southeast Asians, respectively (Siu 1996; Espiritu 1997). Moreover, within these ethnic groups, there is often variation along the lines of nativity status, gender, and class (Takaki 1989; Abelmann and Lie 1995).

The story of educational aspirations is no less complex. More so than for any other racial, ethnic, and immigrant group, Asian parents expect their children to go on to college and beyond, aspirations that are shared by their children (Kao and Tienda 1998; Goyette and Xie 1999). Parents further endorse academic achievement as an avenue of social mobility, and quite possibly as the only available avenue (Hsia and Hirano-Nakanishi 1989; Steinberg, Dornbusch, and Brown 1992, 726). Yet, once again, we know that there is no single effect of "Asian-ness" that operates in the same way for all the groups (Kim 1993; Goyette and Xie, 1999).[14] Asian immigrant parents may indeed share high aspirations, but there are differences along ethnic lines in the types of schools they want for their children and in how they transmit those aspirations.

Researchers seeking to explain the sources of sameness and variation in Asian American academic achievement have engaged in a debate about the relative importance of culture versus structure.

Ethnic Cultures

As I mentioned at the outset of this Introduction, the most popular way of understanding Asian American achievement has been the cultural argument. Asian Americans, it has been argued, draw on ethnic cultures grounded in Confucianism, which values things like family obligation, collectivism, hierarchy, and an emphasis on success as derived from effort rather than from natural ability (Lin and Fu 1990; Rosenthal and Feldman 1991; Chen and Stevenson 1995; Chen 1996). According to this line of thinking, these cultures give rise to high educational aspirations that, when combined with strategic investments, translate into remarkable levels of aspirations and attainment on the part of their children (Siu 1996). Or, to phrase it another way, the ethnic-culture explanation emphasizes the values and beliefs of Asian immigrants, as derived from their homelands, which are seen as playing a decisive role in their children's success in the United States.

The main criticism of the ethnic-culture argument is that in emphasizing what is shared its proponents neglect variation, both historically and in the contemporary era. As discussed earlier, there was certainly no empirical basis for the notion of Asian Americans as academic exemplars prior to World War II. And despite today's image of Chinese Americans as academic stars, their educational outcomes are decidedly bifurcated in the immigrant generation and quite diverse in later generations. Nationally, a bit more than half of Chinese immigrants have received some form of higher education,[15] while nearly three out of ten have less than a high school education, and 15 percent have only a high school diploma. Among the native-born, approximately 60 percent have either a college degree or some college education, but nearly one in four have a high school diploma or less (Weinberg 1997, 7). Similar trends are revealed in data from the Project on the Second Generation in Metropolitan New York,[16] a popular destination for Chinese immigrants: 11.7 percent of the Chinese American adults studied were still enrolled in high school, had dropped out, or had ended their schooling at the diploma or GED level. Another 7.6 percent were either enrolled in or had graduated from a two-year college, and 7.2 percent had some college but no degree. At the other end of the spectrum, more than three out of five (61.4 percent) were enrolled in or had graduated from a four-year college (Louie, forthcoming). Even here, there is considerable diversity in the types of schools they attended, ranging from elite private universities to public commuter universities.

Structure

Writers working from the structural perspective explain these patterns of variation by focusing on the economy and on opportunity structure. It has been argued, therefore, that the nation's need for low-wage workers prior to World War II shaped who came and how they and their children fared. Along those lines, others have proposed that social-class background and selective migration of post-1965 immigrants figure prominently in the Asian American educational success of the last few decades—that, in fact, the children who have done well are from families who were among the educated middle and upper classes in their countries of origin (Kwong 1987; Siu 1992b; Barringer, Gardner, and Levin 1993).

The ethnic economy is another key site of inquiry for structural proponents. The main point here is that the ethnic economy, while largely formed due to the lack of primary-sector labor-market opportunities for Asian immigrants, allows Asians to make substantial gains and to create economic opportunities for the next generation through investment in education (Lieberson 1980; Hirschmann and Wong 1986; Sanchirico 1991). Consistent with such formulations, segmented assimilationists have argued that two groups of second-generation Asian children are positioned to do well in school: those we traditionally think of as succeeding, insofar as they assimilate into the majority, middle-class culture; and those children who come from ethnic economic enclaves that have ethnic capitalist structures and strong educational networks. Although this latter group remains ethnically attached, they nevertheless climb the educational ladder and are likely to achieve mobility in the mainstream economy (Gans 1992; Zhou 1992; Portes and Zhou 1993; Zhou 1997; Portes and Rumbaut 2001a, 2001b).[17] Even in the absence of an ethnic economic enclave, a strong ethnic community can help shield immigrant children from negative influences and can reinforce parental attitudes and educational agendas (Gibson 1988).

This debate over the relative importance of ethnic culture as opposed to structure has come to dominate our understanding of Asian Americans and education, and for that reason, it serves as the theoretical point of departure for this book.[18] For each of these explanations contributes much to our understanding, but they also leave crucial questions unanswered. While the ethnic-culture explanation tells us a great deal about values developed in the countries of origin, it does not make visible the immigrant experience nor differences in socioeconomic adaptation once immigrants arrive in the United States. Segmented assimilation theory does a much better job of incorporating the immigrant experience. Yet it does not give us much insight into children in the ethnic enclaves who are not high achievers, and along with other structural explanations, it does not shed much light on the processes by which Asian immigrant parents, regardless of their social location, come to see education as their children's ticket to success. And neither approach sufficiently addresses the racial incorporation of Asian Americans and their takes on racism in America.

In short, what is needed is a framework that allows us to explore how both ethnic culture and class matter *together*. That is the goal of this book, not to provide the definitive word on the subject, but to raise the subject as something worthy and to illuminate some important parts of it. Thus, rather than focus on ethnic culture and structure as an either/or proposition, I believe that a more fruitful approach is to consider how culture, which we know to be fluid, is transformed by migration, race relations, and the opportunity structure in the United States, and how this interaction informs children's understandings of the aspirations passed on by their immigrant parents.

In this vein, the story told by my respondents is a complex one. As they tell it, their immigrant parents are inserted into an American context with considerable strides made for racial and ethnic minorities, women, and immigrants. The implications for their children proved to be multifaceted. In the case of gender, for example, the varying incorporation of families into the American labor market had little effect on parental expectations for children's education: parents thought it was crucial for both daughters and sons to complete a bachelor's degree. At the same time, some working-class families held on to traditional gender ideologies that were expressed in the realms of the home and social behavior.

The story is not about optimism alone, however. The parents perceive persistent troubling inequalities along the lines of race and immigrant status and believe that higher education will help shield their children from discrimination, at least in part. In some cases, the parents, twice-marginalized migrants, drew on their prior experiences with exclusion as ethnic minorities in Malaysia and the Philippines, which afforded them an additional lens through which to make sense of American racism. In short, the association of higher education with success among Chinese immigrants is as much an acknowledgment of and guarded response to the American racial hierarchy as it is evidence of a heady immigrant optimism.

And, in this respect, the story my respondents tell is quite the *opposite* of the model minority: it is precisely because Chinese immigrant parents see inequalities along the lines of race that they advise their children to do well in school. The accounts constructed by these students speak to their view of social reality as one where race continues to be salient and highly divisive, even for a non-white group thought by some to be faring well enough to be called "honorary whites."

And yet, the ethnic-culture argument is a powerfully shared domain for students, who discuss not only the role of Chinese immigrant parents in their children's education but that of Asian immigrant parents more broadly. How did this happen? Consistent with Kibria's (2002) argument, my respondents believe that Asians in America, while possibly different on other dimensions, share a culture that emphasizes education, family, and work. While some took pains to distance themselves from the model minority image, often because it was so at odds with their own family backgrounds and educational experiences, the ethnic-culture component remained strong.

Each group of students took the ethnic-cultural script and adapted it to their own needs. The Hunter students spoke of structural inequalities along the lines of race and class that corresponded to their own reality. Yet, in the end, they subsumed these elements to the cultural script by identifying themselves, and equally important, their families, as exceptions to the rule. This allowed them to believe that other Asians can and do follow the cultural script to its logical conclusion. At the same time, those Columbia students who grew up in the enclave considered themselves to be the fortunate ones who had overcome the roadblocks that had waylaid their peers. And again, they ended up endorsing the cultural script.

Those Columbia students who had grown up in the suburbs endorsed the ethnic-cultural script because it fit so well with their own reality. A key distinction they drew between themselves and their peers in predominately white suburbia was how their parents were stricter and more vigilant about their education. This impression was only confirmed when they went to college and met and befriended more Asian American students, who shared similar experiences and perspectives.

In sum, among these Chinese Americans, the experience of education is at once illustrative of the opportunities and constraints that derive from the racial, class, and social contexts that my respondents and their families encounter in the United States.

Direction and Scope of the Study

To set the stage for what follows, Part One begins with the journeys of these families to America. In Chapter 1, I focus on the immigrant journey to mainstream, suburban America. In Chapter 2, I turn to the very different immigrant journey to urban-enclave America, and specifically, to the Chinese economic enclaves in New York City. These journeys are both literal and symbolic, and bear upon the identity formation of the immigrants' children.

In Part Two I turn to how the children make sense of education. Chapter 3 looks at how they frame the role of the immigrant Asian family in their understandings of educational motivation and achievement. These children emphasized ethnic cultures, and their vocabulary for describing the learning process (e.g., achievement as derived from effort rather than natural ability) is reminiscent of the way Chinese speak about the learning experience in China, Taiwan, and Hong Kong. Asia, however, does not figure in the narratives of these 1.5 and second-generation children.

The fruits and lingering inequalities of post-civil rights America are what prove to be central to the children's cultural framework for understanding *why* their parents stressed education. On the one hand, children see their parents as subscribing to an immigrant optimism grounded in the widespread availability of quality public education in the United States and in the pay-off to that education in the labor market. On the other, children knew their parents are also pessimistic about their possible futures in the existing American racial hierarchy, which they see as marginalizing the Chinese, especially those who are *without* higher education. As Chapter 4 shows us, this immigrant optimism and pessimism dynamic helps us to understand some of the working-class parents' changing views of gender and education that have worked to the advantage of daughters, who are now encouraged to pursue higher education.

If children understand Asian immigrant parents to be a powerful force in shaping aspirations and motivations, not to mention achievement, how do they then understand their own paths to college? Chapter 5 illustrates that for the Hunter students, all natives of urban, ethnic-enclave America, this question poses a disjuncture between how they understand the role of the immigrant Asian family in education and the experiences they actually have had or have seen their peers and siblings having. To make sense of all of this, these children emphasize a lack of parental resources and voice the idea that their parents did not raise them in the traditional Chinese way. In other words, their parents did not help them *translate* aspirations into reality the way other Asian parents do with their children. The ethnic-culture framework remains powerful, even for these respondents, who would be least likely to subscribe to it, due to their social-class location, and who are in fact pointedly critical of the model-minority image.

Chapter 6 shows that for those Columbia students who are natives of middle-class suburbia, the journey to college was straightforward—they were supposed to be at Columbia and the histories of their families, as well as their parents' involvement with their schooling, all pointed to the near inevitability of that outcome. The Columbia students from urban ethnic enclaves, however, think of themselves as fortunate and often speak thoughtfully of the 1.5 and second-generation Chinese American peers they have left behind, the ones who have dropped out of high school or are not in college even though they may have managed to finish high school.

How does being second generation matter in the lives of my respondents? That is the focus of Part Three. Chapter 7 takes a look at the shared narratives of obligation toward parents among the 1.5 and second generations, and at the role this plays in the children's academic decision-making, specifically with regard to fields of study. But the second-generation experience is also about the processes of Americanization that children undergo that have little to do with mobility and opportunity and that nonetheless also involve their parents in some way. Chapter 8 thus discusses my respondents' diverse sets of interests related to religious participation, choice of mate, politics, and leisure pursuits, interests which oftentimes bring them into dialogue with their parents about the processes of Americanization.

The Conclusion explores the role of race in these children's lives. It is clear that their immigrant parents stressed the existence of an opportunity structure closed along racial lines. But how do their children see this dynamic unfolding in their own lives, especially as their frame of reference has always been the United States and as they are close to obtaining the college degree, the ticket to upward mobility in today's America. Do they see a raceless world, or do they see a world that will continue to be divided by race, and if the answer is the latter, what kinds of implications do they envision for Chinese Americans?

I should say here that my interests in this research have been both professional and personal. As a second-generation Chinese American, I have never been able to find answers, either in the images presented in the media or in the scholarly literature, that speak completely to my family experiences. There were always gaps that were left unexamined. In some ways, my parents are very typical of urban-enclave America. They arrived in the United States prior to the 1960s and lived in Chinatown until the early 1970s, and they have worked mainly for Chinese-owned garment and restaurant businesses. People of my parents' generation mostly have a high school education, and in some cases, only a grade school education. My U.S.-born uncles and aunts fared much better, having attended local commuter city colleges, and in one rare instance, Columbia University. A few in my extended family also went on to advanced degrees. Still, by graduating from Harvard College and then moving on to Stanford and Yale for my postgraduate work, and now as an assistant professor at the Harvard Graduate School of Education, I clearly stood out in my extended family. My older brothers, born in the United States like myself, took quite different paths. They never finished high school, although my oldest brother was accepted at Brooklyn Technical High School, one of the city's best public high schools, and later obtained his GED. In this, they were no different from many of their boyhood friends from Chinatown, some of whom ended up dead or enmeshed in lives of crime, and others of whom found jobs with the U.S. postal service or as janitors in the public school system.

Given that my family is but one example, in many ways particular to the pre-1965 Chinese immigration patterns that shaped all our lives and that are discussed in Chapter 2, I wanted to explore these kinds of issues from an empirical vantage point. This background led me to study post-1965 Chinese immigrants and their children, whose settlement in the United States belongs to a different historical moment than my family's, but whose experiences can hopefully shed some light on the questions that I have had over the years. This book tells their story alone, but the journey is as much mine as it is theirs.

Let me conclude this Introduction by saying that I do not intend this study to be a comprehensive inquiry into the experiences of all Chinese Americans. In the pages that follow, I will be discussing a very specific set of Chinese Americans: they were all enrolled in a four-year college and were 1.5 and second generation; and the majority grew up in the environs of New York City. They cannot speak to the experiences of Chinese Americans who are of another generation, or who live in different regions of the nation, and/or exited the educational system without attending a four-year college. That said, I do believe that this study provides a much-needed window into the complexities of how 1.5 and second-generation Chinese Americans understand the role of the immigrant family in educational experiences.

In that way, their accounts give us a better sense of how the story of exceptionalism surrounding Chinese Americans, and indeed, all Asian Americans, with respect to education must be reinterpreted in light of important family, class, and neighborhood contexts. A central part of this story is how young adults come to understand education in relation to the social contexts in which they are embedded, a process that involves shifting perspectives and cultural outlooks, as happens with migration and a mixing of cultural elements. The different contexts underlying their adaptation—as second-generation Chinese Americans, of a specific class location, as members of racial and ethnic minorities, as young women and men—are themselves shaped by broader historical, social, and economic trends that are an important part of the world in which we live in today.

PART ONE

Family Journeys to America

Chapter 1

MAINSTREAM, SUBURBAN AMERICA

The quintessential markers of American suburban life—the brand-new deck, barbeque grill, and ample yard—lay beyond the kitchen slider doors of the Leong's gray Colonial. It was a warm summer afternoon, and Mrs. Leong sat at the kitchen table, occasionally looking out at the view, and offering me toasty oatmeal raisin cookies as she told me about life in China. China was not an unfamiliar place to me, as I had visited a few years before, witnessing the nation's breathless pace of modernization that seemed to unfold right before me with the construction of new department stores and gleaming skyscrapers. But the China that Mrs. Leong talked about was nothing like the one I had seen; she called to mind a war-stricken, chaotic world that tore families apart.

Mrs. Leong was born in 1949, the year the Communist Party, led by Mao Zedong, finally defeated Chiang Kai-shek's Nationalists, winning a hard-fought civil war and assuming control of China. The effects were immediate and profound. The first thing to go were the men. Mrs. Leong's family village in Toisan in Southern China had long been a village of "male sojourners," a term scholars have used to describe the men, like Mrs. Leong's grandfathers, who had gone to the United States to work, sending back remittances to provide for their families in China. Mr. Leong's father had opted to stay behind in China, but with the Communist victory, that was no longer a possibility. He fled to the British colony of Hong Kong, along with all the remaining able-bodied men in the village. The second thing to go were the Leong family's landholdings and businesses, all the fruits of the patriarch's sojourns to America. With no men and no source of income, the women and children were left to fend for themselves. After years of deprivations, it was decided that the young Mrs. Leong, then seven years old, would join her grandmother and sister in an attempt to escape to Hong Kong. She described the painful logic of who could go, and who had to stay:

> My mother cannot go—cause they only allow, you know, certain people to go at that time. It's not that easy to come in and out, you know? And my—my mother, thinking if I was still with her, it's just like a burden, because I was young, and need somebody to take of. Okay? So she chose my other sister, which is twelve years old.

> I always said, "I don't want to go. I don't want to go." I *tell* them, "I don't want to go." Actually, that night, I sleep, I hold on my mom's hand, you know? And then probably they woke me up at the middle of the night, and I was half asleep, and I remember somebody put me on his back, you know, just go somewhere. And then you're on the boat, and then, you know. And then by the time you arrive the place there, Hong Kong, and they said, "This is your father." I was sad enough to lose my mother, you know. I mean, I don't know anybody as a father, and all of a sudden, they tell you this is your father—"You call him father." I never call him father. I feel shy. You see? I feel shy and this is a stranger. I feel so scared.

Her father, she soon discovered, was still wrestling with his own decline in status—from landlord's son to common laborer—and his jobs were erratic. That meant his children had to work, and worse yet, that there would be no money for formal schooling. Mrs. Leong managed to cobble together an education from the kindness of teachers and eventually became a teacher herself before migrating to Canada and then to the United States. When she and her mother were reunited, thirty years had passed since they had last seen one another: by then her mother was an elderly woman and Mrs. Leong was a mother of three who made her home in suburban Massachusetts.

Given those struggles, and the ones experienced by her husband, another Toisan native, it was important to the Leongs that they provide their two daughters and son, all American-born, a stable, suburban life. It was her husband's training as an engineer with master's and bachelor's degrees from New York University, which landed him jobs at Fortune 500 firms, that ensured this life for their children. Their two-story house, with its two-car garage, spacious eat-in kitchen, and wooden deck out back, blended in with the other homes in the tiny, upscale town of Southborough, Massachusetts, thirty-five miles outside Boston, where, according to the 2000 census, the median family income is $70,989. The family room was filled with poster-sized photographs of the children, the oldest daughter garbed in pink leotard and tutu gazing straight at the camera with a toothy grin. Abstract artwork by the second daughter, Sandra, whom I met at Columbia College, hung in the bathroom and in the hallways. The children all had received years of training in music, tennis, art, and ballet, and summers had been spent in enrichment programs. In short, the Leongs had the kind of typical suburban home and lifestyle that I imagined any other American family in Southborough might have, which meant any other white American family, since the town was close to 95 percent white, according to the 2000 census.

Journeys

Homelands of Political, Social, and Economic Instability

The particulars of the Leong story are their own, but they point to contours experienced in some measure by all the parents of my suburban respondents. Their lives before arriving in the United States were invariably shaped by key moments in the history of East Asia: attempts by the Japanese to establish domination in China and the entire East Asian region, civil war in China, the founding of a Nationalist government in Taiwan amid much resistance after their defeat in China, interethnic strife between the descendants of Chinese migrants in Malaysia and the Philippines and native Malays and Filipinos. In short, had these parents all met one another, they would have had animated conversations about their attempts to survive roiling political and economic instability, and about the hardships that came with living under such conditions, even though their views of the complex geopolitical arrangements in East Asia may have been very different.

Becky Wang's mother, for example, was an ardent Taiwanese Nationalist, a descendant of those Chinese migrants who had settled on the island four hundred years earlier and who thought of themselves as Taiwanese, not Chinese.[1] A Chinese colony for several hundred years, Taiwan was ceded to Japan in 1895, which ruled until 1945. The Taiwanese staged a series of unsuccessful revolts against the Japanese, who are estimated to have killed more than eleven thousand Taiwanese in the years between 1898 and 1902 alone. In the wake of the Japanese defeat after World War II, the Nationalists assumed both control of the island, where they became known as the Mainlanders, and the role of colonizer; the Taiwanese staged an unsuccessful uprising two years later, known as the February 28 incident, that is estimated to have killed or imprisoned well over twenty thousand persons, many of them the sons of Taiwanese elites (Tsai, Gates, and Chiu 1994; Weinberg 1997). When the Nationalists fled China in 1949 and established themselves in Taiwan, relations on the island were still volatile. The transfer of power was difficult, and for many years after, everyday life was soured by conflicting political ideologies and a culture of suspicion.

Mrs. Wang was one of the so-called native Taiwanese who resisted not only Nationalist rule but the very idea that Taiwan was part of China at all. To Mrs. Wang, Taiwan was an independent country and one well rid of the Nationalist stakeholders, as well as the encroachment of Communist China. During the 1960s, she had been a student activist in support of this cause. In those days, public dissent was often tantamount to arrest by the state. To avoid this fate, Mrs. Wang had been sent by her family to study abroad, in Japan, and later arrangements were made for her to migrate to the United States. Although at the time of the study she was a U.S. citizen, Mrs. Wang had never left the cause behind. According to daughter Becky, family conversations often revolved around the political situation in Taiwan and China:

> My parents, like, talk about political issues a lot. I hear about, like, the restrictions that they have in China and Taiwan on, like, education and things like that. How they only teach, this is what my Mom said, so I don't know if it's the same now, but they only teach what they want you to know. And so, like, all the textbooks are like false, not false, but a lot of the history is, like, made up and things like that. To make the leaders look good.

Unlike the other moms in their New Jersey suburb, Mrs. Wang would regularly drive down to the United Nations in midtown Manhattan to protest against China's claim on Taiwan, sometimes bringing her children along.

It was a similar kind of political instability in his native Philippines that pushed Mr. Fong to the United States in 1985, despite having to leave behind a successful business. His family had been in the Philippines for three generations, ever since his grandfather had arrived from Fukien Province in China. The Fong family had done well over the years, trying to blend in with the Filipino mainstream as a way of mitigating the resentment that Chinese sometimes faced as a successful ethnic minority particularly dominant in trade. The family sought to blend in, not through intermarriage but by changing their surname to make it sound more "Filipino." When Mr. Fong came of age, he had the opportunity to attend college and graduate school in Manila before going abroad to study in Scotland.

When he returned to the Philippines, Mr. Fong joined a new startup consulting firm and bought a house attended by maids and cooks; he was generally able to provide a comfortable life for his wife and young son. And yet he never lost sight of the fact that his homeland was under the military dictatorship of Ferdinand Marcos, and that the threat of violence by the state was ever present. He knew, of course, that he was luckier than most. His consulting firm was well connected with the regime in power, and he himself knew important government officials, one of the necessities of doing business in the Philippines at that time. Still, Mr. Fong always had his doubts: What if he someday were to join the ranks of those who had simply disappeared? What would his son's life be like then? As the years passed and his success grew, so did his sense of vulnerability, until the anxieties made life nearly unbearable. Remembering these fears in his book- and paper-cluttered home office in the well-kept Riverdale section of the Bronx, Mr. Fong shook his head wryly and pondered the psychological costs:

What is important is the peace of mind. It seems like, you see, when you are living in martial law, even though I knew a lot of people, life is cheap. If somebody doesn't like you, he can pay somebody a few hundred dollars, and he can wipe you out, just like that. We would go at night, and then there would be checkpoints in the middle of the night, you know you have to pass through checkpoints, these are soldiers with guns and everything, although I had no problem because I had in my wallet cards from my friends, who were generals. But still, you never know. There's that uncertainty. Someone might wake up in the middle of the night, and I'd be arrested for some reason, whatever. So I didn't like that, I didn't like that feeling. So giving up all of that, except that here, I have peace of mind. That's the important thing.

So, Mr. Fong sold off his properties at a loss, gave up his share of the consulting business, and emigrated to the United States with his family. In the United States, he could not afford to hire maids and cooks, and he had to settle for a condominium in a middle-class area of New York City, much smaller than his former villa. But he had peace of mind, in particular, for his children.

Destination: Suburban America

For these parents, the United States was quite simply the promised land. It was a refuge from the instability of their homelands, and because of the way the Immigration Act of 1965 was structured, giving preference to highly educated professionals, they had made it in. Nearly all these parents had at least a college degree, and in many cases a graduate degree as well. More than half of them had earned their degrees in the United States at state and private institutions. Parents who had earned their undergraduate degrees in their homeland had often graduated from the best institutions, like Hong Kong University and National Taiwan University. Rumbaut's apt description of the professional stream of post-1965 immigration as the "most skilled immigrants ever to come to the United States" (1997) very much applies to these parents, many of whom came as international students and never left. They were able to parlay their educational backgrounds into professional jobs in the mainstream economy, as engineers in private industry, as lawyers, and as doctors. Others opened their own businesses, specializing in import-export or technology.

The payoff was the suburban lifestyle that these parents were able to attain. They bought homes in some of the most exclusive suburbs of our nation, like the town of Dix Hills on Long Island, where the median household income is $104,160 and more than half the population has a bachelor's degree or higher. Or the town of Merrick, also on Long Island, where the median household income is $93,132 and 48 percent of the population has a bachelor's degree or higher. As a frame of comparison, the national median household income in 2000 was only $43,163 (DeNavas-Walt and Cleveland 2002), and only 27 percent of the population aged 25 and older had a bachelor's degree or greater (U.S. Bureau of the Census 2002b, March). Nearly three-fifths of my suburban sample, however, lived in census tracts where between 51 percent and 77 percent of residents aged twenty-five and older held bachelor's degrees or greater. And more than half of my sample lived in tracts where the median household income ranged from $79,968 to more than $200,000.[2] In short, the census tracts where my suburban respondents grew up were well above the national norm in terms of income and educational attainment.

A few of my suburban respondents lived in gated communities, bastions of exclusivity in already exclusive areas. The Fans, for example, had purchased a townhouse in Southern California in a subdivision so new that it was not even listed on most maps. To one side of the road, as I pulled up to their Mediterranean-style house, was a stunning backdrop of smoky gray hills. Mrs. Fan pulled into the driveway right behind me, getting out of a shiny white Volvo sedan. Occasionally, as we spoke in the living room amid framed Chinese scrolls of fish and flora, Chinese vases in shades of blue, comfy couches, and an upright piano, something akin to chimes would ring. Apparently, there was an alarm system that was set off every time someone walked through the front door. It was set off when Mr. Fan returned home from work, and then again when he left, minutes later, with their daughter Ava to go swimming in the pool.

In these homes, the parents had been able to leave the hardships and privations behind them, and they gave their children all the advantages that we associate with suburban life in America—good public schools; wide, leafy streets where it is safe for children to play, run, and ride bikes; and a wide array of afterschool and weekend activities.

Growing Up in White Suburbia

Loss of Language

Another defining characteristic of my respondents' suburban experience was race: more than 80 percent lived in census tracts that were predominately white. For the immigrant parents, the suburban lifestyle had few trade-offs, but one was the dilution of ethnicity in the lives of their children. In suburbs that were predominately white, it was particularly difficult for young children to retain the significance of being Chinese in the public sphere of the neighborhood and the school. Even when limited mainly to the home, however, ethnicity still has meaning for people, for example, in the language that immigrant children speak when addressing their parents and siblings. Yet these parents did not want their children to speak Chinese. They feared it would mark their children as somehow foreign and thus inauthentically American. So, in many families English became the lingua franca for parent and children conservations, and Chinese, if spoken at all, was the secret language used by parents when they did not want children to understand what they were saying.

Parents were also concerned that if their children grew up speaking two languages they would become confused about which one should be spoken and would find it difficult to learn English. If that were to happen, the parents had no illusions about what the implications might be, since many had found their career advancement in the United States had been stymied by language barriers. The art of self-presentation, as some parents told me, was crucial in the American corporate workplace. Mrs. Wu remarked on how her former husband, a graduate of a top Taiwanese university, had never been able to handle what she called the "challenge of American society." She observed, "You need to really put yourself in the job market, try to sell yourself; if people question you, you need to answer the questions. You need to really grab the chance that come up to you."

Not only was this a cultural adjustment for these parents, who came from homelands where competency was measured by test scores and output and where there was a tight link between the prestige of one's postsecondary institution and the labor market (e.g., the degree said it all), but language was a further complicating factor. Being a native speaker would not necessarily guarantee success at self-presentation, but not being a native speaker could very well doom the effort. Thus, speaking nothing less than flawless English was the objective for the Ma children. This mandate came from Frances's late father, himself a hospital administrator and nuclear chemist whose career trajectory had fallen short of his expectations. Frances explained: "[My father] spoke with an accent, and he never presented well. He had a lot of ideas, but he could never express them fully. My parents never spoke Chinese to us because my father wanted us to speak English without an accent, and to have a full command of English."

Ethnicity in the Home

Insofar as ethnicity could be a private affair, it was exhibited in the home furnishings that these children's peers did not have. These included porcelain stools, small Buddhist shrines, shoes neatly lined up in the foyer, and the red-and-gold Chinese character for prosperity posted on the doorway. These types of ethnic home furnishings took me by surprise when I visited a few of the families. I was struck, for example, by how ethnically familiar the Leong home was to me, beginning with the chimes that greeted me at the front door and continuing with the Chinese characters for peace and prosperity. Inside, the family room was decorated with Chinese vases that one might find in many a suburban home, regardless of the owner's racial and ethnic background, and some things that one would not think to find, like six-inch versions of the three Star Gods of Happiness, Wealth, and Longevity from traditional Chinese folklore; the Star Gods are typically placed in the dining or living room to attract good fortune into one's home, along with Guan Yin, the equally fabled Goddess of Mercy. I instantly recognized them because my own parents, apparently believing that one can never have too much good fortune, have multiple sets of Star Gods and Guan Yins (and much larger versions: their Star Gods are almost twice the size of the Leong's). In a way, because it was tucked away in a wealthy, suburban slice of America, the Leong's home was very different from my family's; and yet, in the markers of ethnicity the Leong home was immediately known to me.

More generally, ethnicity was expressed mainly in these families in the ethnic foods served at the dinner table and in the sporadic celebration of ethnic holidays. To the children, however, ethnic cultural traditions like the Chinese New Year and the Moon Festival were devoid of meaning and historical context. What they remembered was much more visceral, the taste and shapes of the foods associated with each holiday, like the sweet and salty mooncakes eaten during the Moon Festival; the *dong*—sticky rice wrapped in leaves and consumed during the Dragon Boat Festival; and the Buddhist vegetarian dish typically prepared during Chinese New Year. The loss of meanings attached to holidays that the children reported on was reminiscent of similar patterns that have occurred with white ethnics, albeit this usually took place in the third generation and beyond (Gans 1979; Alba 1990; Waters 1990). In other words, ethnicity, to the extent that it existed, was largely symbolic.

I asked Laura Toy what kinds of ethnic holidays her family had celebrated during her childhood and adolescence on Long Island. She told me her parents had not taught their children Chinese folk songs, nor had they told them Chinese folk tales. For example, Laura had learned about Mulan, the legendary Chinese heroine who disguised herself as a man and helped lead the imperial armies to victory, not from her immigrant parents but, ironically, from the Disney mythmaking machine. Looking back, she was disappointed with the loss of traditions. The only Chinese holiday her family celebrated was Chinese New Year, and with little fanfare beyond the *hong bao*, money given by adults to children in red packets for good luck:

> That's one of the things that I was really upset about, my parents never taught us a lot of stuff, like Chinese holidays. That kind of thing, I feel I found out about by myself. I mean, we got the red packets on Chinese New Year, but we mostly celebrated like seasonal things like Christmas, Easter, things like that. It's only recently because I was talking to my aunt, because the film *Mulan* came out, she was, I actually want to see *Mulan*. And I was like, yeah, I want to see it, too. And she was like, You know the story, right? And I was like, No. And she was like, You don't know it? That's one of the, like, famous Chinese stories. Every Chinese child should know those stories. I can't believe your parents never told you. Your parents probably don't even know. Like my parents are very Western.

The Exceptions: Trying to Maintain a Chinese Identity

Even those parents who were very invested in fostering a strong ethnic identity for their children ran into problems that came from living in white, suburban America. William Jen remembered his parents making the two-hour drive every weekend from their rural hamlet in Pennsylvania to the closest metropolitan center, just so that he and his younger brother could attend Chinese school (which they hated having to do). He was one of the few children who managed to become fluent in Chinese. A more common story was the Leong family's. Minutes into my initial phone call to set up our interview, Mrs. Leong asked if I spoke Chinese. When she learned that we both spoke Toisanese, we ended up conducting the bulk of the conversation in that dialect. Although my interview with Mrs. Leong was largely conducted in English, she clearly relished speaking her native language, even in a small way, to someone of my age and generation. My limited facility in the language (I certainly could not talk about most sociological matters in Chinese) nevertheless amazed her because, like her children, I was American-born and I had essentially learned the language at home from speaking with my mother. Mrs. Leong had also wanted her children to learn Chinese, enrolling them in Chinese school in Boston and teaching them at home. The town of Southborough, however, made reinforcement for her efforts impossible, and eventually, she gave up:

> Because we are always by ourselves, no relatives around, no grandparents around. That is a disadvantage. And the fact that we are the only Chinese family in this town doesn't help. When they [the kids] are home, I teach them how to read, how to write, how to sing, how to recite Chinese poems. But then when you go see a doctor, check up, the doctor speaks in English. So I have to teach them English too. Like the shapes, the colors, the numbers. So you have to teach them also. And then when they go to school, they use the English language all the time. That's how they lose the other one, because there's no use. Even when I talk to them in Chinese, they don't understand, so I end up using English to make sure they get the message. Of course, I regret that I did not insist.

Years later, Mrs. Leong learned there had been other incentives for her young children to speak only English; they were teased unmercifully by other kids about speaking Chinese, being Chinese, having "slant" eyes, and, in general, being "Chinks."

Confronted with the difficulties of transmitting the language, other parents were content to have their children associate with large numbers of Asian American children, regardless of what language they spoke, just so they could have some sense of being ethnic. For that reason, one young woman was signed up by her mother for a regional drum and bugle corps in Sacramento, California, a group that was comprised mainly of Asian American teenagers. Victoria Chang's parents enrolled her in Chinese school briefly (which she hated) and then in music camp, which she liked much better, where most of the other children were also Asian Americans. As a family, the

Changs also attended services at a Chinese church that was a thirty–minute drive from their Long Island home, and Victoria's parents sought out the Chinese American families who lived in neighboring communities, devising an ethnic social network of their own.

> It turned into a huge group, which my parents aren't so involved in now anyways. But it was every month, at somebody's house, everybody would bring food. It would be like a potluck dinner. And then the parents would go talk and go sing karaoke, because that got big. And us kids would play and do whatever we did.

Still, it is worth noting that at the end of these forays with Asian and Chinese Americans, the children all ended up returning to their suburban, predominately white communities, which continued to serve as their primary frame of reference. Victoria's comments below capture the intricate interplay between the ethnic influence that her parents sought to instill and the suburban community that informed her everyday existence:

> I had become involved in outside orchestras and seen more Asian people as opposed to spending most of my childhood in that kind of neighborhood. And also because I spent more time with a lot more Asian people, but then at the same time, my school was like all white people, and I was just trying to figure out who I was.

Just Like Everyone Else

As Erikson (1968) famously proposed, the process of figuring out one's own identity involves a sense of who one is and who one wishes to become. How to do this when one is visibly different from the mainstream along the lines of race and ethnicity presents another layer of complexity in the development of identity (Phinney et al. 2001). This became a central theme in the lives of these 1.5 and second-generation children. Yet, for the most part, the childhoods and adolescence of these suburban, middle-class students followed the script set forth in sociological theories of assimilation (Park 1950; Gordon 1964). That is, for the most part, they remembered growing up with the idea that they were like everyone else, meaning like their white peers, or as Espiritu (1994) found in her study of middle-class Filipino Americans living in largely white suburbs, as "average American teenager[s]." Ethnicity was something that distinguished them only in terms of food and their sporadic observances of Chinese holidays. The general feeling was a sense of belonging. Frances Ma, for example, found that her classmates had their ethnic backgrounds as well:

> When we grew up, our sisters and I were the only Chinese family in our elementary school. It was mostly Italian, Irish, and German, like long time ago American. I grew up with that, and I never really knew I was Chinese. I guess I never really thought I was different. You know, most of them had red hair. I had black hair. I mean, I knew I was Chinese when I was in elementary school because my Mom would, like, for culture day, we would bring in dumplings, and someone else would bring Irish soda bread, and someone would bring in cannolis. But it was never something that set me apart from other people.

Even those who remembered early incidents in which they were singled out minimized their significance. Victoria Chang was made fun of when her family first moved to Garden City, Long Island, for its superior schools. She was the new girl in the fourth grade, and everyone already knew each other from kindergarten. There was a racial element, too, she says, with kids pulling their eyes to the sides to imitate what they thought Asians looked like, and talking sing-song to mimic what they thought Asians sounded like. The incidents passed, and those same kids became her friends as Victoria became one of the group.

Or, if my respondents had anger about the situation, they sometimes repressed it so they could get by. William Jen, for example, does not remember dwelling on the fact that he was usually "the only Asian" growing up in his small town. It was only when he arrived at a diverse urban campus like Columbia's that he allowed himself to reconsider his past and to admit feelings that he had previously put to one side:

> I didn't feel it was too bad (being the only Asian), but looking back in retrospect, I really didn't like it at all. I guess where I grew up, people aren't really as open to different ethnic groups. I mean some of my friends, you know, they're cool with it. But other people are very biased. So they really didn't keep an open mind. So I guess those are the reasons why I wouldn't have liked it. But at the time, when I was going through it, I just ignored it. Just kind of thinking they're kind of naive or whatever.

A few respondents said they understood they were different and always would be. The realization was a deeply painful one, and marked by longing to be "like everyone else." Melinda Wu, for example, desperately longed to be white as a child, "to be like the Brady Bunch," as she described it, and knew quite clearly that she was not. This longing was wrapped up with the desire to have a mother like everyone else's, who dressed like other mothers and who knew the cultural lexicon of mainstream, middle-class America. This desire was particularly intense when she was living in Nevada and the South, where everyone seemed to be blond and blue-eyed. And yet, Melinda knew even at such a young age that this was impossible, given that her family's physical characteristics and cultural background were so different:

> And my first memories of elementary school were in Nevada, when I was Asian among these other white people. And I guess that was a typical thing. I just thought they looked prettier. I liked the blond hair and blue eyes. I liked Barbie. And, and their parents, I thought were cooler. Like, for example, their mothers sometimes would come in and help my class. They would know all the latest TV shows. My mother, on the other hand, wouldn't know anything, you know. And all the latest songs. And that was why I wanted to be white.

For Brenda Hsieh, the issue was not so much wanting to be white as not wanting to be Chinese. Even while she felt accepted by her white peers, Brenda did not want to feel in any way connected to being Chinese. She was never made fun of by her peers, but Brenda saw on television all the representations of Chinese as some sort of "Other," as busboys in restaurants, as hapless foreigners unable to speak English, as gang members that she wanted no part of in her life. Brenda's observations hearken to the negative portrayals of Asians in the media that are legion and often gendered and contradictory, from the subservient Chinese laundryman or manservant to the villainous Dr. Fu Manchu, from the subservient Lotus Blossom female to the evil Dragon Lady (Hamamoto 1994; Espiritu 1997). In the context of such images, some Asian American youth seek to reject anything associated with Asian-ness (Min and Kim 1999; Sue and Sue 1999). In Brenda's case, she resented having to do "Chinese things," like visiting Chinatown every few months to eat and shop for groceries.

> Like I remember as a child, I'd be like, oh, I hate being Chinese. It's so annoying. I have to do stuff, like, I have to go to Chinese school. I have

to do this and this. I was never really made fun of personally, but I mean, you see it on television, you see it. I know when I was much younger, I used to, I hated going to Chinatown, you know, it was dirty, it was smelly.

In their story of this journey to suburban, middle-class America, the respondents were very clear about who they wanted to be and to become, namely, part of the (white) mainstream. But this story could not be told without reference to another part of America, one that my respondents did not want to be part of, in actuality and in the perception of others, and that was the urban, ethnic enclave. Yet the urban enclave was always a point of reference for these suburban families. It was the mirror image of their lives, what life would have been like had their parents not gone on to higher education. No matter how settled they were in suburban America, with their airy houses and well-tended lawns, they were acquainted with the existence of the other Chinese in America. They knew about the lives of labor of those other Chinese, or as one mother put it, the "menial jobs" that could be found in Chinatown. A few parents had a more intimate knowledge of this other world, as they had worked briefly as waiters in Chinatown restaurants to support themselves in college and graduate school. Now, though, Chinatown was just a place to pick up groceries and have an occasional meal, and thankfully so. Their children knew they were different, too. As one young woman described her years growing up in a small town in coastal Maine, she observed: "We were not the poor immigrants. My dad was a doctor. Everyone knew him, everyone knew I was his daughter." It is to the urban, ethnic enclave that the next chapter turns.

Chapter 2

URBAN, ETHNIC-ENCLAVE AMERICA

Paul Chen had never been to China. China for Paul was the rattling of the sewing machine pedals in the garment factory where his mother worked, the pungent smells of whole fish sold fresh on vats of ice along Canal and Grand Streets, the fast-paced tones of Cantonese, and the sweetly fragrant incense in the Buddhist temples and funeral parlors whose scent stubbornly clung to one's clothing long after leaving. The China that Paul knew was in New York City.

This other version of China greeted Paul's parents when they arrived in the United States in 1971, having left the *real* Southern China via Hong Kong. In some ways, it was as if the couple had never crossed an ocean into a new world. In Chinatown, the Chinese language was everywhere and the Chens never had to learn English. Even if they had wanted to, the Chens did not have the time, because as they quickly discovered, the jobs that were everywhere in Chinatown, in the restaurants, the small shops, and the garment factories, all required grueling hours. They had three sons in quick succession, and to get by, the Chens had to work six, seven days a week, twelve hours a day, at the minimum, with few of the benefits that most Americans take for granted, like sick days, paid vacations, retirement funds, or health insurance.

Like the suburban parents in Chapter 1, the Chens also saw America as the promised land, especially for their children, but with only a grade school education, few skills, and virtually no English, they had to settle for life and work in Chinatown. And life in Chinatown turned out to be a series of compromises: the comfort and familiarity of immigrants like themselves, who provided valuable information about how to navigate their new country, versus the long hours and scarce benefits of manual labor; crumbling tenement housing and narrow, congested sidewalks. One could also see the trade-offs with the next generation, in whom many parents invested their hopes and expectations. Chinatown was full of academic preparatory schools for young children, to help them get an inside track to doing well in their regular classes; all one had to do was open up one of the local Chinese newspapers to see the dozens of advertisements for such schools (Zhou and Cai 2002). Education was the talk of the town at family gatherings, garment factories, and restaurants, where immigrant parents traded information about the best public schools and how to get access to them, and talked up their children as star achievers.

The other side of the story, however, was decidedly less optimistic and involved the children who did not do so well. The Chens, for example, could not afford to send their sons to the ethnic academic preparatory, or so-called cram schools. In fact, two of their sons, Paul's brothers, struggled through public school, spending their teenage years on the fringes of Chinese gangs. The Chens were lucky, though. They were able to intervene, sending the two boys to relatives in Hong Kong and Baltimore; one son managed to graduate from high school, the other received his GED, and both eventually made it to college. Other people's children were not so lucky, as they dropped out of high school or never went to college. These children turned to the underground criminal economy or ended up working in fish markets or warehouses, in immigrant jobs the Chens knew well but never expected the generation born and raised in America to have.

But the journey faced by the 1.5 and second generation was not an easy one. While the Chens were protected by the familiarity of language, customs, and norms they shared with other immigrants like themselves, their son Paul, for instance, was required not only to abide by the "cake of custom," as sociologist William Graham Sumner would have put it, but also to navigate the journey to mainstream America without a clear road map. Paul felt the tension in his everyday life. He was born in the United States and he quite obviously spoke English. Yet he also knew his cultural compass was calibrated to a particular ethnicity that set him apart in many aspects. He observed:

I grew up using chopsticks. People find out I use chopsticks, it's shocking to them. You use chopsticks? Really, you do? (laugh) I'm like, yeah, I do. Funny thing is, when I grew up, I thought everybody used chopsticks, and when I found out they didn't use chopsticks, I was like, word? You use forks? That how I saw it as.

Complete strangers would often feel entitled to let Paul know that he was different, and at first, he was at a loss as to how to respond. Over time, he developed his own coping strategies: "People actually come up to me, and ask me, do I speak English? I was like in English, 'No, I don't speak English.' (laugh) I walk away." And, over time, Paul came to recognize the peculiar markers of status in the world outside of Chinatown—the briefcase, the suit, the shiny new car, and the office job. The ticket to this world required at least a college degree; Paul came to understand that, too. Otherwise, Paul figured it would be back to the plumbing jobs that his father did after years of working the counter at various Chinatown stores.

Chinese Immigrants in New York City

New York City has historically been a key destination for Chinese immigrants, and never has this been more the case than today. New York City is the destination for about one in five Chinese immigrants entering the United States, and more than one in four arriving from mainland China (Zhou 2001). Today, Manhattan's Chinatown is the largest Chinese enclave in the United States (Ong and Umemoto 2000), and is joined by two other enclaves, Flushing in Queens and Sunset Park in Brooklyn, along with other neighborhoods that have large numbers of Chinese immigrants, such as Elmhurst/Corona in Queens, and Bensonhurst in Brooklyn (Wallin, Schill, and Daniels 2002). These five neighborhoods are or were home to about 62 percent of the students whose experiences I explore in this chapter. Their accounts speak to life as it is lived in such enclaves and in those residential neighborhoods with substantial numbers of Chinese immigrants.

The key to understanding the experiences of these families is Manhattan's Chinatown. As any New Yorker can tell you, every corner of Manhattan exhibits a distinct personality. The Upper East Side is certainly notable for its museum mile and diplomatic residences, and the West Village is known for its beatnik culture and sidewalk cafes, but few areas of Manhattan are as unique as Chinatown. What distinguishes Chinatown from other New York City immigrant enclaves dating back more than a hundred years is that the neighborhood has not given way to the pull of suburbia. Chinatown remains where it always has been, except it is larger and still expanding in the shadow of Manhattan's skyscrapers and outward into other boroughs. To understand why this has occurred, we need to look briefly at Chinatown's history, and at how it has been shaped by immigration policy and contexts of immigrant reception.

The Historical Roots of Chinatown and the Lower East Side

The Lower East Side of Manhattan has been home to Chinese immigrants for more than a century, since the 1870s, when it was the endpoint of an arduous journey for the early migrants who had left Guangdong Province in Southern China bound for the American West. In Guangdong, the inroads of European colonialism, coupled with a failing and corrupt Chinese monarchy, bitter local disputes, and natural disasters created the conditions for large-scale immigration. Men in the region were ready to leave behind the devastation wrought across the entire nation by the T'ai Ping Rebellion (1850–64), and, more locally, by overpopulation (the number of people in Toisan County, the key sending area, had quadrupled in the years from 1838 to 1920), interethnic hostilities, and an unrelenting succession of floods, typhoons, droughts, and famines (Hsu 2000, 25). News of the discovery of gold in California in 1848 set off the chain migration. Male laborers crossed the Pacific Ocean, heading for California with hopes of earning enough money to return to China and take care of their families. The success stories of the return migrants of the 1850s and 1860s did much to nourish the promise of these hopes and to maintain a steady stream of labor migration to the United States, which became known in Guangdong Province as Gum Shan, or Gold Mountain (Hsu 2000).

It is a matter of debate among scholars whether the early Chinese were welcomed in San Francisco, their first port of call, only later, as their numbers increased, to become targets of resentment (Nee and Nee 1973; Wong 1988), or whether anti-Chinese sentiments predated their arrival (Kwong 2001). Regardless of when such sentiments appeared, what is unequivocally known from the historical record is the depth of anti-Chinese hostility and its pernicious effects, for the migrants' hopes of earning a living in a country free from the unrest that was plaguing their native land were met with threats. In the labor sector, individual and collective attempts were made to drive the Chinese out of the mines. The Chinese nevertheless persisted in their efforts to find work, and by the time the gold mines had been exhausted in the late 1850s, they had moved into other sectors of the economy, most notably, construction of the transcontinental railroad. Hostility did not abate, however. Chinese railroad workers were caught, on the one hand, between railroad employers, who oftentimes hired them for dangerous jobs that whites were less willing to perform and who paid them lower wages, and on the other, white laborers, who viewed the Chinese as a cheap labor pool that depressed wages (Takaki 1989).

The Chinese fared little better in other economic sectors, where they met with violence, boycotts, and outright exclusion. Chinese workers found themselves steadily driven out of farming, shrimp and abalone fishing, and boot and cigar making, as well as woolen mills and factories; they were also barred from operating certain types of businesses, denied the right to testify in court against whites, and physically attacked where they lived (Hsu 2000; Kwong 2001). In their depictions of Chinese immigrants as a "subordinate race" and a yellow peril that could never assimilate, media reports from these years fed such hostilities (Nee and Nee 1973; Zhou 1992; Glenn and Yap 1994).

In response to escalating anti-Chinese sentiments, the U.S. Congress passed the first Chinese Exclusion Act (1882), which suspended the immigration of all Chinese laborers, skilled or unskilled, for ten years. The only exceptions were diplomatic officers, scholars, students, merchants, and short-term travelers. A decade later, in 1892, the Act was extended to further prohibit the entry of all Chinese laborers. The laws had the desired effect. In the 1880s the number of Chinese immigrants admitted to the United States fell to 61,711, down from 123,201 in the previous decade. The laws also prevented laborers already in America from bringing over their wives, thereby creating an entrenched Chinese bachelor community (Zhou 1992). Still, Chinese continued to come through legal and extralegal means.[1] Despite harsh conditions in the United States, the earnings from their labor that were sent back as remittances were enough to provide their families in China with a middle-class status, complete with land ownership and new homes (Hsu 2000, 30).

The origins of New York City's Chinatown, geographically far from the tensions in the West, can be traced to this confluence of hostility and marginalization, as Chinese immigrants sought refuge and less visibility. Between 1880 and 1920, the West Coast share of the nation's Chinese population plummeted from 83 percent to 55 percent. At the same time, the Chinese population rose in urban centers in the Midwest and along the East Coast. The Lower East Side of Manhattan, in particular, emerged as a thriving hub for the Chinese (Kwong 2001, 38). What had been an enclave of only 120 in 1870 had grown to 5,042 residents, still mostly male, by 1920. Hand laundries and restaurants catering to non-Chinese clients became the mainstays of the economy (Wong 1982).

It was not until 1943, with the repeal of the Chinese Exclusion Act, that this community began to see substantial change. Concerns over the United States's international image and the wartime alliance between the United States and China led to the repeal and opened up new channels of legal Chinese immigration (Wong 1988). These included many new kinds of immigrants: Chinese women who were the wives of both Chinese resident aliens and U.S. citizens, many of them veterans of the war; some five thousand "stranded scholars" who remained in the United States after the Communists won the civil war against the Nationalists in 1949; and Chinese refugees, who entered the country under relief acts that were issued during the 1950s and an executive order that was issued in the early 1960s. Only some of these trends directly affected Chinatown, notably the arrivals of war brides, whose presence restored some of the skewed gender imbalances and led to the rise of family life.

Still, there were fears that as the old-timers passed away and as opportunities to move into the mainstream economy were finally made accessible, along with the chance for families to move into more integrated neighborhoods, that Chinatown would decline (Sung 1987; Kwong 2001). Indeed, that fate befell many Chinatowns across the United States by the early 1960s (Alba and Nee 2003). But as we shall see, the Immigration Act of 1965 belied such predictions and gave rise to a diversity and expansion in New York City's Chinatown that few would have imagined possible.

Post-1965 Diversity and Expansion

Increased immigration after the 1960s and the influx of foreign Chinese capital transformed what had been an ethnically homogeneous immigrant residential enclave (Zhou 1992; Hing 1993). According to figures from the 2000
U.S. census, the Chinatown in the Lower East Side has a current population
of 66,053 residents, 60 percent of them foreign-born (Ong 2002). Having
long outgrown its original ten-city-block area, Chinatown has taken over
much of Little Italy to the north, and now extends on the Lower East Side
below Houston Street. Within this reconfigured geography, the dominant
ethnic origin can change from one block to another. Immigrants come from
Hong Kong, the People's Republic of China, Cuba, Burma, and Indochina
(Sung 1987; Wong 1988; Pan 1990). Thus, Kwong has noted that the "western rim of Canal Street" is home to a Vietnamese Chinese community; East
Broadway is dominated by the Fuzhounese; Chaozhounese are dispersed
throughout the community; and hawkers of sidewalk snacks and souvenirs
are typically from Wenzhou (Zhejiang Province) (2001, 160). Added to this
mix is a continuing stream of immigration from Guangdong Province, but
one that is no longer exclusively from Toisan. Evidence of this ethnic and geographic diversity can be found in the restaurants serving non-Cantonese
cuisine and, indeed, non-Chinese cuisine (Wong 1982). A popular grocery
store, a mainstay of Mulberry Street since I was an infant, now has an awning
that proudly reads, "Chinese Grocery Store," but the message is accompanied
on either side by the words "Vietnam," "Thailand," "the Philippines," and
"Malaysia," and for added visibility, by two additional signs depicting those
nations.

The economic transformation that has accompanied large-scale immigration and the influx of foreign capital has been profound. The previously
"small-scale ethnic subeconomy" has been recast as a diversified and expanded economy with more pronounced class distinctions (Kwong 1987;
Zhou 1992, 91, 94).[2] The twin engines fueling this growth have been the
restaurant and garment industries; it is estimated that in the early 1980s
twenty thousand people worked in the four hundred garment factories in
Chinatown (Kwong 2001, 159). Today, about 60 percent of the women in
New York City's Chinatown work in the garment industry (Zhou and
Nordquist 2000). In such a diversified context, it is less likely that the dis-

tinctions between laborers and small business owners will be blurred. Since the late 1960s, the Chinatown labor market has become increasingly segmented, with the major players being capitalist owners of large-scale businesses, including pricey real estate, a professional class of physicians, lawyers, and accountants, and small shopkeepers and manual workers (Chen 1992).

The expansion of Chinatown into the Lower East Side has been accompanied by the stunning rise of similar Chinese economic enclaves across borough boundaries, notably in Sunset Park, Brooklyn, and Flushing, with each enclave bordered by rings of residential neighborhoods with concentrations of Chinese. Zhou has noted that "between 1970 and 1980, Queens County's Chinese population more than tripled and Kings County's [Brooklyn] more than doubled" (1992, 84). Nor can the influence of the ethnic economies be measured exclusively by their geographical boundaries. Both the garment industry and, to an even greater extent, the restaurant business extend into different parts of the city and the suburbs, and even into other states. The enclaves, however, remain the anchor and hub of the labor force working in Chinese businesses, including those outside of New York City (Zhou and Logan 1991).

There are important ethnic, linguistic, and socioeconomic differences among these enclaves. Chinatown, for example, has attracted the greatest percentage of legally admitted immigrants from mainland China, and most of them have low levels of education and must work long hours at low wages to make ends meet (Wallin, Schill, and Daniels 2002). It is estimated that 65 percent of the working-age population in Chinatown either do not speak English or speak it poorly (Ong and Umemoto 2000), and that 70 percent of the adults have less than a high school education, as compared to only 25 percent in the nation as a whole. Moreover, while the employment rate in New York's Chinatown approximates the national average, the hourly wages paid are only 50 percent of those paid in the region (Ong 2002). The median household income of $22,000 in the Lower East Side and Chinatown is well below the $33,000 that was the median annual household income in New York City in 1999 (Wallin, Schill, and Daniels 2002). Poverty is another pressing issue (about 25 percent of Chinese are living in poverty, or about double the national average), as is housing (nearly 95 percent of the Chinatown population lives in rental housing) (Ong 2002).

Sunset Park, while also home to immigrants from mainland China, has a higher median annual income, of $25,000. Flushing, meanwhile, has drawn comparatively well-to-do immigrants from Taiwan (*New York Times*, 21 September 1999, B3). It is not surprising, then, that the median annual income in Flushing/Whitestone is $39,000, substantially higher than in Chinatown and Sunset Park (Wallin, Schill, and Daniels 2002). Flushing's poverty rate, which stood at 12.3 percent in 1999, is also notably lower than in the other two enclaves.

Additionally, the rate of homeownership is higher in both Sunset Park and Flushing, as Chinese immigrants with relatively low incomes have been able to purchase multifamily homes, collecting rent to make their mortgage payments (Zhou and Logan 1991). The residential neighborhoods of Elmhurst/Corona in Queens and Bensonhurst in Brooklyn have also attracted Chinese immigrant homebuyers in search of multifamily homes; compared to Chinatown, these neighborhoods are characterized as well by higher incomes, lower poverty rates, and racially and ethnically mixed populations, with significant proportions of whites and Hispanics, many of them post-1960s immigrants from Latin America, Russia, and Israel (Wallin, Schill, and Daniels 2002; Zeltzer-Zubida, forthcoming). Another attraction in all of these neighborhoods for Chinese immigrants is their relative proximity to Chinatown by subway, a commute that can take as little as thirty minutes from some points (Sung 1987; Zhou and Logan 1991).

The parents of my urban respondents were very much a part of this post-1965 social and economic milieu. Although mainland China was the homeland of close to 38 percent of the parents, others were from Japan, Malaysia, Hong Kong, Taiwan, and Burma. The key sending areas within the People's Republic of China were also diverse: in addition to Guangdong, they include capital cities like Beijing and Shanghai, and coastal cities like Fujian, Zejiang, and Shangdong. Still, most of the families spoke Cantonese in addition to their native dialects, mainly because Cantonese has been the traditional dialect spoken in Chinatown and in Hong Kong, which is often an intermediate point in their journey to the United States.

In New York City, 42 percent of the respondents lived in census tracts that could be described as very low and moderately low income.[3] These were predominately Asian American (with the next largest groups being African Americans and Hispanics), and 10–23 percent of the residents aged twenty-five or older had a bachelor's degree or higher (as compared to the average in

New York City, which was 27 percent). About 30 percent lived in census tracts that had median household incomes between 84 percent and 120 percent of the city's, and thus could be defined as middle income, and in these areas the proportion of college-educated adults was higher, ranging between 16 percent and 40 percent. However, the racial and ethnic makeup in these tracts still tended to be about at least a third minority, with most more than half minority, predominately Asian and Hispanic. Another 27 percent lived in census tracts that were greater than 120 percent of the city's median household income, and thus can be described as upper income. Once again, these census tracts tended to be either predominately Asian or Asian and Hispanic. More simply put, the enclave respondents, even those who lived in better-off neighborhoods, still lived in areas that did not approach the high income and educational levels of the suburban respondents, whose neighborhoods tended to be predominately white.

Enclave Lives

Immigrant Lives of Labor

A strong bond among many of these parents was their working relationship to the ethnic economic enclave, mainly in the restaurant and garment industries. It was in the workplace, in fact, that most of these parents spent their days. When asked to recall their years growing up, my respondents consistently spoke of the loneliness they felt because their parents were continually at work. Even when left in the care of relatives, these children were keenly aware of their parents' absence. Hank Chiang could not tell me exactly where his father worked, only that it was in New Jersey and that his father had to spend most of the week living there to perform his job as a chef in a Chinese restaurant. His mother stayed behind in New York City, but she was out of their apartment on the Lower East Side for 12–15 hours a day at her own job in the garment factory. Not surprisingly, Hank, who at the age of twenty-eight still lived with his parents, called to mind the emotional distance he felt from both of them:

It was lonely, I think I told you before. My father's away, I only see him twice a week and mostly the day that he's off, he just stays in bed and reads his newspapers. I don't bother him, you know, even now when he's at home. It's hard for me to talk to him, you know. We just really don't know what to say to each other.

A similar story was told by Susan Chu. During her adolescent years, Susan was either fighting with her father about high school and boys or not speaking to him at all; otherwise, she remembered him hardly ever being around. Susan's father worked as a chef at a Chinese restaurant in Upper Manhattan seven days a week, a schedule that meant he was asleep when Susan woke up for school and still was not home when she went to bed. One of Susan's strongest memories of her father was waking up in the middle of the night and spying him in the dimly lit kitchen as he intently carved strips of carrot into the intricate miniature flowers and dragons that would be taken to the restaurant to be used as decorative edibles.

Other children, like Jannelle Chao, saw more of their parents because they helped out at the family business. Jannelle's time after school and on the weekends was spent at her mother's delicatessen in Flushing, where she helped out with pouring coffee, taking the lotto slips, ringing up purchases at the register, and where she had unlimited access to chips and candy. It was fun work for Jannelle, who still regards the store as a second home, but tough work for her mother, who managed the business with only occasional hired help and whose days started long before sunrise and lasted till the store closed at 8 p.m. Yet despite spending lengthy stretches together, Jannelle and her mother rarely used the time to share thoughts of their interior lives. The intense labor that goes into running a small business of this kind did not allow the occasion and emotional space for much meaningful conversation (Song 1999).

Not that either of her parents was very willing to discuss the homeland or their adjustment to life in the United States. Jannelle did not push, because she understood her parents' lives had not turned out as they had hoped. The Chaos finally divorced, after years of arguments about why there was never enough money, who was working harder, and whose idea it had been to come to the United States in the first place. After the divorce, though they had wanted to live apart, the Chaos stayed together simply because they could not afford to sell their house. Divorce was certainly never in the couple's plan when they migrated to the United States; nor did they quite envision that Mr. Chao would go from being a member of the Taiwanese army to working as a car service driver, or that Mrs. Chao, a bank teller back in Taiwan, would be running the family store for fourteen years, which they still could not afford to sell. Explained Jannelle: "It's depressing to talk about these things. I'm sure they have tons of regrets about coming here. And you just don't want to open that. They don't really talk to me that much."

Most respondents told me that the internal map of the world that their parents brought with them remained very much their own. If a child wanted to learn the particulars of this map, he or she had to find it out for him/herself, sometimes through indirect means. Hank Chiang, for example, pieced together what he assumed to be the details of his father's journey to the United States from a chance conversation with his brother-in-law and from fragments of childhood memories. Apparently, the wife of a Chinatown community leader had helped Hank's father with getting settled in the United States. It did not seriously occur to Hank to consult his parents about whether this version was actually correct. Family history was not the stuff of parent–child conversations:

Okay, so I think he was caught and he was going to get deported until a wife of a (Chinatown) Tong leader heard about the story and helped my father. Okay, because there was this one old woman that, like, sometimes stayed with us, in fact, when I was still a kid. I never knew who she was and why my parents gave her so much respect. Because, you know, they would do everything for her when she would come. So it was like, I never ever knew, you know, so I found out if this was the girl. So, you know, basically if it wasn't for her, I wouldn't be here.

When parents did talk to their children, it was frequently to issue directives about what to do to succeed in the United States rather than to relate stories of life back in the homeland. Paul Chen, for example, often attempted to take the initiative in asking his parents about the family history, only to find that his efforts would be thwarted or would be met with minimal response. Instead, he would find the spotlight shifting from his parents back to himself.

Occasionally I ask. I initiate the conversation, but for the most part, it's about like, you go to school, don't go out that late. I ask, what's that word mean? What's that? A couple of months ago, I asked them, where exactly is Hoiping, where the village is exactly in China. It's right next to Toisan.

The few times Lily Gong's parents voluntarily called forth stories of the homeland, they did so in the most general of terms and as a way of reminding their children of the opportunities they have in the United States. According to Lily: "Sometimes they use it against us—we worked so hard and you guys don't do anything. We used to labor in the fields for eight hours under the hot sun. I guess they feel like we don't appreciate hard work, and we just take everything for granted."

Generational Disconnections

Due to the long absences of parents at work and their reluctance to speak of the homeland or share their thoughts about life in the United States, the children experienced a disconnection with their immigrant parents. The children felt a strong sense of obligation to their parents, which I will discuss further in Chapter 7, but at the same time, they felt very much removed from the world their parents came from and the world they inhabited in Chinatown. Their parents' homelands were quite literally distant places, since parents could rarely afford even low-season airline tickets, which can still cost several thousand dollars for an entire family, and just as important, they could not spare the week or two of unpaid leave from work that would be necessary for a family trip.

And while the children were well acquainted with the everyday world of their parents in Chinatown, they lacked an understanding of its deeper significance. Often, other immigrants from their parents' generation characterized the ignorance of my respondents as common to *jook sing*. This is a derogatory Cantonese term which, literally, means "the shallow end of the bamboo stick" and is used to describe American-born and/or -raised Chinese (cf. *jook kak*—"the knot of the bamboo stick," which refers to foreign-born and -raised Chinese). With a mix of amusement and frustration, Lois Wei vividly recalled the reaction of a family friend visiting from Hong Kong:

She kept on talking to me really slow in Chinese and like using like a lot of [British] English phrases that I have no clue what she was saying. But when I turned around and I said something in Chinese, I said, "Oh, I like this and this."

Even the Chinatown waiters came in for criticism. The children ate at the same restaurants as their parents, but, often, the initial assumption of waiters was that the 1.5 and second-generation children did not speak Chinese, and they would place a fork and not chopsticks in front of the young people. In fact, it was the case more often than not that the children were unable to read the Chinese-language menus well enough to order on their own, although they had memorized how to order their favorite dishes in Chinese, which, as Lois said, was key to getting "the food that other Chinese people get."

At home, the 1.5 and second generation followed their parents' rituals, so at special times of the year they lit incense to honor the Kitchen God or Guan Yin, the goddess of mercy, and bowed as their parents uttered barely comprehensible words of blessing. They participated in their parents' ancestor-worship rituals at the cemetery by laying out a boiled chicken, roast pork, and buns as offerings, as well as burning incense and paper money and paper clothing before spilling sweet rice wine over the grave.

But it was without much insight into the meanings of these elaborately scripted rituals that my urban enclave respondents performed them. Parents told the children what to do but provided no framework for why they were doing it. As Ling Choy observed: "We were never taught the meaning behind the holidays, so they lost meaning." In some cases, the disconnection between the holidays and rituals and their meanings reached the point that respondents thought of them solely in terms of food. Douglas Chan ventured this response: "Moon Festival? Is that the one with the cakes?" Only a few realized that such rituals were calibrated by the Chinese lunar calendar, and that the dates thus changed from year to year, making the processes that much more confusing to them.

The ethnic language schools were another marker of this generational disconnection. Chinese immigrants, anxious for their children to retain the Chinese language, sent them to these schools mainly to learn how to read and write Chinese, exactly the kinds of skills that parents could not easily teach their children at home. To their children, however, the schools were about being forced to spend weekdays and/or Saturday afternoons stuck in a classroom while other, non-Asian children were playing outside or watching cartoons. At the schools, they were forced to memorize endless lists of ideographic characters that made no sense and that they promptly forgot once they left the building. Instead of transmitting knowledge, the Chinese schools were all about discipline—teachers trying to manage unruly children throwing temper tantrums and the passive-aggressive children hiding in the back row, playing video games. Greg Zhang and his brother finally got to quit after literally staging a boycott and hanging up posters in their Chinatown apartment that said "No More Chinese School." By the time I spoke to the children, they were young adults, and many regretted the loss of the ethnic language (but they still thought of the schools as a waste of time).

1.5 and Second-Generation Chinese Identities: "Made in the USA"

Nonetheless, my urban-enclave respondents reported themselves as easy speakers of Chinese and strongly identified themselves as Chinese. The answer to this apparent paradox has to do with the world that the 1.5 and second generation made for themselves within Chinatown. In fact, their language fluency was not derived from everyday conversations with parents, as these tended to focus on whether the children had eaten, tended to their chores, or where they were headed. Rather, their fluency came from daily interactions with peers. Together with fellow 1.5 and second-generation Chinese, they developed a hybrid of Chinglish, complete with slang, that even their immigrant parents could not understand.

In a very real sense, then, the 1.5 and second generation inhabited a social space that was uniquely theirs, an American-made product though one that was situated in an ethnic economic enclave. As Portes and Rumbaut (2001b, 302) put it, second-generation identities, in general, "do not represent linear continuations of what their parents brought along. They are rather a 'made in the U.S.A' product born of these children's experiences of growing up American." My respondents' world in Chinatown was one of Chinese pop music and Chinese serialized soap operas on video and cable TV, all imported from Taiwan and Hong Kong, along with Chinese pop concerts held in Atlantic City, New Jersey. Their markers were the local CD stores, the pool halls, the Hello Kitty store, the Shisheido store, or the hot hair stylist with the latest hair dyes on Elizabeth Street. A popular video/music store at the corner of Elizabeth and Bayard Streets exemplifies these generationally bounded social spaces within Chinatown. In low-slung jeans and form-fitting T-shirts, the youth milled about the tight confines of the store, rifling through the CDs and speaking to one another in English, while the old-timers, graying men in their sixties garbed in polyester pants, strolled down the aisles alone, silently clutching Chinese opera CDs. The youth gravitated to CDs and videos recorded by either pop stars that were mainly known in Asia, like Steven Chow, Aaron Kwok, Nicholas Tse, and Leslie Cheung, or by stars who have crossed over to the United States, like Jet Li, the late Bruce Lee, Jackie Chan, and Michelle Yeoh.

Consequently, despite their lack of Chinese literacy and insight into the rituals they performed with and for their parents, my respondents still grew up realizing they were Chinese. When asked whether she considered herself a member of an ethnic group growing up, one woman replied: "Yes, definitely. Because I was in Chinatown. I lived in Chinatown. Everybody was Chinese." Those respondents who grew up outside of Chinatown remembered being taken by their parents into the enclave to attend Chinese school while their parents went grocery shopping, ran errands, or caught up with friends and relatives. Now that they were young adults, these respondents voluntarily traveled to Chinatown for their own "ethnic fix."[4] It is important to note that this "ethnic fix" did not have much to do with the cultural practices that their parents raised them with—for example, visiting the cemetery and honoring the dead, attending Buddhist temples, and lighting incense at home. As I have noted, the meanings behind those rituals were increasingly becoming lost, making it difficult for respondents to incorporate them into their personal lives.

Nor were their identities necessarily the same as those of Chinese immigrants who had come to the United States as adolescents. Even though these immigrants could be considered their peers, there were still important cultural gaps with respect to childhood and adolescent socialization. In other words, having been born in the enclave in the United States, the lexicon and norms of their youth culture did not have much in common with the youth culture known to first-generation immigrants of their age group. Grace Li thoughtfully remarked on such differences:

Like I work with another girl, she was not born here, when we were talking about things, she would mention Cantonese terms, she would mention phrases and sayings, and I would be like, What are you talking about? Things like, let's say, relationships, we don't ever talk about relationships, we don't talk about love. It feels like there is a stop where you can't ask her to talk about stuff. They won't go there.

Winston Woo was the only American-born member of a Chinese-Christian fellowship group at Hunter College comprised almost exclusively of Chinese immigrants who had arrived in their teenage years. In addition to the spiritual bond, Winston turned to the group's everyday cultural practices as a learning tool into traditional Chinese practices. As these were adopted by the younger generation, they were very different from what he knew. According to Winston:

The food they eat, it's not McDonald's or Burger King. It's stuff that they bring from their homes and eat, and some of the stuff is very curious. Like one of my friends would buy candy or potato chips, or something, and she would say, real food, real food for Winston. And I was like, yeah, real food. . . . I learned how to do certain things, like a Chinese banquet, I didn't know you had to give money. I thought it was optional. But they're, like, it would be good if you just gave enough money. I was about to put in forty bucks. But they were like, no, no, four is an unlucky number.

And just as the urban enclave served as a frame of reference for my suburban respondents, so did the suburban Chinese serve as a foil for their counterparts in the enclave. For example, Paul Chen's detailed descriptions of Chinatown evoke feelings of isolation and alienation, or what he called the "ghetto mentality":

I was born and raised in Chinatown, which is like a totally different culture. I mean, there are certain ways of doing things in Chinatown, you know. You expect certain things in Chinatown, and when you go outside, it's not the same, it's totally different. Like if you want to hire someone for a job, or for plumbing work, or something, it don't matter whether you have a license or not, truly, for Chinese people. But when you go outside to another community, sometimes they ask for it, they expect you to have a license. It's totally different. Another example, all the money that's made in Chinatown tends to stay in Chinatown with Chinese people. It's like that. We spend on our own, we buy our own people's food. I mostly buy outside clothing. That's about it. But everything is so tight-knit, it's closed.

Paul explained that the community's "closed" character would have important implications for the ability of the second generation to leave the community to join the wider world, where he felt they would be marked and possibly stigmatized. Asian Americans who grew up outside Chinatown would not face such struggles. He observed:

> It really handicaps you when you get outside. That's the way I see it. In terms of getting a job, or meeting outside people. It's handicapping, holds you back. I know I won't starve because I could get a job doing some stupid plumbing work (laugh). I could do that, but if you compare me to a person, another Asian, who wasn't raised in Chinatown or born in Chinatown, it's different. They have another outlook. And I guess that makes them more competitive than I would be, than it would make me. They're more tolerant, more willing to accept, and to try new things. The people in Chinatown, that's all they know.

And the fear was that they themselves might not make it out. Greg Zhang had this to say about the *jook sing* who stayed in Chinatown:

> I don't want to be like that. I just want to go out. Maybe not even live in New York, like go to another state and another country or something. They don't seem very successful, the *jook sing* who stay in Chinatown. Maybe that's why they stay in Chinatown, they're like losers or something. I don't know too much about them. But maybe I see a couple working in a toy store, a family business or something.

The urban-ethnic enclave shaped my respondents' awareness of who they were, namely, the generation raised and/or born in the United States. At the same time, the enclave reminded them of the very real gulf that divided them from mainstream America, and the challenges they faced in becoming enough a part of that other America to get the professional jobs that would be their ticket out of Chinatown. Higher education, of course, was the key. In the next section, we explore how not only the children of the urban enclaves but their counterparts from suburbia actually made sense of education.

PART TWO

How Children Make Sense of Education: A Family Matter

Chapter 3

ETHNIC CULTURE, IMMIGRATION,
AND RACE IN AMERICA

During the late 1980s, Garry Trudeau, the creator of the popular comic strip *Doonesbury*, introduced a character named Kim, a young Vietnamese refugee girl growing up in the United States. Kim quickly emerges as a prodigy, earning stellar grades and a National Merit Scholarship, along with several other students of Asian descent. Kim's achievements make her a figure worthy of admiration and a lightning rod for controversy. Some of her white classmates and their parents claimed that Asians were unfairly breaking the academic curve and taking up slots at colleges. The alternative view was expressed by her black principal, who applauded Kim for setting an example that discipline and personal motivation are all one really needs to do well in school. At one point, a classmate says outright that Kim's success must be related to her growing up in an Asian family. Kim responds that she is in fact adopted and that her parents are Jewish, to which the classmate answers, "Jewish? Yo! Say no more!" Kim replies, "I wasn't planning to" and returns to reading her book (Trudeau 1989, 80–81).[1]

Trudeau brilliantly captures the dominant explanation in popular and academic circles for understanding Asian American educational motivation, aspirations, and achievement—namely, that ethnic cultures are mediated by the family. He never mentions the term "model minority," but Trudeau's gift is that he does not have to, since it is understood that Kim and the other Asian students are the model for others to uphold, much as Jews, another ethnic group historically and popularly associated with academic success in the United States, were the model before them.

This explanation carried great weight with my student respondents, despite their awareness of the rich variability in the Chinese American population. My respondents believed that the Chinese and, indeed, Asians in general, while inhabiting different worlds in the United States, shared at least one thing—the ethnic cultures they drew upon within their families to value education and to do well in school. As I will discuss in Chapters 5 and 6, this is not the same as saying that my respondents endorsed the model-minority stereotype. Their takes on the model minority were much more varied and complex. However, my respondents did subscribe to the cultural script, with culture defined here as shared norms and values (Erikson 1976), or, to borrow from LeVine, as "the framework of ideas from which they view and act upon the world" (1984, 72). This script is a key component of the model-minority stereotype and in considerably more nuanced fashion serves as a crucial perspective in the field of education, in particular, for how to understand educational differences along the lines of race, ethnicity, and immigrant status. We can see this shared script at work in the two accounts below.

It's All about Family

Jeffrey Yao, stocky and muscular, has the look of someone who lifts weights. Back in high school, weightlifting helped him navigate the "bad" elements in his neighborhood of Sunset Park. The fact that he had grown up in Sunset Park and had thus gained the acceptance of his black and Hispanic neighbors also helped. The Chinese moving into the neighborhood in recent years had not been so lucky, as he wryly noted in this exchange:

A: Chinese people constantly running home at night. I just look at them, they are constantly running home at night.

I: Running where?

A: To their house. (laughs) Running home to their house at night-time. Summer time, they are always running. Wow.

I: Oh, because they are afraid?

A: Yeah. Because they get beat up so many times so they get afraid. I grew up in that place, so they all know me. Oh, constantly running home.

It was still a source of amazement to Jeffrey, a third-year student at Hunter, that he had been able to survive Sunset Park and then Fort Hamilton High, which he characterized as a tough, inner-city school, when many of his Hispanic neighbors had not. Jeffrey's theory was that Asian students like himself valued school in a way that other groups did not. He observed: "For Asians, school first. They can't go out before school, whatever. Can't cut school. Can't ditch school. I know because I used to have a lot of Hispanic friends, never come to class, you know, do really bad in school and stuff."

When I asked him to elaborate, Jeffrey brought up the idea that Asian parents are more exacting of their children than American parents, a category which he understood to include non-Asians. In other words, the emphasis on school came from the family.

> A: Our family background, the way the family taught them how to be, how to grow up. They're more strict on the children than the American parents are. American parents, they're more lenient, they give them ways, go out. Where Asians, you have to do good in school, no matter what. (laughs)
>
> I: Why do you think that is?
>
> A: Huh? I don't know. Because parents all tough on me and my sister. Basically that. I don't know about the other families, but I know my parents has been tough on me. My American friends, their parents not really, just like, (You) want to do something? Go ahead.
>
> I: Did your friends go on to college?
>
> A: Uh, some of them. The rest were in jail, died, something like that. (laughs) That's my neighborhood. It's a bad neighborhood.

Later in the interview, I asked Jeffrey why he thought his Hispanic friends were not interested in school. Again, he cited the role of the family, in this instance, the negative influence of his friends' parents.

> Just the way they grew up around the surroundings, the way people acted. And the way their parents raised them. Their parents were too, you know, bummed out from alcohol and drugs so they didn't care about school, started working. Yeah, that's about it.

Jeffrey articulated the idea that his parents were crucial to why he was able to make it to a four-year college, while most of his Hispanic friends dropped out of high school. According to Jeffrey, however, the reasons did not have much to do with the educational level of his parents, or the kinds of jobs they held—factors, along with income, that are thought to influence educational attainment. The Yaos, in fact, completed only high school in Vietnam, and in the United States they worked at unskilled and low-wage jobs, his father as a supermarket manager and his mother as a cashier. Rather, Jeffrey's explanation had to do with the rules his parents imposed on him and his siblings: about going out, cutting school, and the very importance of school itself.

Brenda Hsieh's childhood and adolescence occurred in a setting that was worlds apart from Jeffrey's. Brenda grew up in Lincroft and Warren, comfortable New Jersey suburbs, where people, indeed, did run in the streets, but their running was part of their physical exercise regimens, not a strategy to escape street crime. Here, going to college was the norm for children. College was familiar to Brenda's parents, although they had experienced it in a different national context. Her father had graduated from Taiwan's premier National Taiwan University (Taida) before coming to the United States to get a Ph.D. in electrical engineering, and her mother held a bachelor's degree earned in Taiwan. Brenda herself was a freshman at Columbia. Yet, much like Jeffrey, when it came to education, Brenda pointed to the Asian family.

> A: And then there is all the well-known Asian parent stereotypes, which are all true. (laughs)
> I: And what are those?
> A: You know, work, work, work. School is everything. Don't go out on the weekends.

The striking parallel here is that two students from such different worlds talk about Asian Americans, education, and family in the same ways. These two students have never met, and probably will never meet, despite the fact that both grew up in the New York City/New Jersey region and that both attend colleges within a four-mile radius. Yet there is a high level of consensus between them in the vocabulary they use to describe the role of the Asian family and the taken-for-granted approach they have on the subject, as if it is something that they know well and that I, as the interviewer (and fellow Chinese American) must also know. This comfort level extended well beyond our dynamic in the interview, as they understood themselves to be tapping into a wider, shared cultural understanding, or what one might call, the common sense about Asian American families. As Brenda observed, such understandings are "well-known." Both she and Jeffrey typified them as stereotypes, but stereotypes that had a degree of empirical truth to them. It was not surprising, then, that neither Brenda nor Jeffrey spoke of this dynamic as being isolated to only their families or even to the bounded spheres of their kin and social networks; rather, they immediately framed it as something much broader, as something common to Asian families (Kao 2000).

The theme of the Asian family as the reason why Asian children surpassed their peers educationally came up in all my interviews. It is important, however, to understand how my respondents used the term "Asian American." My respondents were all well aware of the Asian American label, which as Espiritu (1992) and Kibria (2002), among others, have richly documented, results from American processes that racialize ethnicity. This was construed positively by some of my respondents, who thought it gave them access to another cultural identity besides the ethnic one. For others, the term transcends ethnic boundaries and signals a commitment to social-justice issues pertaining to the civil rights movement from which it first emerged, notably, to a definition of Asian Americans as a racialized minority that shares interests with other minority groups. Yet this process of identifying as Asian American does not come without active contestation, as my respondents realize that being Chinese can very well be different from being Asian, that the very term "Asian American" means many different things to many different people, and that there might always be a struggle to embrace the various constituencies who claim the label (Kibria 2002).

At schools like Hunter and Columbia, where Asian American students make up about 17 percent of the student body and where multiculturalism is a part of the institutional culture—from Asian American Studies programs to ethnic student clubs—the term had everyday resonance for my respondents. Even if they did not take a single class in ethnic studies or participate in the clubs, they nevertheless had to confront the Asian American concept and situate themselves in relation to it (Kibria 2002; Louie 2003). The issues of belonging that they grappled with in school are common to identity politics across race and ethnicity, not to mention gender and sexual orientation, among others. In other words, a key part of their college experience was the expectation that they should develop some kind of stand on what the Asian American concept meant to them. A few of the respondents even anticipated that I would ask them about their participation in ethnic clubs and their views on being Asian and/or Chinese American.

Yet, regardless of how they defined being Asian and Chinese American, my respondents believed that one could legitimately speak of an Asian American familial ethos of education, one that the Chinese American experience was firmly a part of. This was one of the few places where students felt very comfortable using the terms "Chinese" and "Asian American" interchangeably. In this, they deployed what Kibria has called ethnic pan-Asianism, an identity that emphasizes a shared "Asian culture, marked by certain orientations and values, such as an emphasis on education, family and work" (2002, 121). The way my respondents voiced this idea highlighted how given and undeniable it was to them, to borrow Clifford Geertz's apt phrase. Geertz tells us that in its historically constructed nature, common sense serves as a cultural system "capable of being empirically uncovered and conceptually formulated" (1975, 25). In the rest of this chapter, I parse out the presuppositions that my respondents' constructed framework was based on, or, in other words, *how* it became common sense. First, though, we need to understand what exactly about Asian American families and education was so normal and natural to them.

Asian Parents Push Hard

When asked to describe her father's expectations for her education, Elizabeth Wong simply said: "I was telling you before: college, college, college." Most of my respondents similarly describe their parents as having high educational aspirations for them, with the bachelor's degree as the minimum requirement, a finding that corresponds to national survey results.[2] Additionally, children are expected to go to not just any college, but to aim for the elite schools. It follows that schools like Harvard, Yale, and Columbia are commonly discussed within families. This was a unifying theme that cut across neighborhood, family background, and gender lines.

As a way of making sure children stayed focused on school, most parents were described as imposing strict rules on children's attendance rates, dating, and going out, especially daughters'. Or, to borrow another phrase that commonly came up in interviews, Asian parents simply "pushed their children." In short, Asian parents were seen as ever vigilant against potential distractions to school for their children, and against potential challenges to their authority.

Susan Chu brought up the subject when I asked her about high school. Susan had started at Edward R. Murrow High in Brooklyn, which was close to the family's Bensonhurst home, and she had finished at Hicksville High School in Long Island. Susan told me that until high school she had followed the routine that her parents had laid out for her: school every day, coming right home afterward, Chinese school on Saturdays, and housecleaning on Sundays. Once she started high school, however, Susan had her own thoughts of how to spend her time, and they included hanging out with some fellow-Chinese American classmates, mainly boys, grabbing a snack after school, playing handball, talking on the phone. She saw these habits as normal, adolescent rituals. Her parents, she said, "freaked out." There were fights, as Susan's parents took to eavesdropping on her phone conversations and spying on her and her male friends as they approached the house.

This drama continued until the day Susan's parents announced that the entire family was packing up and moving to Hicksville, Long Island, a predominately white neighborhood. Their new house had been purchased courtesy of loans from friends and family. For the next two years, Susan refused to sit at the same table with her father. Five years after the move, Susan was still angry:

> They *claimed*, that I was not doing good, well, in school; they claimed I was hanging out with gangsters, cutting class. I loved it there [at Murrow]. Yeah, I mean, of course, every school has their gangs and bullies. But that's high school. How are you going to take that away from somebody? That's just not right.

What made Susan feel a bit better was her awareness that her Chinese American friends, even those in their early twenties, were having to deal with similar parental conflicts. Or, as she put it, they "were also pushed by their parents."

> A: Yeah, they were definitely. They were like, I can't do this. I have a friend, she's older than me, she can't go anywhere, and she's still hiding her boyfriend from her mother. She can't hang out late, you know, stuff like that, till twelve, one.

> Q: Why is she hiding her boyfriend?
>
> A: Her mom would flip out, probably. Because they think that her boyfriend interferes with schoolwork.

Parents living in urban enclaves or, like the Chus, in neighborhoods with substantial Chinese immigrant populations, were especially watchful of challenges to their authority from negative peer influences, notably the temptations of gangs. The parents were not trying to ward off the temptations of black and Hispanic gangs, which are widely perceived to be the source of juvenile delinquency in our nation's cities. Rather, they sought to protect their children from Chinese or pan-ethnic Asian (mainly Chinese, Vietnamese, and Korean) gangs. Moving out of the neighborhood, as Susan Chu's parents did, is one strategy. Another is sending the child out of the neighborhood, especially useful if the parents themselves cannot move for reasons having to do with employment or finances.

One such example is Robert Ong's account of his six-month "exile" to the tiny town of Redford, Michigan. Robert's parents sent him to live with some Michigan relatives in the hopes that he would straighten out. Robert, then an adolescent, had started dating at the age of thirteen and had been hanging out with the kinds of Chinese kids in Bensonhurst, Brooklyn, who regularly cut classes—in short, the kinds of kids his parents feared would someday turn to crime because they had used up all their educational opportunities. Robert recounted his unhappy experience in Michigan, made worse by the fact that students and teachers there proved to be closed minded, especially around matters of race and ethnicity, and that he had been quickly labeled as a troublemaker.

> A: And I was the only Chinese kid in the school. The school had three black kids, one Asian kid, me, everyone else was white. You know, chink, duh, duh, sometimes the teacher would say something, and I was like okay. Me being a New Yorker, cursed them out. They flipped out, can't say the word "fuck," but all the cheerleaders were pregnant. So it was like, that was cute, that was cute.
>
> I: So what would your teachers say?
>
> A: My social studies teacher once told me, like, "Oh, I heard you Asians are really smart." Uh, we're smart except for those Jewish kids,

who are like, smarter. It was like, okay. Mind you, this was a social studies teacher.

After only one semester, Robert was shipped right back to New York City. But the experiment worked because upon his return Robert quickly set about improving his grades. In his mind, poor academic performance had become equated with being sent away from New York City, a prospect he certainly did not want to confront again.

While parents living in suburbia did not face the same fears that their children would lapse into delinquency, they nevertheless pushed their children to keep their minds focused on school. Judy Lai's account captures the essence of this intense parenting, as she spoke of the goals of her childhood and teenage years:

> Work, school, grades, doing well. [My mother] was very rigid in terms of my schoolwork when I was younger. When I had tests or exams, she always expected 100s. And if I did badly, I would definitely get punished.

Judy learned to fear the "scolding, or hitting with chopsticks," and, sometimes, the corporal punishment, like slapping, when she did not meet her mother's standards. It is not surprising, then, that she remembers her childhood as being shrouded in anxiety, contrasting it to the "carefree" childhoods of "non-Asian kids," who did not face the same kinds of pressures.

The ever-present possibility of failure was Joseph Pang's dominant memory of childhood:

> I remember when I was young, my mom would tell me, "Oh, you know, you have to study hard, you know, be successful in life, so that you can drive around in nice cars." That's when I was five, she would tell me that. And I would think about it. Sometimes at night I would kind of cry, thinking, "Oh, what happens if I don't make anything of myself? I'll be a bum living on the streets."

An-Huei Hum remembered her parents as being very different from the white parents in her Long Island neighborhood. Things that other children took for granted, like sleepovers, were matters of contention in the Hum household:

> Well, they are really strict about who I like, hung out. Like in elementary school, I would never be allowed to go to someone's house first.

They would have to come to my home first so that my parents could see what they were like. And like, for the longest time, I wasn't allowed to sleep over at someone's house. God forbid, like, I get corrupted there. (laughs) But that was when I was young. As I got older, they just really had like, academic expectations.

Still, my respondents generally spoke positively of the net effect of Asian parenting, despite the pressures, because they believed the push by parents stimulated them to do well in school. Children who were raised in the suburbs believing they were like everyone else, and children who were brought up in urban neighborhoods believing they were somehow marginalized, all came to the same conclusion: growing up in an Asian family provided them with an educational advantage that other children did not have. As Melinda Wu explained to me, it was the power of expectation in Asian families, as opposed to hope, that mattered:

I really believe that. Instead of saying, "I hope you go to a good school," Asian parents are, "You *are* going to go to a good school or else." And even though it may not feel very good emotionally, actually I think it kind of works. It actually makes you kind of do it because it's more expected.

Melinda went on to talk at length about the motivational force offered by her mother, a computer programmer and a graduate of National Taiwan University. She told me her mother filled the void left by peers who were not especially interested in school and teachers who were not especially interested in teaching:

Generally speaking, the standards between my mother's expectations and other Asian parents' expectations is much higher than those of many Caucasian friends I have or Hispanic friends or non-Asian friends. For example, I went home and I got a 99 on a test, and my mother's reaction is like, "Why not 100?" And other parents are like, "Oh good, 99." Without them, I don't think I would have had the drive myself, because in elementary school, especially, my friends were not doing so well. But generally speaking, the environment wasn't toward school.

At the time, though, Melinda sometimes balked at the "pressure" coming from her parents. Looking back, she could see the logic in their actions. As she said:

To me there's a very close tie between Asians and education. I'm un-happy that my mother puts so much pressure on us for school because it made me miserable, but looking in hindsight, though, it was for a very good cause.

The Ethic of Hard Work

Another key piece of the familial ethos described by my respondents is the ethic of hard work. Children were indeed expected to earn perfect grades, as Melinda said, but the key was not thought to be natural intelligence or abil-ity. Rather, hard work was the key to achievement, and Asians were thought to work a bit harder than everyone else. Some were a bit apologetic about it, as Ling Choy was when she shared this family perspective: "Well, I mean, they say stuff like, have you ever seen a homeless Chinese person? There's a reason why. Because we work hard. It was more like jokingly."

Others subscribed to this idea without apology. Jeffrey Yao, for example, discounted the stereotype that all Asian Americans were achievers in math, a key plank in the model-minority image; at the same time, he upheld the be-lief that Asians did better in the subject because they worked harder than other people. It was this learning style, not a natural affinity for the subject, which actually made the difference. He observed: "We do good in math probably because we study more than they do. That's why. You know."

Melinda Wu again had much to say on this subject, describing the so-called work ethic as an ethnic advantage:

I felt like I had an advantage because I was Chinese because I felt that I was coming from a better work ethic. And I know I sound so conde-scending. I'm like, "Nobody else worked." It's not my fault. I just feel like I know the values that my mother has instilled in me and the values I see other Asian parents have instilled.

According to my respondents, while college students of other racial and ethnic groups had more freedom to indulge in the "drug scene," or at the very least, to slack off, there were no such luxuries for Asian Americans. Paul Chen argued that Asians were more willing to make the sacrifices necessary to completing their studies:

I'd say [Asians have a] work ethic. . . . I have seen so many people. I

mean, Asian people are lazy, too, sometimes. . . . . I have to admit, everyone has their lazy people. But I see so much other races, Hispanics,
blacks, whites, they're lazy. I mean, someone who says like, "Oh man, I
got this due, and this and that to do. I can't study for this . . . when I get
home, I got to sleep, I'm tired," this and that. I've been tired before. I do
get tired, too, but I still force myself to study. It's something that's required. You want to graduate, you want to pass, it's what you do. Other
people just don't do it. It's terrible, actually.

Conceptions of Learning: Hearkening Back to Homeland Cultures

In their views of education as embedded in the family nexus and learning as
derived from effort, my respondents hearken back to the cultural norms of
their parental homelands. Both concepts can be traced to Confucian ideals.
For instance, not only in traditional Chinese society but in a number of East
Asian societies with strong Confucian imprints, the individual self is seen as
being rooted within the collective (Hsu 1971). The family ideal type is thus
multigenerational, in which ancestors are ever present and "the individual
alive is the manifestation of his whole Continuum of Descent" (Baker 1979,
27). When it comes to achievement, then, the accomplishments of the individual are strongly grounded in familial obligation and prestige (Gardner
1989). In short, in such a system, family and education are interwoven phenomena, as Whyte writes:

> Chinese family life created strong family bonds and a sense of security as
> well as indebtedness; such sentiments could be a powerful force in moti-
> vating individuals to work hard, study diligently and take risks—all for
> the welfare of the family. (1971, 298–99)

The link between effort and academic achievement also dates to the days
of the Chinese Empire (Siu 1992a; Cheng 1998). Until it was formally abol-
ished in 1905, the Chinese imperial examination system channeled scholars
into plum civil service positions that brought material rewards and prestige
to themselves and their families. Aspirants spent years sequestered in exclusive preparatory schools studying the Four Books and Five Classics that made
up the core of the examinations, a time-consuming process that relatively few

families could afford for their sons (only men were allowed to sit for the exams) (Weinberg 1997; Cheng 1998). The irony was that even as these select few pored over the nation's literary canon, much of the rest of the population remained illiterate. Indeed, some scholars estimate that at any one time at least 80 percent of the population could not read or write (Siu 1992a).

Despite these inequities, the examination system was nevertheless imagined to be a meritocracy, in which success was derived from achievement, not ascription. Cheng, for instance, notes that "the uniformity and simplicity in the desired mode of study was a sign of 'fair competition.' It was applicable to all individuals regardless of their background and abilities. It was a means of increasing the likelihood that effort and hard work would be rewarded in the learning game" (1998, 17). Such ideals, stressing success from effort (as opposed to natural ability) and respect for teachers, so crucial to the learning process, were key to Confucian ideology. They found expression in the observances of Teacher's Day (a tradition that continues today in some Chinese communities) and in Chinese folklore tales about "poor children who made it because they studied hard, and sayings such as, 'A gold mansion and a beautiful girl await you in your books,' and 'Compared to scholarly pursuits everything else is lowly'" (Siu 1992a, 8). These sayings reflect the social logic with which people went about their lives, even as social forces made their chances for upward mobility through education extremely unlikely. This educational ethos extended even to the peasants, the group least likely to benefit from the examination system (Rawski 1979).

Although the imperial exam is long obsolete, the examination system as a stratifying mechanism in education lives on in contemporary China, Taiwan, and Hong Kong, among other East Asian nations where education is still regarded as the principal route to upward mobility (Cheng 1998). There is evidence that Confucian norms continue to exist as well (Brinton 2001). Among the most well-known accounts in support of this claim is Stevenson and Stigler's (1992) comparison of failing American schools with the Japanese and Chinese systems of education. While Stevenson and Stigler's analysis focuses on the counterpoint between American models of learning that privilege natural ability and East Asian models that stress hard work, Cheng (1998) astutely points out that their argument actually underscores differences in the "cultural norms, values and assumptions of the particular societies." For instance, there continues to be an extensive repertoire among the

college-educated in mainland China for thinking about, expressing, and referring to learning along with a view of learning as "enduring hardship" (Li
2001, 130; Li 2003).

A central thread of the several interviews that I conducted with middle-
class, suburban parents was their homeland cultures and how these had instilled a preoccupation with "good schools" combined with a respect for
learning, discipline, and teachers. Thus, while their children spoke interchangeably of a Chinese and Asian American phenomenon with regard to
education, these parents spoke of it in solely Chinese terms. Although the
parents I spoke with came from different parts of East Asia, they described a
similar world in which schools taught by rote memorization, teachers could
physically discipline their students for giving a wrong answer or speaking out
of turn, students had tightly structured daily schedules that included hours of
homework, and everyone knew which were the "good" schools and the
"bad" schools. So when I asked Mrs. Wu how she had learned about
Stuyvesant High School, the top New York City public high school attended
by her daughter, she was puzzled. To her, the answer was so straightforward
that the question seemed unnecessary. Mrs. Wu had heard of Stuyvesant before ever coming to the United States; as she explained, the school's reputation was common knowledge in her native Taiwan:

> Stuyvesant very famous in Chinese society because we have a writer, his
> son is from Stuyvesant. So he wrote a book about his son, and then the
> cultural difference between father generation and son generation. So that
> school is very famous in Taiwan. And that school is very famous, I think
> all the Chinese parents know this school. Get a copy [of the book] in
> Taiwan.

It was understood on the part of my respondents that such cultural norms
had been brought by their immigrant parents from Asia. What was less clear
to them was how these norms had actually manifested themselves in Asia. As
1.5 and second-generation immigrants, my respondents' frame of reference
necessarily rested within the United States. This emphasis on an American
frame brings home the ways in which cultures, ever fluid, are transformed by
migration. The world of the immigrant family, as my respondents described
it, was, to borrow from Nancy Foner's insights, one "where there is a dynamic
interplay between structure, culture and agency—where creative culture-

building takes place in the context of external social and economic forces as well as immigrants' premigration cultural frameworks" (1999, 257).

That my respondents understood the cultural norms of learning transmitted through Asian immigrant families to be an ethnic American phenomenon thus speaks to this rich interplay of structure, culture, and agency, or what I call cultures-in-transition. Immigrant parents, while transmitting these norms, did not instruct children on their historical and cultural underpinnings, except to say, as we shall see, that the examination system served as a stratifying mechanism in many homelands. Parents did tell their children, however, about what it was like to be Chinese in America, and that higher education was central to that identity. In our interviews, my respondents spoke explicitly and quite eloquently of the American social and economic forces, or structural contexts, that made education so important to their immigrant parents, and such a central touchstone in how they were raised. As we shall see, the parental discussions of the American opportunity structure and all its many rewards and roadblocks, particularly along the lines of race and ethnicity, loomed large in the consciousness of my respondents and helped them explain why education was so important to their parents, in particular, and to Asian ethnics in general.

Why Education Is Important: The American Context

Access and Payoff to Education

According to my student respondents, their parents stressed higher education because it was so accessible to their children, at least in the United States. Many of the immigrant parents came from Hong Kong, China, and Taiwan, which, as I have mentioned, all maintain rigorous examination systems that govern access to the universities.[3] In Taiwan, for example, there is a nearly universal transition from elementary school to a local junior high school, assigned on the basis of where one lives. However, the transition from junior high school to senior high school is more stratified, as students must take competitive examinations that channel them into schools varying in prestige and curriculum. The stratification at the top of the educational hierarchy (we might think of it as a pyramid), namely, at the university level, is even greater. To complete this transition, students must take the national entrance examination, lasting several days, the results of which determine their placement into particular schools and departments within them. It has been found that the father's educational attainment plays a central role in the student's transition from one level to another across all levels in this system (Tsai, Gates, and Chiu 1994).

By comparison, the American system of education is a remarkably open one, with public universities offering opportunities for an excellent and affordable education. It is important to remember that these Asian parents raised their children in the post–civil rights period, a historically transforming moment that lifted the educational restrictions that had been imposed on earlier generations of Chinese immigrants, not to mention African Americans, women, and minority groups in general. The result is that, today, even elite universities in the United States, both public and private, are open to the children of immigrants, whose chances of acceptance into comparable institutions in their parents' homelands would be much lower.

There is even speculation that the desire to provide children with an American education has fueled the high levels of post-1965 immigration from Hong Kong and Taiwan (Weinberg 1997). In fact, this desire proved to be a common theme relayed by the students. For some, it was a driving force in the immigration narrative that their parents shared with them (Portes and Rumbaut 2001a). Jannelle Chao remembered:

> My parents say they came here to give us a better education. Cause you know in Taiwan, it's so hard to get to college, you have all these tests. They thought, here, we could get further. Not that we could get further, but we wouldn't have all that pressure. Because in Taiwan, you start having tests when you're in junior high.

In contrast, there are seemingly inexhaustible occasions for higher learning in the United States. The very existence of community colleges and the chance to reenter four-year colleges after one has been away for some years affirmed to parents the fluid character of American higher education, one where second, third, and fourth chances are always available. In their homelands, only a select few made it to higher education and the process was strictly sequential and tied to age, with no second chances offered. In the words of Mrs. Wu:

> This is the part I love the best about the United States. Like I have a

younger sister, she graduated from a very bad school, she was only a high school graduate, a very bad school. She just not good in academic field. But she never stop continuous education. Taiwan, they don't have community colleges where you can go. In Taiwan, school is only for the young people. After you are married, have children, no such thing.

Milly Lin spoke of her father's disappointment with several male cousins in Taiwan who did too poorly on the national exam to place into college and who started working immediately following their compulsory Army service. Mr. Lin's advice to them was to come to the United States and start over again:

> And like, my dad goes, "You have to get an education. You know, [your cousins] are working, but I told them." My dad would tell them, advise them, "Why don't you go to the U.S. and go to New York and get a degree?" And he would lecture like other people's kids. They don't want to listen to you. So they're working. He thinks that's the worst thing. He thinks you won't get anywhere. There's a point where you'll hit, and you'll never be promoted no matter how good you are. You have to have your education.

Of course, this is not to say that all immigrant children end up at elite universities, or that the American educational system is without its own deeply felt share of problems having to do with immigrant, racial, gender, and class-based inequities. Clearly, neither is the case: immigrant children can be found at both ends of the educational spectrum, as both academic achievers and as at-risk students (Suarez-Orozco 2001). And American public schools largely remain segregated along de facto, if not de jure, lines (Ong 2002).[4] My point is merely that Chinese parents came from countries with relatively closed systems, compared to the American one, and that, as a consequence, they viewed their children as having greater opportunities in the United States, a conviction which had some basis in fact.

The second powerful message relayed by parents to children was the compelling economic payoff to schooling in the American labor market (Murnane 1994; Wilson 1999). Speaking of her parents' view on the route to success, Brenda Hsieh had this to say: "There is no other route. It's just middle school, high school, college, maybe grad school, career. That's pretty much the way it goes." The parents of my respondents became aware of the payoff to higher education from their particular vantage point in the labor market. So,

Chinese working-class immigrants knew this to be true from the limitations of their own lives. With few English skills and little schooling, they had found the ethnic economy to be their only option. While some met with success, all knew it to be an arduous path that none wanted for their children. For them, the ethnic economy might have been the only option, but their children would have much more, notably a path to the good jobs in the mainstream economy—provided they did well in school. This close link between higher education and mobility was at the heart of the counsel regularly imparted by Lan Jong's father, who ran a Chinese restaurant:

> He always says, I have to work so hard. But if you get a good education, you can find a better job. You won't have to work like me in the restaurant, sweating. Every day, I mean, he says it over and over, it's in our head.

Other children whose parents worked in the ethnic enclave economy recalled hearing similar messages. They were never in doubt about the import of the college degree to the world beyond the enclave economy.

Suburban parents who had jobs in the mainstream economy recognized that higher education was the reason they were not working in the ethnic economy to begin with. As I mentioned in Chapter 1, most had little first-hand knowledge of the enclave, work- or kin-related. A few, like Mr. Leong, had worked in an enclave business when they first arrived in the United States, an experience they did not care to repeat. According to Mrs. Leong, her husband's years working his way through college and graduate school at his uncle's Chinese restaurant only reinforced the idea of higher education as his way out of the enclave economy.

> We all have a tough life. You know, you are a new immigrant, and at that time, there were not that many things available. You are not as well edu-cated, you really struggle a lot. He finished [the Master's degree] in one year because he said that he do not want to stay in the restaurant for all his life.

There was also the idea that education opens new vistas of opportunity in that it is a highly transportable good that never declines in value, and, equally important, that it can never be forcibly taken away (as opposed to tangible items like cash, jewelry, business, or real estate). In common parlance, educa-tion is something that you can use anywhere and do anything with. The following story, told by Mrs. Liu, a single mother who raised two children on her own, underscores the self-assurance that she believes higher education gave her, that is, her faith in her ability to overcome life's obstacles. As she recounts, her decision to divorce from her husband could not have come at a worse time, as she was still relatively new to this country. And yet, her educational background gave her hope that she would get through:

> When I got divorced myself, I didn't have a degree in this country. I didn't have a green card. I didn't speak English. I didn't have working experience. I think I got the nerve to divorce is because of the self-respect, and the self-respect through my educational background because I graduated from a very good school [in Taiwan], and I know that I am worth that. I have nothing. I mean, I really have no background that I can divorce at all. That is the education that makes me more responsible, makes me see that I can make it.

In sum, the accessibility of higher education and its payoff in the labor market were actual structural conditions that proved to be the basis of what Kao and Tienda (1995) and others have described as immigrant optimism. Regardless of their own socioeconomic positions, parents taught their children that higher education would be their route to mobility in the United States. However, this was not the only lesson parents taught their children, as we shall see in the following discussion of another American context that influenced their perceptions of education in a decidedly less optimistic fashion.

Racialized Ethnicity as Liability: The Specter of Discrimination

My interviewees told a story about Chinese immigrant families and education that was of opposing strains: immigrant optimism, with its underlying idea that anything is possible in the United States, and immigrant pessimism, with its underlying idea that despite the opportunities that can be found, not everything is equitable in the United States and, in fact, some people find that they are blocked from taking advantage of the opportunity structure. The sources of the pessimistic strain can be found in the third structural condition that students said their parents frequently mentioned—racial discrimination. Parents taught their children that there is a clear racial hierarchy in the United States that privileges whites and positions the Chinese not at the top of the ladder but rather in a potentially vulnerable location. Education, then, becomes necessary as a credentialing mechanism to safeguard against potential discrimination.

The conception of education as a way to circumvent racial discrimination is, by itself, not a new phenomenon. Sara Lawrence Lightfoot (1978) has richly documented that the earliest blacks in the United States saw education as "preparation for emancipation." From such beginnings, this has continued over the course of our nation's history and has given rise to a tradition that persists among blacks today, namely, a view of education as a vehicle for their children's economic and political survival and advancement, or, in other words, assimilation into mainstream society.

What *is* interesting is that members of a group held up as a model minority frame their understandings of the importance of education along the lines of racial discrimination. While much scholarly work supports the parents' understanding of American education as more accessible than in their countries of origin, and as an increasingly necessary condition for economic advancement, the role of race in Asian American socioeconomic outcomes represents more contested terrain.[5] Still, numerous studies indicate that Asian Americans have not gained parity with whites. Rather, they receive a smaller return on their educational achievement than whites, and they bear higher costs for comparable material rewards (Sue 1973; Suzuki 1989; Hsia 1988; Hurh and Kim 1989; Hsia and Hirano-Nakanishi 1989; Barringer, Takeuchi, and Xenos 1990; Schneider and Lee 1990; Kim and Chun 1994; Wong 1995b; Hune and Chan 1997; Bankston and Zhou 2002). Other studies have shown that Asian Americans tend to have fewer chances for career advancement than their white counterparts with comparable training, skills, and experience (U.S. Commission on Civil Rights 1988; Tang 1993; Woo 1994; Woo 2000).[6] This has led Sue and Okazaki (1990) and others to propose the so-called blocked opportunities thesis, which argues that Asian American parents invest in their children's education to give them a head start in what they fear is an unequal society.

Certainly, the Chinese immigrant parents in my study did not come to their realizations about the importance of race through social scientific research, any more than they used such research to make their conclusions about the accessibility and payoff of higher education. Rather, they based their beliefs on their own experiences, on hearsay from friends and family members, and, for the urban Chinese, on the occasional article that might appear in a Chinese newspaper. That their beliefs were based on folk knowledge rather than social science evidence, however, does not make them any less real.

As their children tell it, the majority of the immigrant parents were acutely aware that they had entered a society with a prevailing racial hierarchy that not only privileged whites but grouped others in rigidly defined racial categories that belied distinctions based on national origins. Chinese immigrants from Hong Kong, Taiwan, China, and a host of other Asian countries saw their very different national identities disappear into a narrow ethnic categorization, itself subsumed by the Asian American label. In the United States, they all became Chinese, and they soon discovered that being Chinese was a liability. Parents saw it in their own lives, and they foresaw it for their children. Their hope was that education would blunt the edge of discrimination for the next generation (Sue and Okazaki 1990; Tuan 1998). It is within this context that we can begin to understand how a tradition born under completely different historical circumstances was transformed and adapted. Historically speaking, Chinese cultural identity was tied to academic achievement—"to do well in school is to be Chinese" (Siu 1992a, 8). But once the parents arrived in the United States, they found that this folk-saying gained another kind of force that inverted its original meaning, so that to be Chinese was to *have* to do well in school.

A small number of the parents were, in fact, twice-marginalized migrants, as they or their families had first left China, Hong Kong, or Taiwan to settle in other countries, mainly in Southeast Asia but also in such Latin American nations as Cuba and Brazil. Their experiences as members of the Chinese diaspora, and, in some cases, their encounters with discrimination thus predated their arrival in the United States. The legal protection of minorities like the Chinese, for instance, became a highly contentious issue in post–World War II Southeast Asia. As leaders proceeded with nation building, they often perceived the ethnic Chinese populations as linked to the external threat posed by mainland China (Wang 1988).

Thus, for Mr. Chin, it was his marginalized status as an ethnic Chinese in his native Malaysia, where the Chinese made up nearly half of the population after World War II (Wang 1988), that taught him the lesson about discrimination:

We (Chinese) were not allowed, even though you are born there, you're not allowed to be the prime minister or be in a very high office in government, basically because you are Chinese. Whereas if you are a Malay man, you're allowed all these privileges regardless of whether your education is as good as another Chinese. The one reason why I don't like to go back to Malaysia is because I would always be regarded as a second-class citizen.

In many ways, this unequal treatment prepared Mr. Chin for the racial hierarchy in the United States. It was a lesson that he wanted his daughter Diana to understand as well:

I made sure that we told her right from the beginning, right from day one, you know, when she was able to understand the issues. We say, "Look, let's face it. You're a minority. You're Asian. You're Chinese. You're a minority. There aren't too many of us here. And when you get on in this world, you have to get on with these people, you have to have a certain way of surviving. You've got to know how to get around it."

For other parents, the American context was their real first brush with racial discrimination. Mrs. Chang was one example. She had earned a Master's degree from Columbia University, and her husband was a graduate of National Taiwan University and the medical school at the State University of New York, Stonybrook. These credentials notwithstanding, Mrs. Chang described their status in the United States in marginalized terms, especially around the constraints of physical characteristics, culture, and English-language facility. On the one hand, Mrs. Chang, seated in the sunroom of her Long Island home, understood that she and her husband had done well and tried to rationalize the sense of marginalization that they had experienced by claiming that it was "natural" to discriminate against an unknown group and she realized this. On the other hand, her resentment that they had constantly to prove themselves was quite clear, as the following comments reveal:

I think there is discrimination, okay. Why we said discrimination, I think it's very natural because people don't understand us. When people see people, we look different, and we certainly have a distance, okay. So don't try to walk away from them. Try to know them or try to let them know you, okay. I think this is very important but I think this is a long process.

In the real world, like for business lawsuit or whatever, I think they take advantage of us, like we don't speak English that clearly, okay, or that correctly. Or like, the basic thing is they don't know you. Like once my husband had a lawsuit, like Taida is considered to be like Harvard. They don't know that here. So my husband's sitting in a courtroom like, very stupid. And they're like, like that. Actually, most Chinese people who came here to study, came for higher education, they are the elite of our society. But people here, they don't know. They talk to you like dumb-dumb. You don't understand, you don't speak English as well as we do. But we reverse that. You Americans go to Taiwan, they're dumb-dumbs, too.

This passage is particularly illuminating for what it says about the migration process and social class background. By all indicators, the Changs belong to the highly professional stream of the post-1965 immigration. Yet their incorporation into the American middle-class mainstream has not been entirely seamless. Despite all the trappings of incorporation, the grand house in the suburbs, the ability to provide their children with private music lessons at Julliard, the renowned school of music, and the successful medical practice drawing patients from many different racial and ethnic backgrounds, the Changs still felt that they were viewed and treated as foreigners in everyday interactions, with foreign being equated to inferior. This was true despite the elite status they had enjoyed in their homeland; migration had involved a loss in status, in some ways, despite their very real success here. To borrow Mrs. Chang's usage, they felt they could never claim the status of "the elite of American society." Regardless of their impressive incorporation in other indicators, the door to elite status remained closed because they were visibly marked as different.

This was evidenced in the "respect lessons" that Mrs. Chang gave to her daughter Victoria while the girl was growing up. The theme of parents preparing children for the racial hierarchy lay at the root of these "respect lessons." In the words of Victoria:

A: My mom would say to me, you know, you have to have respect for yourself because when you grow up, you may not have respect in society because you are a woman and you are Chinese. And she would prepare me for all of this and so I got a lot of respect lessons.

I: Did she ever say why she thought that you wouldn't get respect because you were a woman and Chinese?

A: Yeah. Because this is a white man's world. That was basically it.

The twin burdens of foreignness and marginalization are illustrated in the account of Milly Lin. Milly's father had struggled with odd jobs in the ethnic economy to support himself through graduate school, but he found that there were more adjustments to come in the professional workplace. Recalled Milly: "He still laughs when he says, 'When I was in New York, starting out, everyone in my company would laugh at me. Where did you get the monkey suit?' You know, what you wear. But, he was like, 'But I always gave a better comeback line. I always had the last line.'" Milly's father understood these comments to mean that he was not a part of the group; his clothing, his demeanor, and his very cultural lexicon marked him as different and, therefore, lacking.

He and his wife eventually decided to return to Taiwan, where they obtained high-income jobs in finance, comparable to the work they had had in the United States, but where there were more possibilities for advancement. An added bonus was that in their homeland they did not have to confront daily reminders from coworkers and supervisors that they looked too foreign or lacked a firm grasp of the prevailing cultural norms, and then later at home reflect on whether this would or did impede their chances for climbing the corporate ladder. Milly explained:

> I mean they eventually worked fine jobs [in the United States], but it wasn't like anything big. It's like, there's no chance, you know. There's like no point, and they, if they had stayed here, there's nothing. That's what they felt. They eventually moved back, and it was so easy, you know. Everything just works out.

While Milly's parents represent the extreme case, in terms of their decision to leave the United States altogether, parental perceptions of racial discrimination were a common theme voiced by my student respondents, and in fact, they transcended many of the class and neighborhood differences among them. Physicians and lawyers living in posh suburbs voiced the same kinds of fears to their children as garment workers and cooks working in the enclave economy and living in urban neighborhoods. Consider the following vignettes shared by four respondents from very different backgrounds.

Sandra Leong, the daughter of an engineering consultant, grew up in a small, predominately white, suburban town outside of Boston:

> My parents said if you want to get ahead in the world, being an Asian

American, they always look at you, they always think, you're not as good, so you have to be twice as assertive, you have to make your voice be heard.

Frances Ma, the daughter of a hospital administrator and physicist, grew up in a mostly white suburban community outside of New York City:

The way my father felt was that you need to be smart because you'll never be accepted or given the chance because you're Chinese. That's how my father felt. Being Chinese will never be a plus, it will always be something against you. . . . My father wanted us to be smarter, you have to be smarter than other people, than the majority, because unless you have 110, they're not going to take you. If you have 88, you know, they're not going to look at you, and say, "Oh well, we'll take them anyway." It'll be like, "We've got to take this guy because he's the smartest person." Your acceptance through merit, merit-based acceptance, you'll make it in because you have the criteria, not because you're what they're looking for.

Paul Chen, the son of a contractor and seamstress, grew up in Chinatown:

I have a Chinese name, but it's not on the record. Officially, on the birth certificate is Paul, my Chinese name, then Chen. We asked them that, "Why did we get American names instead?" My Mom goes, like, "It's not acceptable to have a Chinese name as much as it is to have an American one." It was her way of pushing us to get accepted by society. But she does know that, you know, they don't like Chinese people. And a lot of people don't. And it happens. My father works, he gets around a lot, so he sees a lot of people saying things to him, commenting about his race and ethnicity.

And Winston Woo, the son of an electrical technician, grew up in Rego Park, in Queens, New York, a racially and ethnically mixed neighborhood with a number of immigrant Chinese:

My dad would say, "There's not a lot of opportunities for Chinese," or "You're not going to get this job because you're Chinese." "You're going to be limited from this and that." "You can't do this because you're Chinese." "People expect you to do this because you're Chinese." "People aren't going to expect you to do this because you're Chinese." "You have to work harder because there is a lot of expectations about Chinese people, and they're going to look down on you." Yeah. Like you have to be much better than whites.

The general tone and language with which these respondents described their parents' messages about discrimination were strikingly similar. In Paul's case, his mother chose an Anglicized name for him because she sought to spare him the stigma of being labeled Chinese. She was only too aware of the hostilities or slights that might confront him, even without a Chinese name, but she was powerless to change any of that. This conscious strategy to suppress ethnicity through naming supports the findings in Tuan's (1998) study of multigenerational Asian ethnics. The parents highlighted the disadvantages they saw that came with being Chinese in the United States and sought to impress upon their children the reality of racial stratification. The message was more or less the same, despite the parents' different trajectories of socioeconomic incorporation and varying ties to the ethnic enclave (ranging from marginal to very strong). In short, the parents taught their children to be mindful of racial discrimination, to work harder than other people for the same results, and to pay particular attention to education as a way to level (somewhat, at least) an unequal playing field. These themes, of fear and vigilance, appeared in the majority of my interviews.

Not that speaking of issues related to race was easy for parents and children. Milly Lin remembered how awkward those conversations were, even though she knew her father had much to share from his own experiences in corporate America. Milly raised the issue with her father before she started college at Columbia. At the time, she was thinking that she would move to Taiwan after college, just as her parents had done. She feared that she would face the same barriers, despite the fact that she had been born and raised in the United States.

> I: Did your parents tell you that you had to do better than whites to get ahead?
> A: My dad says for him, yes. For men, not so much for women. But he really doesn't know what's going on nowadays. Because I asked him this before I went to college. Sat together talking about this with him. He doesn't like to talk about these things, like, like the whites and the blacks.

To sum up, my respondents' reflections on family and educational expectations show that culture is a fluid entity and that migration and settlement constitute a key time of upheaval and adjustment. As migrants incorporate into the complexities of American social and economic contexts, the cultural frameworks they bring with them necessarily take new forms and meanings. In the next chapter, I explore how such processes of cultural transformation and transition influence the meanings attached to gender.

Chapter 4

CULTURES-IN-TRANSITION:
GENDER AND MIGRATION

Along with its stunning diversity along ethnic and socioeconomic lines, a hallmark of post-1960s legal immigration has been the predominance of women, arriving singly or with families (U.S. Bureau of the Census 2002b).[1] Numerous writers have shown how gender relations structure migration decisions and flows and are themselves reconfigured by migration processes (Tienda and Booth 1991; Pedraza 1991; Hondagneu-Sotelo 1999).[2] This chapter is about the gender roles transmitted by immigrant parents to their children, with a particular focus on education, and the investments parents make in the schooling of daughters and sons, processes that further highlight the interplay between culture, structure, and agency in immigrant families.

My respondents' reflections on family and education pointed to a common theme of parents generally having the same educational expectations for *both* daughters and sons. That did not mean that gender was insignificant, however. Parental expectations for daughters and sons to obtain a college degree, while the same across families, unfolded in very different ways according to family background. A family's take on gender boundaries pre-migration, combined with their incorporation into the American labor market, were two strong factors; the result was a mix of old and new cultural norms in response to American economic conditions and opportunities (Foner 1999). In the urban working- and middle-class families, gender-egalitarian educational expectations frequently coexisted with gender-specific socialization in the home; this was a dynamic that was at once contradictory and challenging to daughters. The picture that emerged from my respondents' accounts was one of the structural and cultural transformations associated with migration encouraging change, continuity, and contradictions in the meanings attached to gender.

Theoretical Perspectives on Gender and Migration

Discussions of gender and migration have often focused on the ways in which patriarchal norms are altered with migration and settlement. It was once commonly held, for example, that migration afforded immigrant women enhanced economic opportunities, along with a greater voice in household decision-making and more independence, processes that transformed patriarchal norms within the home. Researchers have since complicated the so-called relative resource model, finding that more nuanced processes are at work. The sense of empowerment that comes from laboring outside the home and earning a regular wage is indeed a common theme among women across different immigrant groups. In the case of working-class families, survival itself makes the two-income proposition a necessity.

But the turn to waged work in the United States also has less than positive consequences for immigrant women that belie the optimism of the relative resource model. Working conditions for many immigrant women are difficult: they earn low wages, lower than what men generally earn, work long hours, and receive few benefits. Then there is what some sociologists have called the second shift (Hochschild 1989)—the demands of childcare and the burdens of housework that immigrant women must bear in addition to doing paid work outside the home. There can be conflicts between husbands and wives about the women's increased financial authority and independence, especially tricky when immigrant men are unemployed or do not fare as well at work yet still insist on dominating the household and holding a privileged position (Foner 1998).

In short, like other immigrant traditions and practices, patriarchal norms neither continue unchanged in the United Stares nor die out. Rather, they are redefined and renegotiated. In fact, migration brings both benefits and burdens to immigrant women, and gender relations reflect a mix of the old and the new (Foner 1998, 1999). Nazli Kibria's (1993) work with the Vietnamese immigrant community in Philadelphia is a fine illustration of this phenomenon, as she writes about a process that she describes as "bargaining with patriarchy." Kibria finds support for the resource model: Vietnamese women in the United States contribute a greater share to the family household economy than do men who were formerly middle-class breadwinners in Vietnam and who find themselves either unemployed or in low-wage, unstable jobs that do not provide enough to support the family household. This set of economic circumstances leads to a redefining of the patriarchal bargain. There is greater informal family power for Vietnamese immigrant women, who band together socially to protect against abuse of authority exerted by husbands over wives. And yet, the patriarchal bargain is never seriously challenged, and in fact, there are advantages for women in keeping the "old bargain." The women are careful to preserve the traditional boundaries of family and gender relations, in contrast to the American family system which they view as being less cohesive and privileging the individual, and they are aware of the economic constraints that would make the loss of the men catastrophic to the household budget.

Turning to studies of the 1.5 and second generation with respect to education, we find examples of gendered parenting practices. Yet, just as there is no single effect of Asian-ness on the educational aspirations parents have for their children, so the research reveals no single pattern of Asian parenting along gendered lines. Gendered parenting takes many forms, with varying consequences. During the 1970s immigrant families in New York City's Chinatown, for example, invested more in the education of sons than daughters, and there is some evidence that this may be happening today with other working-class Asian groups as well (Sung 1987; Hune 1998). Mau's (1995, 244) study of Filipino American, Native Hawaiian, and Samoan American girls finds that "traditional socialization in home and schools" had girls cooking, cleaning, and caring for younger siblings and taking less rigorous courses, and thus self-selecting themselves out of contention for high-paying, high-status jobs. Coming from a different perspective, Kim (1993) demonstrates that Korean immigrant parents stress the importance of education and attendance at prestigious institutions to both their daughters and sons; the difference comes with career expectations: the Korean parents orient their daughters toward less stressful careers, since they will need to care for future children and balance work with family. How did my respondents conceptualize and experience gender in Chinese immigrant families? That is what we turn to next.

Chinese Family and Kinship:
The Role of Gender

My respondents clearly identified certain patriarchal norms as being derived from traditional Chinese culture, such as the subservience of women to the authority of men and the favoring of sons over daughters. Their knowledge, however, did not extend much beyond this common sense understanding. In fact, in traditional Chinese culture, and by that I mean before the founding of the People's Republic of China in 1949, the role of women in the family was unambiguous. Confucian ideology prized a set of hierarchies: the collective over the individual, the elderly over the young, and men over women. Descent in the Chinese kinship system was traced exclusively through the male line. Women could neither inherit from their parents, nor could they sufficiently honor them in ancestor worship rituals.

It followed that in raising daughters, parents were supporting a child who was destined to leave the natal unit upon marriage to join the family of her husband.[3] Due to this lowly and outside-the-family status, there was little incentive to educate women. Unequal gender relations was also evidenced by the existence of concubinage: married men, if they were wealthy enough, could bring in secondary wives, or concubines, to join the household. The inferior position held by women found expression in popular sayings, such as "May you have a hundred sons and a thousand grandsons." And as Baker points out, it is elegantly rendered in the famed eighteenth-century novel *Dream of the Red Chamber*, in which a servant compliments an elderly woman's granddaughter by saying, "Her whole bearing, madam, is such that she seems to not be your granddaughter on your daughter's side, but rather your granddaughter by your son" (Baker 1979, 24).

In contemporary times, such gender ideologies have played out in different ways across East Asia. In the People's Republic of China, the government formally enacted a marriage law in 1950 that, in theory, eliminated the system of male privileges, weakened filial piety, and offered protections for women and children (Baker 1979). This represented an attempt by the government to transfer the power of familial obligations away from the family unit to the state (Ikels 1996). In practice, however, change was slow to occur, as Whyte (1991) and others have pointed out. The end result was that patrilocal marriage and patrilineal inheritance were never effectively challenged by the state (Stacey 1983). Additionally, state policies that reduced infant mortality rates, increased the average lifespan, and strictly policed internal migration inadvertently strengthened the family unit and traditional kinship roles (Davis and Harrell 1993, 1).

In Taiwan the traditional Chinese family structure remained evident as late as the early part of the twentieth century. The Japanese colonization and, later, the Nationalists, set Taiwan on a very different path to modernization as compared to the mainland, which saw the opening up of educational and work opportunities to women. In particular, the scarcity of educated male labor from the late 1970s through the 1980s led to the dissolution of barriers against the employment of educated married women, as employers became eager to hire them (Brinton, Lee, and Parish 2001). At the same time, the high ratio of wage levels to household expenditures has meant that married women have had to work outside the home (Yu 2001). Nevertheless, a strong patriarchal culture still exists in Taiwan, in which the gendered ideology of home and hearth are commonly expressed in "a saying that wives should manage domestic affairs while husbands are in charge of business outside" (Thorton and Lin 1994; Yu 2001, 73).

That such traditional gender ideologies were still meaningful to immigrants was eloquently expressed by one suburban, middle-class father. Mr. Chin, a native of Malaysia, had led a cosmopolitan adult life. Having gone to college in Boston and law school in Great Britain, he now lived in a Boston suburb. And yet, when discussing Diana, his only child, his frame of reference remained the traditional gender ideology he had grown up with in the ethnic Chinese community of Malaysia. Mr. Chin: "I wanted a son, but that's obvious. You know, Chinese men always want this. But I did not treat her like a daughter. I always treat her like my descendant. I always treat her like a son. So I treat her as an equal, I do."

It is quite telling that my respondents had a very limited knowledge base about the particulars of Chinese patriarchy, namely, its origins, history, and functional manifestation. Similar to their understandings of educational expectations, as transmitted by parents, their version was very much a distilled 1.5 and second-generation product that was commonsensical. The actual ideological and empirical scaffolding of this commitment to men over women that I briefly outlined here was not available to my respondents. In other words, they could identify the "gender issue" and explicitly link it to their parents' homeland cultures, but they could not elaborate extensively on how the gender issue played out in traditional Chinese culture or in contemporary East Asia. Instead, what was more visible to them was how migration interacted with gender in their own families in the United States, and that is what I turn to next.

Gender Equality in Educational Expectations

In Chapter 3 I demonstrated how my respondents spoke of particular American contexts, conveying to parents the utility of higher education for their children. Two of those same American contexts also played a crucial role in parental understandings of higher education as being important for both daughters and sons. These were the accessibility of education in the United States and the advantages that come with it in the labor market, and they represented the goals parents envisioned for both sons and daughters. This was grounded in their realization that in the United States their daughters would most likely have to work as part of a two-income couple for at least some period of time to maintain a viable standard of living for their families (Foner 1998; Bankston 1995). Thus, there was a material incentive for parents to encourage their daughters to pursue higher education, both in the payoff for the daughters and in the minimal investment on the part of parents, since higher education was more available to begin with.

Another important point is that few of my respondents reported any gender inequities in the arrangements parents made for their children's college education. The fact that parents might want both daughters and sons to go on to college does not always mean that they invest in their children's education equally; the potential for gender inequities can still exist in a number of domains. These include how much parents are willing to pay for their children's schooling, how far away from home the college can be, and how much prestige value the college has (community versus four-year college, public versus private, and the various ranking tiers within public and private institutions).

What was striking among my interviewees was that there was little evidence of any gender distinction in these areas. Suburban parents, for exam-

ple, did not have any qualms about sending their daughters to prestigious colleges, even if that meant their daughters would live hundreds or thousands of
miles away from home. This is in contrast to what Wolf (1997) found with
middle-class, highly educated Filipino parents, who did not necessarily want
their daughters to attend competitive colleges if that meant living away from
home, and who were more inclined to allow their sons that opportunity. At
the other end of the spectrum, my urban parents did not expect their daughters to attend only community colleges while reserving the bachelor's degree
for their sons. Nor did they reserve private college as an option only for sons,
relegating daughters to less expensive public universities.

In the few instances where there existed tensions in my urban families,
their source could not be traced explicitly to gender, as can be seen from Julia Lau's account. The youngest of three children, Julia was also the only
daughter. And yet, she was the one who broke the family mold and went
away to college. Located in a Westchester suburb only sixteen miles from
Chinatown, the distance to her college was more psychological than real—
Julia boarded at the Catholic college rather than commuting. Nonetheless,
this was a first within the Lau family—a child going away to school, and the
only daughter at that. Julia recalled how her mother had initially worried
about her: Without her mother there, how would Julia get enough to eat?
Who would look after her daughter? Enlisting the support of her older
brother, the young woman eventually prevailed. The key was her brother's
strategic presentation of the educational and professional benefits that going
to this particular college would provide. This is how Julia described those in-
terchanges between mother and son: "He said, 'Look, this is the opportunity
for her to go to a good college and get her degree, and when she graduates,
she'll be, you know, doing nursing. And then she'll be able to find a good job.'
And so because of that, she let me go."

None of this means, however, that such egalitarian expectations developed
in the same way for all the families. As Chapters 1 and 2 reveal, these were
parents with varying levels of education and socioeconomic backgrounds.
Their own experiences with gender norms in their countries of origin necessarily spanned a wide range, and their incorporation into the labor market
was also very different. All of this influenced how they approached issues of
gender and education with their children in the United States.

Continuity

Among the suburban, middle-class families, there was already a firm foundation for egalitarian expectations. These daughters reported that they were in fact the beneficiaries of gender battles that had been fought and won by their mothers, many of whom had college degrees themselves.[4] Gender inequalities, to the degree that they existed, were associated with their parents' experiences of growing up in their homelands. Chloe Gao, for instance, traced her mother's views on women and education to her active contestation of the family norms that valued sons more than daughters. Chloe's mother had graduated from college in Brazil and had worked as a computer programmer in Northern California, achieving more than Chloe's grandparents had ever expected of her. Thus, Chloe remarked:

> Like, she's working, you know, she's always worked throughout my whole life and she did the school thing. So I don't think that she would expect any less of females, you know, she knows like, ideally, there aren't differences between males and females. But then, well, talking to her, I mean she recognizes that this society is dominated by males, and especially in like, Chinese culture. I mean, and she'll talk to me about our grandma, and how my grandma really still practices like, Chinese beliefs and, you know, expecting more of her sons. And treating us grandkids, she'll kind of favor the kids of her sons, as opposed to the kids of her daughters. Yeah, so I think my mom has really, she's really like gone away from those beliefs that she was probably brought up with, you know.

In my interview with the parents of Diana Chin, I heard a similar story. Higher education, said Mrs. Chin, was prized in her family because her father had fled to Hong Kong from Communist China with only a fourth-grade education. Although he was able to build a successful construction business without a college degree, he wanted his children to pursue higher education. So when Mrs. Chin's older brother came to the United States to study at MIT during the 1960s, she arrived to join him. She soon discovered, however, that her parents' definition of higher education for daughters was quite different. To her parents, it was inconceivable for a woman to obtain a bachelor's degree and to pursue a "masculine" field. Women were to have more modest goals, as Mrs. Chin recalled:

My parents wanted me to study secretaries college so that I could go home in one year. I said, "I don't think so." They were, "Just do your thing, come back and get married." I said, "I don't think so. I think I want architecture." [They were like]: "No, but this is a five-year school." I said, "We'll see." But anyhow, my bottom line really is just in America, getting an education. You know, my whole goal was to get a degree. [My father] wanted his children to have a better education, the boys, not the girl. Still very traditional. But after me, I think my sister had a much easier time.

Mr. Chin, her husband, added:

You know, they never thought of her as being equal to her brother who attends MIT, and who's a civil engineer, you know. That even her mind or even her intelligence might be as high as her brother's. They never think of that.

Although this idea had come late to Mrs. Chin, she went with it and obtained her bachelor's degree from Boston University, and later a professional accounting degree.

In the Toy family, the parents explicitly told their son and two daughters that traditional Chinese gender ideologies would have no place in how they would be raised. In comparing the experiences of the three children, Laura, who is the middle child, found little different:

We took the same high school classes, and we all took the same lessons, like tennis lessons, piano lessons. Like we always did things as a group. As far as gender hierarchy goes, first there's an age thing, the oldest kid gets more freedom, gets to do stuff first. But it's not really gender, because my parents make a point of saying all our kids are equal, we know a lot of Chinese families who see sons as more important, but we're like no. Like my parents get upset when they see families who favor one child over another for whatever reason.

Change

Gender egalitarianism was more of a marked shift among the urban Chinese families. The mothers typically had low levels of education, and few children reported that their mothers had ever challenged patriarchal authority in their own families. In fact, the reverse was true: a few of my respondents described their mothers as believing in the inferiority of women, in terms of intelligence (at least those in the immigrant generation). And although nearly all the mothers worked outside the home, it was evident that they *had* to work because the family could not survive on only one income, especially in those families where both parents worked in the low-wage enclave economy (Kwong 1987).

In contrast to the suburban families, parental expectations for their daughters to get a college degree rested on two survivalist assumptions specific to the family's socioeconomic location: one was that their daughters, even when married, would also have to work outside the home to make ends meet, and two, that their daughters would need to work so as to have financial independence, just in case their marriages turned sour. It was important to urban parents that their daughters not be left stranded by husbands without any financial resources of their own; since it was not likely that the parents would be able to step in to help, their daughters would need to provide their own safety net. For all of this, higher education was crucial.

In exchanges with their daughter, Ling Choy's parents underscored such fears, as she pointed out: "My parents stress, since I'm a woman, I'm a female, that I should be independent. That I should be financially independent. My father would want me to get married, but I should be prepared. I shouldn't depend on my husband."

Bonnie Tai also grew up with this message very much in mind:

My mom thinks that it's important, even if you're married, to have a good education, to have your own career. She always said that even if you're married and no matter how good your husband is, it's always good to have something solid under your belt. That's what she believes in. She said that you can't, you can't depend on anybody but yourself.

The few exceptions were mainly female respondents whose college career had been interrupted by five or more years. Kathy Zhao, a reentry student at Hunter, shared memories of a recurring argument she had with her mother about her plans to finish college after a long hiatus. When Kathy decided to drop out of the first college she attended, her mother had opposed the decision; but now that Kathy was in her late twenties and back in school after having worked full-time for some years, her mother was more ambivalent.

She presented marriage as a more pressing and perhaps faster way for her daughter to become financially secure. Kathy:

> She was telling me how, "Well, you're a woman, you're female, so it's not important for you as it is for a man to make it in this world, because you can marry a rich husband and then you're set for life, right." That's her way of thinking, and so I had to constantly tell her that I want my own thing.

There was an irony to this story. Kathy's mother herself was divorced, and afterward had had difficulties supporting herself and the children. This fact was not lost upon Kathy: "So, I constantly told her, 'No, I want my own career, I want to make my own money and not depend on a man.' And I tell her, 'Well, you should know, you're divorced. You should learn from that.'"

Another exception was Linda Eng, whose mother was not sure if Linda's plans for study beyond the bachelor's degree would necessarily be the best thing. Linda had graduated from SUNY Old Westbury and was getting additional credits at Hunter to apply to Master's programs in occupational therapy. According to Linda, her mother had "up-to-date" Chinese friends, also immigrant women, who told her things were different in the United States and that women should have as many years of formal schooling as they could get. These friends chastised Linda's mother for having allowed her older daughter to drop out of college, marry, and have a child by the time she was twenty-six:

> I eavesdrop on their conversations, and my mom will say, oh, about my eldest sister, about her marriage and stuff, and her friend will criticize her and stuff: "You really shouldn't let your daughter marry so early." "It's really not that beneficial to her cause she's so young, and she's already tied down with the family." "You should really, really advise her to go back to school." Yeah, that's why she let me study, too.

On the other hand, Linda knew that her mother still had mixed feelings about her plans to pursue a Master's degree:

> I guess she's caught in the middle as well. She still has this idea that men protects the women financially, emotionally in a household. And that's what she would want. But at the same time, as an understanding mother, she said to me, "If you really want to study, why don't you marry someone now, and then I'm sure he will let you study." . . . But she does sup-

port me. If I tell her I need five years to study, she would say, "Okay," and she support me emotionally, financially.

As Linda observed, her mother's views have to be understood in the context of the migration process and how it complicates conceptions of gender. Her mother is reminded of the economic opportunities available to her daughter in the United States but is still conflicted about whether her daughter should forge an independent work life or rely on a husband, the arrangement that she knew from China. It is important to note, however, that Linda already had the undergraduate degree and thus had already met a significant criterion for having her own career and supporting herself. From her mother's perspective, a Master's degree was something extra that might not be necessary, especially if her daughter could find a wealthy husband. Ironically, Linda's mother was the financial force and "prime decision maker" in their own family. Nevertheless, she still advised her daughter to pursue a model of marital relations that obviously had little bearing on her own marital relationship.

Gender Contradictions in Urban Families

Cultural traditions and practices privileging sons over daughters, however, still persisted among urban working- and middle-class families. The fact that these parents expected their daughters and sons to get a college degree did not actually shake their belief that there were appropriate standards of female behavior and a gendered division of labor to which their daughters had to adhere. My respondents often spoke of parental favoritism toward sons. This is how one female respondent described the "traditional" gender relations in her family: "I think my mom pays more attention to my brother because he is the son, and because he will carry on the family's name." Rachel Larsen saw a similar kind of inequality in how her father treated Rachel and her younger brother. Both she and her mother, who was Swedish, made note of this favoritism:

My Mom tells me, "Your father never, never really wants to make it obvious." He can't help favoring my brother. I see it, inside I know he is. Because I see little things that he does, such as if he makes dinner, he'll make a plate for my brother. Put everything on it. "What do you want to drink?" He gets him a drink, puts it on the table, then he calls, "Rachel, food is ready." I have to do it myself. You know, it's like okay, like that. Sometimes he's nice. Like yesterday, he made a plate for me. I think it's because he's Chinese.

In these families, it was the role of parents to ensure that their daughters learned about what my respondents described as "women's work and the woman's role."

Women's Work

In urban working- and middle-class families, daughters were more likely to help out around the house, and one might argue that structural location in the economy could explain this finding since their mothers worked outside the home in full-time, often labor-intensive jobs. In suburban families, mothers either did not work, or if they did (typically in professional jobs or office work), they were able to hire household help such as nannies, babysitters, and cleaning ladies. Economic location alone, however, does not explain why girls in urban Chinese families were expected to help around the house to a greater extent than boys. To better understand such gender dynamics, one must keep in mind traditional Chinese gender ideologies that maintained that "the whole training of a daughter by her family was aimed at fitting her to be a wife, mother and worker for another family" (Baker 1979, 41).

The (unequal) division of labor in the home was a particularly vivid memory for my urban female respondents. Consider the following responses to a general question about household chores performed when growing up, and how those experiences compared with those of their siblings:

Grace Li

> [I had] a lot 'cause I lived with my grandma. She made me cook, I didn't mind learning to cook. Every Saturday was scrubbing the floors, sweeping. I remember summers, every morning, I would have to wake up at nine to go with my grandma to buy groceries. I mean, I had a lot because I lived with my grandmother, and I didn't really make much friends, so I was never really out of the house. My main purpose was to help out my grandma. They wouldn't really let (my brother) because he had asthma. I didn't mind. I was very tolerant.

Lan Jong

> Like sometimes, I have to, you know, help out, you know, do the cleaning and stuff like that, and the woman's role, chores and stuff like that. And my brothers don't have to do anything. And I'd kind of get very upset. They say, you know, tell me, especially my Mom, you know, she tells me, "Girls have to do this, do that. You have to do this. It's the woman's role."

Julia Lau

> I was always told be the woman, which meant that you set the table, you had to do the laundry, you had to help cook, you had to help do the housework. Whereas my brothers would just sit and watch TV. And I never understood that. I used to fight with my Mom because of that. She's like, "You don't understand that you're a woman."

Mary Sing

> I had to wash the dishes. Chores, women's work. And I was the one that needed to learn how to cook. They always made my brother take out the garbage and stuff like that. But for me, I had to learn to cook.

These passages capture the pervasive view among urban working- and middle-class parents that daughters had to learn how to do women's work, which included but was not limited to the following tasks—washing dishes, doing the laundry, sweeping, stocking up on groceries, and, of course, cooking. By grouping these tasks as specific to women, immigrant parents were attempting to socialize their daughters into traditional gender norms. The message was clear: parents were merely tapping into the natural order of the world. Even if daughters did not end up performing these chores (and some refused to do them consistently, if at all), they ought to know how to perform them, and it was the parents' duty to ensure that those lessons were learned. It was not necessary for sons to learn these tasks because being a man meant being served and being at the head of the family structure relative to women.

Ivory Miao, for instance, called herself "my brother's second mother," even though she was only older by a year. Since her parents worked "24/7," she became responsible for her brother's well-being when she was still a young girl. The obligation, however, was not reciprocal. Although we might assume that older siblings might have to assume more of the household burdens regardless of their sex, birth order made little difference among the urban Chinese. Women who had older brothers were just as likely to say they had to do more as their counterparts with younger brothers.

The Woman's Role

Gender-specific conceptions were also expressed in the types of behavior that were considered appropriate for boys as opposed to girls, and in the different sanctions the children might receive for misbehaving. Daughters, for instance, were supposed to be sexually pure. Thus, parents made the threat of sexual transgression particularly relevant to the lives of these young women, whereas their brothers did not have to live with the same fear of "getting into trouble." Or, as this exchange with Ivory Miao indicates, there was a clear "double standard" that allowed her brother to live with his girlfriend, a Japanese national whom he met over the Internet, in their parents' house:

> A: Yeah. Speaking of double standards, if I had ever done that, I would be disowned. I'd be called a whore. Everything. Yeah.
> I: Did you ever talk to your parents about this double standard?
> A: I've yelled at them for doing this.
> I: And what do they say?
> A: Oh, you're just jealous.
> I: Jealous of what? That he has a girlfriend?
> A: Jealous of his girlfriend, that they're treating her so nice.

Susan Chu did not even have brothers, but her mother still framed her rules as being gender-specific. Certain forms of behavior, like "hanging out late, sleeping over a friend's house" were fine for boys but not for girls. According to Susan: "My Mom would be like, no, you're a girl. You cannot hang out late. If you were a boy, it's a different story. Because girls, you know, can be taken advantage of, are easier to be taken advantage."

Daughters also had to be respectful of their elders and keep to their place. One woman I interviewed had this to say about her father's advice to her: "There were times when my father would say, you know, you have to be a good Chinese girl and not talk so loud. Be more neat." As Deborah Ow told me, boys were given greater latitude, whereas girls were expected to obey the dictates of their parents without question, and faced greater punishment if they did not:

Well, I got punished, they were very strict on me but they were very easy on my brother. Like very strict. Anything I did wrong would get punished and the form of punishment was very different. Mine was much harsher, much stricter. His was just like, a little slap on the wrist and, you know, "Oh, he's just being obnoxious, he's a boy." That type of thing. Talking back. Talking back was a really big issue with my mother and me. If I questioned, and, you know, I was pretty sassy, I would really get [reprimanded]. I mean I would get the [duster], you know, the stick. Yeah, a big punishment. But when my brother talked back, it would be just brushed off. It would be okay, she just allowed it.

Rachel Larsen remembered chafing against similar restrictions imposed by her father. She sensed that they clashed because they were too much alike — two people who spoke their minds, except that she was a woman and was not supposed to speak her mind, and certainly not to her father. She remembered gleaning further insights into the dynamics of their relationship from her father's sister:

When I went to Malaysia, I spoke to my aunt because she saw us get into a little fight, and she told me, "Rachel, I know that you live in America. That you have your opinions, and you stand up for it, but your father is a typical Chinaman, so just be quiet." She goes, "What do you think I've done all these years?" I'm like, "I can't stay quiet, that's the thing, I just can't."

In Rachel's case, gender relations in the family were complicated by the fact that her Chinese father and Swedish mother had very different conceptions of womanhood. Rachel's mother, for example, believed that women should speak their mind, a belief at odds with Rachel's father's values. The marriage turned out to be an inversion of the traditional Chinese husband and wife roles, as Rachel noted:

See, my father's very contradicting, you know, he's very contradicting. He's the one who cooks and cleans and does the laundry. But still, he favors the man, and the woman should, you know, be in their place. But my Mom isn't in her place. He's so contradicting.

However, this "untraditional" arrangement proved to be a cause of friction that would contribute to the couple's divorce, and to the father advising Rachel, "Believe me, I wouldn't take anything back, but it makes life easier if you stay within your own race." Although her father was unable to pattern

his marriage on traditional Chinese gender norms, he tried to do so in his relationship with his children, much to Rachel's chagrin.

But even such traditions were redefined and renegotiated with migration
in some families. Mai Liao, the eldest in a family of three daughters and one
son, is an example. The family left the countryside of Toisan, China, because
of the government's one-child policy which sanctioned families who had
multiple children. Mai's mother had had her first two children (both girls)
before the policy was enacted, and afterward she was fined for having two
more children (a girl and, finally, the long-awaited boy). Growing up in
China, Mai noticed how her brother was favored in the family, and also how
that came to change in the United States:

> He had to be taken care of, you know. He wasn't yelled at as much as we
> were. He was like the baby. So he was very much spoiled. And whenever
> we had food, my grandfather would always give him the most. But now,
> it's different. Now everyone has to do chores, same way, same amount,
> same food.

Benny Sen, one of the few men who paid a great deal of attention to matters of gender, remembered that his brother, the eldest child, never had to do
the dishes or the laundry (and still did not, despite the fact that he continued
to live at home with their parents). Benny, however, grew up with the same
rules as his sisters because his older sister protested and his parents responded
in kind:

> When I was growing up, same rules, same rules. I do the dishes, I do the
> laundry but that's after the women's lib in our family. Because my
> twenty-seven-year-old sister is very outspoken about equality and all
> that. So, you know, when I grew up, no, no difference. She asked for
> equality, and she got it. So, no difference for me.

In short, most of these parents directed contradictory messages at their
daughters—they were to graduate from college, at the least, but they also had
to do "women's work" in the household and fulfill the "woman's role" by not
openly challenging parental authority and by not leaving themselves vulnerable to sexual transgression, both of which were non-issues for sons. In other
words, traditional Chinese gender expectations for daughters in the division
of household labor and social behavior existed alongside the new educational
expectations that emerged in the United States for both sons and daughters.
What was common sense to these immigrant parents, however, was cause for

resentment for their 1.5 and second-generation daughters. My women respondents often found themselves in conflict with the gendered norms their parents brought from the homeland and tried to retain in the United States despite the change in their social and cultural circumstances (Kibria 1993). The common resolution on the part of the daughters was to very grudgingly perform the "women's work" as a way of accommodating their parents, but not to acknowledge the implicit message that they could not go as far in life because they were women. Hence, the daughters did not self-select themselves out of contention for high-status jobs that required postsecondary education. They still sought the college degree (if not more) because they understood the parental message about educational attainment as the key to mobility in the United States to be valid and highly relevant to their lives.

Suburban Families: There Are No Differences

Gender was generally a non-issue in suburban families. The sense that daughters had to do women's work, which was quite different from men's work, was largely absent from these respondents' lives. Boys and girls typically took turns performing the same chores. Or, if boys and girls performed different household chores—for example, boys taking out the garbage and girls washing the dishes—they were not accompanied by the message that boys took out the garbage because they were boys and girls washed the dishes because they were girls. This was a lesson that suburban middle-class parents did not think important to impart to their daughters or sons.

This is how Daniel Fong described his parents' expectations for his younger sister: "For my sister, get a good job, do well. I certainly have no sense that they're bringing her up in the housewife mode. I mean, my sister's never done the dishes, she doesn't do the laundry, doesn't cook. Sort of like, what else is she going to do?" As we have seen, younger sisters in urban families generally ended up taking care of more household chores because they were female; in suburban Chinese families, they took on less of the burden because they were younger. Birth order, more than sex, differentiated sibling experiences in these families. Chloe Gao is one example. Her brother, who was two years older than she, became the caretaker, responsible for cooking, for example, while their parents were still at work, and he was the one who complained about favoritism: "In terms of chores, he'd always say, 'Well, when

I was her age, I was already like doing the yard work and things like that.' And so I think I was even favored because I was younger."

While a few of these female respondents reported gendered parental expectations, they operated differently than in urban families. Melinda Wu, for instance, reported on her mother's adherence to "the traditional stereotypes of women should learn to cook." Melinda, however, never did learn to cook, which casts doubt on the depth of her mother's commitment to that cause. Additionally, the chores that Melinda and her younger brother shared had an equitable cast to them. According to Melinda: "He has to do the garbage. I have to do the dishes. He set the table. I cleared the table. Laundry, I was responsible for doing, but then he had to, I forget what was his thing." And when Melinda left home for college, her younger brother ended up doing her old chores in addition to his own.

Margaret Wang, the daughter of well-to-do Taiwanese immigrants, described her parents as "traditional, Chinese-wise," who "weigh[ed] guys and girls differently." According to Margaret, her parents had made it clear that their sons would inherit substantially more than their daughters. This unequal distribution of inherited wealth had led the parents to stress their daughters' education. Since the girls would inherit less from their parents, the hope was that they would marry well (e.g., by marrying into wealth), and according to this rationale, a prestigious university would be the perfect place for them to meet suitable partners. Paradoxically, since the boys would take over the family business, school for them was less important. Margaret observed: "[My parents] view college as something my brothers just have to get, just to get the degree, like in name. It doesn't matter where they go to school. Just as long as they have a degree, and later on they can carry on the family business, you know what I mean."

So far, the story I have recounted here is of my respondents' commonsense understanding of the Chinese immigrant family playing a crucial role in their children's paths to college. At its core is a cultural script that has immigrant Chinese parents valuing and investing in their children's education more than other parents, which explains why their children do better in school. It is logical to ask, then, how did my respondents understand their own experiences with school and paths to college in light of this cultural script. Did family ties work to the advantage of the children's experience of education in their own families? It is to this question that I turn in the next two chapters.

Chapter 5

"ENDING UP" AT HUNTER

As elaborated in Chapter 3, a common theme characterizing my student interviews was the educational goal they remembered their parents having for
them: to earn an undergraduate degree, preferably at a prestigious, private
university. My Hunter respondents were all too well aware that their undergraduate institution was not the kind their parents had had in mind for them.
In recent years, CUNY has been the subject of numerous cutbacks in funding and has been mired in very public controversies about academic standards. It can safely be said that the public perception of CUNY, justified or
not, is one of underachievement. And yet, while not currently a top-ranked
institution, CUNY was once known as the Harvard of the proletariat.[1] Un-
fortunately, my Hunter respondents generally had no idea of this. Their perception of CUNY derived from the barrage of media attention that characterized CUNY as an institution that symbolized the pitfalls of the open
admission process.[2] Hence, because they attended a public commuter university, not to mention one that was the focus of such negative publicity, my
Hunter respondents believed that they had fallen short.

How did my Hunter respondents rationalize their having "ended up" at
Hunter, as many of them put it, especially since, by their own accounts, as
children of Chinese or Asian immigrant families, they were supposed to have
exhibited the high levels of achievement that would lead them to Columbia,
Harvard, or Yale? In this chapter, I show that, as a way of explaining this dis-

juncture, my Hunter respondents pointed to a lack of parental resources, one result of their parents' labor-intensive jobs and low incomes. Paradoxically, the emphasis my respondents placed on socioeconomic status did not allow them to challenge the cultural explanation itself.

Alienation and Failure

There were many reasons that my respondents felt themselves to be alienated from Hunter. First and foremost, they did not think that the school was prestigious enough in the academic hierarchy set forth by their parents. Second, most had struggled with school before ever coming to Hunter. Their difficulties, for some in the high school years, and for others in college, would hardly have qualified them as superachievers to begin with. About 18 percent of the Hunter respondents had attended a community college; two had dropped out of the first four-year college they had attended and had worked for a few years; two had entered the labor market between high school and college. These respondents, a third of my Hunter sample, were hopeful but by no means certain that they would ever finish college.

Regardless of their actual paths to Hunter, my respondents expressed a similar kind of alienation that was amply reflected in their take on the school. Few reported that Hunter had been their top choice for a college. Offhand comments, like "It was near a subway line" and "It was convenient," were among the reasons my respondents gave for why they attended Hunter. Some believed that by not going away for college, they were missing out on the authentic collegiate experience. Hunter, lacking the grassy quadrangle of the archetypal college campus, would never be a real college to them. It was more the case that Hunter was seen as a stopping place between work and family. As one twenty-one-year-old male said, "I go to school and go home." Consequently, few respondents reported having many close friendships based at the school. Their friends went to schools in the State University of New York system, and not necessarily the elite private universities. Still, these residential schools were considered a step above a commuter university like Hunter by my respondents.

There were many ironies to this, of course. First, by even getting to college at all, my Hunter respondents were already achievers and belonged in relatively select company; nationally, 58.2 percent of persons between the ages of twenty-five and twenty-nine have some college or more, and an even smaller proportion, 28.2 percent, have a bachelor's degree or more (U.S. Bureau of the Census 1999). Second, Hunter is one of the best of the City Colleges and can indeed be called a centerpiece of the system. Still, my respondents felt that they just "ended up" at Hunter. It was not where they wanted, hoped, or were expected to be.

Paul Chen was one example. I met Paul for our interview in the Skycafe at Hunter. As students around us were grabbing sodas and yogurt, on the go between classes, Paul told me about his parents' expectations for him and his two brothers. I mentioned that they must have been happy that after many travails (both brothers had dropped out of high school for a time; Paul had taken six months off between high school and his enrollment at Hunter) all three young men were enrolled in four-year colleges. To my surprise, Paul did not agree. He believed his parents felt quite the opposite; more to the point, he did not feel particularly good about how either he or his brothers had done in school. The following exchange reveals this feeling of inadequacy on Paul's part:

> I: You're all in college. That's good.
>
> A: Yeah, I suppose so. But there are like a hundred other people out there who did so much better than that in school, standard of living, I suppose.
>
> I: People you know?
>
> A: Family friends. And they always compared us to them. It drives us mad.

Paul then took special delight in telling me about the fate of one of these family friends, a young man whom his father had always compared (unfavorably) to the Chen boys. When the young man took a drastically wrong turn, Paul's parents had been proven wrong (and the Chen sons had thus looked better as a result). Paul said: "And he ends up killing somebody and killing himself. We had such a field day. 'We told you he was not a good kid, but no, he was always better than us.' So we always talk back. 'He was a good kid alright.'"

On another occasion, I was talking to Beth Liu in the Hunter library about why she kept a journal when the young woman suddenly broke down in tears. When we resumed the conversation, Beth explained that writing was an outlet for all the feelings she could never express to her parents. The journal was her way of working through her feelings of having failed her parents by not yet completing college. Beth was a twenty-five-year-old Hunter reentry student who had attended several other colleges and had waitressed for a few years in between schools, trying to figure out what she wanted. Beth was keenly aware of her parents' disappointment at her choices: "When I didn't go straight to college, my father died. They think it's really important if you want to get a halfway decent job, you have to graduate college. And not just like a B.A., but you have to go and get more."

Nor were respondents like Beth and Paul alone in their struggles with school. Despite the strong emphasis they attributed to Asian parents in education, about 21 percent of the Hunter respondents had brothers or sisters (mainly brothers) who had dropped out of high school or college, or had received their GED. These siblings typically had ended up waiting tables (either at Chinese or non-Chinese restaurants) or engaging in what the respondents suspected were illicit activities. The percentage of respondents who had seen their childhood friends leave school was higher still. When asked why this had happened, my respondents pointed to apathy toward school, difficulties with schoolwork, and the desire to make money. Waiting tables, plumbing work, warehouse jobs, odd jobs here and there, typically within the ethnic economy, were the lot of these friends and siblings. Downward mobility, rather than the upward mobility we typically associate with the children of Chinese immigrants, seemed to be the path they were embarked upon.

Certainly, their accounts complicate Ogbu's (1995) characterization of the Chinese as having positive views on schooling because they are a voluntary immigrant minority. It is true that my Hunter respondents did not speak of this alienation from schooling on the part of their peers and siblings (and, in some cases, themselves) along the lines of the oppositional identity that Ogbu proposes African Americans adopt to cope with racial barriers and limited economic opportunities. Nonetheless, their comments were much closer to the negative frame of mind on education that Ogbu associates with African Americans than to the optimistic one he associates with voluntary minorities (Goto 1997).

The Model Minority: Another Expectation to Live By

It also became clear that this sense of failure was not solely an individual matter. Two social phenomena heightening my respondents' sense of inadequacy made them feel even worse about being at Hunter. One of these was the model-minority stereotype. The prevalence and importance of stereotypes to everyday life has been well-documented (Schuman et al. 1997; Dasgupta et al. 2000). In the case of second-generation Asian ethnics, Kibria has argued that the model-minority stereotype functions as "an idealized and evaluative yardstick of achievement" which Asian ethnics believe they do not and can never measure up to (2002, 135). Consistent with this, my Hunter respondents roundly criticized the model-minority image as being unrepresentative, one that imposed a set of psychological burdens on them. The common complaint I heard was that the model-minority stereotype was very much at odds with their own family backgrounds and experiences with school.

Deborah Ow was particularly vocal on this point: "The media is always portraying [Asian Americans] as people who have it well off. Always talking about people who make it to Princeton, Harvard, or Yale. And if you have kids in Yale or Harvard, you must be doing well." Such a presentation of wealth and stellar academic achievement was certainly inconsistent with Deborah's status as the daughter of a garment worker and a restaurant worker living in Chinatown, and as someone who had struggled in high school before finally obtaining a GED. When we met, Deborah was completing her bachelor's degree at the age of thirty-one. As she observed, "Maybe it was me—I just didn't find the schooling experience productive for me."

According to my Hunter respondents, the model-minority stereotype powerfully informs their everyday lives, by shaping how people of other racial and ethnic groups view and interact with them, especially in school.[3] Explained Julia Lau:

> Americans sort of have this stereotype of, "Oh, you're Chinese. You're supposed to be smart. You're supposed to be an A student, and stuff like that. So what happened to you?" It's like, "Excuse me?" I've gotten special treatment from professors because they figure I'm supposed to be smarter. And it's really another standard that you have to uphold. And another expectation you have to live by.

Susan Chu had a similar perspective:

> I remember when I was in high school and junior high school, I missed a homework, and they're like, by God, gee, you *missed* a homework. You *failed* a test. 'Cause it's like that Asian or Chinese thing, you don't do that. It's just not in your genes or something. But it's not true.

The frustration expressed by these students indicates the psychological costs of having to fulfill a prescribed image (Toupin and Son 1993). Benny Sen, for instance, talked about how the model-minority stereotype shaped a critical voice within that assessed and, ultimately, judged the actions that he thought about taking. Embedded in the notion of Asian Americans as model minorities is not only the idea of academic prowess but that of passivity as well, as Benny indicated to me:

> A: I mean, I'm Asian, but sometimes I don't feel like doing anything, nothing. Just eat, eat, sleep, survive. Listen to the radio. So that stereotype. And the stereotype that they're not assertive. Sometimes, I try to be assertive, but maybe it doesn't work all the time. How do people view me? Is it just because I am Asian that I'm not assertive, or is it because I'm shy? And I know stereotypes are not the ideal way of looking at yourself and what you represent. But I'll admit that I think about it sometimes. Am I speaking coherently?
>
> I: Yes.
>
> A: It places a burden, it places a definite psychological burden on who I am, on my daily life, occasionally, whenever I choose to think about it, I think about it. And it's just one added distraction.
>
> I: How does it become a daily burden? In what ways?
>
> A: Because whenever I perform, I do something, I prepare for a test, prepare for a paper, or even prepare myself for a presentation, I do something where I will be judged. Whenever I judge myself, I'm thinking in terms of those stereotypes, they are definitely on my checklist. Do I fit the stereotype, in addition to the basic checklist I have when I judge myself in performing a presentation, or performing on a test. Did I do well? Did I study well? Did I do enough but did I do enough?

As Benny's comments suggest, his attempts to distance himself from stereotypes of Asians as passive superachievers still did not shake off his critical internal voice. Being Asian American meant that he did not have just an individual set of criteria with which to assess how he fared in school or in the world at large. He also had to confront an inescapable set of criteria imposed by others on the basis of racialized ethnicity, criteria that he himself had internalized.

Ethnic Networks: "Bragging Rights"

The ethnic networks that these respondents' parents engaged in also prescribed a compelling image of academic achievement for them. Min Zhou has argued that these ethnic networks serve as an effective channel of shared information among Chinese working-class immigrant parents for how to navigate the infamously Byzantine public school system in New York City.[4] Certainly, the accounts of my urban-enclave respondents, regardless of whether they had gone to Hunter or Columbia, speak to the vibrancy of such networks. While the respondents' parents were mostly unable to move out of neighborhoods with low-performing public schools or to afford private or even parochial school tuitions, they could draw on such informal ethnic networks. Thus, much as Stanton-Salazar (1997) theorized, institutional agents, in this case, kin, friends, and coworkers living in better-off neighborhoods and with varying resources and lengths of residence in the United States, came together to provide an invaluable source of knowledge about school programs and general academic help. My respondents reported that their parents had relied on such networks to learn about New York City's public-school rankings (not just in their neighborhoods but in areas relatively distant in relation to where they lived).

In some cases, parents had exhaustively followed up every lead, however happenstance. While their intentions had been sound, their children remembered that the result was they had had to attend a myriad of elementary and junior high schools, sometimes too many to count. Grace Li, for instance, attended a seeming whirlwind of Chinatown schools that her mother had heard about through the ethnic networks. Grace also spent some time at a Catholic school, even though the family was Buddhist:

> I went to a Catholic school, the Catholic one on Mott Street. I went
> there from fourth grade to eighth grade. My mom kept changing me. I

remember being changed to a lot of public elementary schools, like the one behind Allen Street, the one near Pathmark, near Pell Street, and [P.S.] 124, I went all over. I went to all the public schools.

Another strategy to improve the educational odds for children through ethnic networks was taking the address of a friend or relative who lived in a more upscale neighborhood so as to gain access to the better school district. Mary Sing provided one such example of this "fake address" tactic:

> I went to Forest Hills HS in Queens. My local, zoned high school was Newtown, but that's not a very good school. Forest Hills is a better school. So my dad wielded his way for me to go there. Lucky me. He knew a friend that lived in the Forest Hills district—am I going to get arrested? I'm kidding. With a notarized letter saying he would be my guardian for like a little while. And then they do that whole scam thing. I don't know how my dad knew it was better, actually. I guess through word of mouth from other parents. And Forest Hills is a better neighborhood than Elmhurst, income being higher, therefore it's probably a better school. It looked better.

Forest Hills High School was not the marquee high school enshrined through these networks, however. The prizes to be won were the city's specialized public high schools, namely, Brooklyn Technical, Bronx Science, and Stuyvesant. Each year, more than twenty thousand eighth and ninth graders vie for a spot at these three schools by taking a three-hour entrance examination in math and verbal skills. The stakes are high. Stuyvesant High School, which moved in the mid-1990s to a posh new site in Lower Manhattan that cost an estimated $150 million, generally has only about seven hundred spots available (*New York Times*, 3 December 1995, sec. 1, p. 51). The payoff is also high. Bronx Science boasts more finalists in the acclaimed Westinghouse science competition than any other high school in the nation, and five Nobel Prize winners are among its alumni (Forero 2000). Unsurprisingly, given such statistics, my respondents reported learning from their parents that gaining admittance into one of these schools could ensure their future. As my respondents told me, this was just something "everybody knew."

Ethnic networks served another purpose as well: they were a venue where parents could engage in a status hierarchy that buffered them from the pressures and losses of working-class immigrant life. According to my urban-enclave respondents, the ethnic networks did this by making the academic performance of children central. In allowing parents to gauge their children's performance relative to other people's children, the networks provided parents with "a source of emotional support and psychological comfort" (Zhou 2001, 167). Even if parents found the migration process to be difficult and psychologically draining, they could at least talk up their children with their friends, coworkers, and family. In short, talking about the accomplishments of the next generation became a way for parents to enhance their own social status and to make up for the daily challenges of survival that they faced in the world of the enclave. Several of my respondents accorded this parental dynamic its own name, calling it "bragging rights." Grace Li described "bragging rights" in this way: "Well, my parents have a lot of pride. 'Cause, you know, she works at a factory, and at the factory there is a lot of competition between the mothers in order to make themselves look good."

Ethnic networks, however, have a negative side that is not much reported on by scholars. Previous accounts of ethnic networks have highlighted the benefits derived from them, insofar as they support distinct ethnic-class strategies to promote generational mobility through education. This is not surprising, given that such accounts are largely derived from the perspectives and experiences of parents seeking to manage a notoriously complex public educational system. In contrast, the viewpoints of children, and in particular, those children who do not do well in school and/or do not have a linear trajectory to college, have largely gone unexplored.

Most of my Hunter respondents belong in this category of children, and the ethnic networks that their parents relied on often brought them psychological costs along with benefits. This is because an unintended but very real consequence of the ethnic network dynamic is for parents to compare their respective children, one against the other. Even those children who have done well often feel uncomfortable with the current of competition. Ivory Miao, for example, a senior at Barnard, related how "bragging rights" unfolded in her family. It is noteworthy that the members of Ivory's family refer to her college as "Columbia," the better-known (at least in their ethnic circles) name that connotes an *Ivy League* institution. In Ivory's case, using "Columbia" instead of "Barnard" is a slight shading of the truth:

> My grandparents are actually proud of me, but they're only proud of me because they can boast about the name of the school. "Well, you know, she goes to Columbia." Just kind of drop it. And automatically, their

friend would be like, oh, we have a son at, and as soon as this person is not from an Ivy League school, they'll shoot them down. Oh, she's too good for your son. He goes to Stonybrook only. We want somebody from Harvard or Yale. Oh, stop, stop. They use it to boast, as opposed to not they're proud of me per se but they use it as bragging rights.

Ivory's parents fixated on one young Chinese American girl, in particular, intent that their daughter should outdo her:

And, ultimately, when it came to high school, our parents started talking again, first thing out of her mother's mouth was, what college is your daughter going to? And my mother's like, oh, Columbia. Don't even talk. Your daughter is going where? Syracuse what? And I was just like, Mom, you're so rude. Shut up, you know. We both worked hard. We're going into different fields, you know.

It was this kind of competitive atmosphere that left those children who were not meeting the established community norms for academic excellence feeling, in the best-case scenario, rather left out, and in the worst case, alienated. It is not difficult then to understand how children who do not get into the city's specialized public high schools or who simply do not like school very much can feel like failures. As my respondents told me, one's performance is never merely an individual matter, but one that is weighted against dozens of other children, "so and so's son or daughter," who always seem to fare better. That a child has not met the prescribed community standards means that their parents have nothing, or nothing positive, at least, to report on in these networks. Consequently, a child believes that she is letting down her parents, both privately and publicly, with all the attendant burdens that implies.

This was evident when Julia Lau talked about the drawbacks of growing up as the child of Chinese immigrants. Hunter was the third college that Julia, who was twenty-five, had attended. Her first college experience had been at Mount Saint Vincent, a Catholic four-year school in the Bronx where Julia had spent her first two years "partying" rather than studying. Julia soon left the school to regroup at her parents' home in Chinatown, and eventually matriculated at the Borough of Manhattan Community College before transferring into Hunter. Along the way, she had switched fields from nursing to education. Julia spoke thoughtfully about the pressures she felt from her parents and the community, and about how they affected her sense of self:

There's this way of thinking for Chinese Americans that you have to do better, and you have this idealized look on life that you should be doing, and if you don't achieve that, it's like, "Okay, well, then, I'm garbage. I can't do that." And you are expected to do a lot of things, being a Chinese American from Chinese, traditional China parents. You know, they come here and they expect you to do certain things so. Education to them is really important because they didn't have it. And for us, for all three of us [kids] to finish is like a miracle, you know. And since I'm the last one, and they feel like I'm taking a long time, it's a lot of pressure. And the only thing I would say is the bad thing about being Chinese Americans is that they put a lot of pressure on themselves. And I've encountered a lot of Chinese American kids that are going through the same thing.

Peggy Teng thought the issue lay more with the parents and wished for a more "caring" kind of parenting rather than one centered on the weight of expectation. It was the hope that children's academic performance would both impart prestige to the family and, equally important, improve the family's socioeconomic status that became the focus of the parent–child relationship. And children do not necessarily have an easy time of it, as Peggy recalled:

A: I think that the emphasis like on the progeny being the savior of the family or something like that, in terms of they're the ones who are going to push everyone forward, and so therefore, you have to succeed, you have to do everything. Not enough unconditional support. Maybe that's too much to ask. . . . I think that they could provide more support for us. I mean, when you compare it with a Western family, where they're much more kind of physically open with each other, I think that's another lack. Even the language is harsh. You know, maybe, there aren't the words to show that, to show the caring. But there are too many words to show the criticism.

Q: Like what words?

A: Maybe phrases, not so much like words. I remember getting very upset because I thought I failed a test. And instead of saying, well, you tried your best, they said, or my mother said, I don't know, she criticized me. She reprimanded me. She was angry that I was upset. Perhaps, I mean, she didn't know how to deal with it. On the other hand, I felt that she was like angry at me for, you know. . . . So yeah, there's this kind of comfort thing that's lacking.

The Path to Hunter

I Could Have Gone to Yale

Given all this pressure, one central dimension of my interviews with the Hunter respondents was their take on how they had ended up there in the first place. A few of the male respondents I interviewed adopted an attitude that was part bluster, yet nonetheless grounded in the idea that doing well in school depended on effort, not natural ability (Chen and Stevenson 1995). In other words, they reported that they certainly had the capability of making it to an elite college; they had just slacked off. Douglas Chan, for example, a Hunter junior, was the only one of his high school friends to go to Hunter. His friends, whom he described as "nerds," had gone to schools like New York University, Queens College (another centerpiece of the CUNY system, but with a more traditional campus setting), Columbia, and Cornell. As to why this had happened, Douglas argued that he simply had not worked hard enough. In his mind, he was certainly gifted enough to have made it to a "better school." As he observed of his parents' views on his education: "Well, they know if I would have put work into it, I could have probably gone somewhere like Yale. I really didn't put much effort, but then they knew I could." Dean told me his teenage sister, also a "nerd," would definitely go to a better college.

Jeffrey Yao, a Hunter junior, also drew upon bluster to explain why he was not doing so well in his classes. When we met, Jeffrey was carrying only a 2.3 grade point average out of a 4-point scale. He explained this away by saying that his classes were too easy and that they ended up boring him into a lack of effort. He definitely believed that his grade point average should have been at least a 3.4:

> If the class is too easy for me, I don't pay attention and [I get] too cocky with the class. I just don't pay attention. This summer, I am taking some classes that I might be interested in, so [I'll] get my GPA back up. Where it supposed to be, belong. Which I had 3.4, but it just dropped because I'm too lazy. Sometimes, classes are too easy for me, I can't take it.

What Jeffrey gave short shrift to were the demands of his schedule. In addition to a two-hour round-trip commute each day from school to home and back again, and taking four courses, Jeffrey worked between twenty-seven and thirty-six hours a week as a sales associate to pay for expenses and tuition and to help out with household expenses for his parents and siblings. When I expressed amazement at how he was able to manage such a crammed schedule, he explained: "I don't sleep a lot, that's why. Four hours, maybe, tops. So tired. I sleep at work during my break time, so tired." Although Jeffrey was trying to cut back to working only eighteen hours a week, he never made the connection between his schedule and his school performance. Other students, however, were more inclined to cite the lack of parental resources as the key factor in their path to and performance in college, as we shall see in the next section.

Limited Family Resources

The K–12 Years

That their parents were constrained by socioeconomic status was the dominant explanation voiced by my Hunter respondents on why they were not "typical" Asian American overachievers. It was true enough that their parents had held high educational aspirations for them (as they believed all Asian parents did for their children); the only difference was that their parents had lacked the resources to help them translate those aspirations into reality. For those living within the tight confines of Chinatown tenement housing, where voices and smells overwhelmed thin walls and ceilings, it was difficult enough to find a quiet place to study; there was no room in the apartments themselves and there was certainly no quiet.

Overall, when comparing their experiences to the Asian or Chinese American "standard," these respondents believed that the push for education in their families had been weaker, due to the challenges faced by their immigrant parents—coping with limited education, limited fluency in English, jobs in manual labor, and a low standard of living that could lead to marital strife and financial stress. Such conditions, my Hunter respondents argued, were not conducive to academic success. Equally important, my respondents believed that their families did not represent the norm for Chinese Americans, even within the enclave. It was this kind of belief in their own exceptionalism that allowed the notion of the centrality of the Asian immigrant family in children's outcomes to go unchallenged. This is similar to Wendy Luttrell's (1997) nuanced analysis of how working-class women, black and white, made sense of their disengagement from schooling by citing their mother's lack of involvement and inadequate parenting strategies. In this way, the institutional mechanisms of social inequality that inform both the mothering and schooling these women received were obscured in favor of an individualist account.

Kathy Zhao, the daughter of a seamstress and car service driver, was one example. Kathy was aware that she and her younger brother were far from academic superstars. The twenty-seven-year-old junior at Hunter College had dropped out of the first college she attended and had then worked for six years. Her brother was a high school dropout, and she suspected he was now relying on petty crime to make ends meet. In thinking back to the paths she and her brother had taken, Kathy pointed to her parents' divorce as a pivotal moment, one that set them apart from other Chinese families, whom she believed gave more motivation and direction to their children. According to Kathy, she and her brother had been the victims of the emotional and financial fallout from their parents' bitter breakup:

> They weren't strict parents. We were able to go out and do whatever we wanted. I grew up lying and so did he, you know. We didn't grow up in that typical Chinese household. You know, they didn't instill the culture, the tradition, and the language. Like, we didn't go to Chinese school, you know what I mean. And I understand why, because, you know, they were divorced and they had their own problems and issues. And so in a lot of ways we were kind of like left to the side, you know.

The Zhaos nevertheless had the same academic standards for their children as other Chinatown parents did. Kathy remembered their distress when she decided to drop out of college. And yet, even as she related this, Kathy asserted that her parents' childrearing practices had been lax compared to other Chinatown parents and had led to the problems in school that she and her brother faced:

> They didn't like it, totally opposed to it, but it was my decision. I didn't want to be in school. They didn't like it. Yeah, because I think I am the first one in our family to go to school, to go to college. And so I guess honestly they wanted to see me, you know, finish college and everything.

But like I said, they weren't strict to the point where, if they were strict, my brother and I would have turned out a lot better, you see what I mean.

Ling Choy, another daughter of divorced parents, was different from Kathy because she and her brother had done well in school. She had gotten into Brooklyn Technical High, a specialized high school, and her brother was then at Baruch College in the CUNY system. Yet even she thought her parents had been "not very traditional" and "not very strict" when compared to the parents of her Chinese American friends. That she and her brother did well was in spite of their parents' lack of attention to their schooling and overall development. Thus, Ling observed:

> They did struggle a lot, probably that's why they didn't pay a lot of attention. Maybe if they paid more attention to developing our other kinds of interests, besides just school, 'cause we did really well in school. But I have friends, now when I talk to them, they tell me how they were like young, they went to gymnastics, whatever activity. I guess, just to research stuff, why didn't they provide that for us? That wasn't important, maybe. They didn't really think that contributed to being well-rounded.

Ling was one of the few respondents who said her parents did not emphasize education, again linking this attitude to their social class background. Ling's mother, for example, had only gone as far as middle school in China, and she was presently managing a store in Chinatown. Her father, who had attended some high school in China, was a restaurant worker. Although her father had been able to buy a three-family house, using the rental income to pay for the mortgage, money had always been tight in the household:

> My family is like all working-class people. They've made it through life without education, so they don't stress it that much. Like I talk to other friends, and their families do. But I think mine is a little different. Like if I tell them, I'm going to take a year off to work, they wouldn't mind it. They wouldn't say, you have to finish school.

However, a much more complex picture of her parents' views on education emerged later in the interview:

> They definitely want me to finish college. But they haven't really pushed me, I don't think. Like even since I was young, I would do well in school. I think my mother was really involved, but my dad was not

that involved. I think they'd rather me go to business school, mainly go into business, because they've dealt with business all their lives, like they've worked in restaurant businesses. They haven't said it to me directly, but they'll brag, oh, so and so's daughter goes to Stern Business School, whatever, you know. They want me to be really successful, but they haven't really stressed how, what way, which I think is different.

Like her earlier comments, this one pointed to Ling's belief that her family was somehow different from other Chinese families who may have placed more stress on education and who were more involved in their children's schooling. Yet the passage also suggests that Ling's parents do, in fact, have clear ideas of what they would like her to pursue (e.g., business), and, indeed, that they have specific schools in mind, based on what their friends' children have done. The difference is relative rather than absolute—her parents seem to stress education less than other Chinese parents.

Another theme voiced by my Hunter respondents was that the ethnic networks, while noteworthy for providing parents with a crucial venue for sharing information about schools, are limited in their actual effect. To borrow from Baker and Stevenson's conceptual framework, ethnic networks represent "one crucial point of parental influence" in children's schooling (1989, 165). However, the cumulative influence that Baker and Stevenson have identified with effective parenting is absent. This is due to the very disadvantages that parents sought to overcome through the networks, for example, time constraints imposed by their labor-intensive jobs, their own lack of education and lack of financial resources, and poor English-language skills. As a result, parents are not able to help their children with school by all the traditional measures that educational researchers have identified: meeting with teachers, going over homework, reading a book to children, enrolling them in enrichment programs (other than for Chinese language, which my respondents disliked). Some of my respondents said their parents did not even know how they were doing in school because they could not understand the report cards that were sent home. It was easy for them to circumvent their parents, since they were more likely to be found at work than at home. Thus, for all the benefits derived from the ethnic networks, my Hunter respondents still felt very alone in making their way through school.

For instance, Deborah Ow reported that her parents used the networks to learn about some of the "better" local elementary schools and the specialized high schools. But when it became clear that their children would not get into the specialized high schools, the networks could provide no further information. Left on her own, Deborah had followed some of her Brooklyn friends to Canarsie High School in Brooklyn. As she elaborated, she had not counted on the hour-plus commute from Chinatown to Canarsie; by the time she had realized about the long commute, Deborah's options had narrowed to Seward Park High School, the last-choice option for Chinatown children because of its reputation back in the 1980s as being an academically deprived and violent school:

> I jumped around a lot. I went to school [at Canarsie] and I didn't find the atmosphere really good. I had friends there and I was still living in Manhattan and I made the trek all the way there. Yeah, I was young and impressionable and they were like, yeah, come to my school, so I went. And that's probably why I did not do well because it was such a long trek there, it was like an hour, I don't know, it was over an hour-long trip and we still had to take the bus. Then I went to Seward Park in Chinatown.

Looking back, Deborah acknowledged her parents' high educational aspirations for her and her brother. At the same time, she pointed out that doing well in school was more than a matter of parents expecting it. According to Deborah, parental involvement was also key. Her parents, for instance, simply lacked the time, energy, and background to become involved. Deborah voiced ideas that are consistent with what educational researchers have found, namely, that parental involvement acts as a powerful mediating variable in how family socioeconomic status matters in one's attainment, through influencing students' experiences with school and, ultimately, their achievements (Baker and Stevenson 1986; Lareau 1987; Useem 1992). Thus, Deborah remarked:

> I think that my parents, they want us to succeed and have an education or whatever we choose to do but there wasn't a big push for it because I think they weren't pushed and also they were too busy with their jobs. I mean there was nobody to sit there and read a book with you or check your homework or stuff like that.

Children whose parents were able to use the networks to better effect nonetheless reported that their parents were unable to be greatly involved in their schooling. Parents did not have the necessary knowledge to help their children with their assignments or even to understand what their children actually did at the school they had worked so hard to place them in. Mary Sing, the woman whose father managed to place her in Forest Hills High School, spoke to this:

> Besides my father trying to get us into like the best schools possible, they weren't very involved with our schoolwork. Partly because they were always working, but also they don't have the working knowledge of the English language. So basically we had to fend for ourselves in regards to homework and assignments and stuff like that.

Alberta Tao was another example. Her story underscores that while the enclave Chinese encouraged their children to strive for a specialized public high school, they could not facilitate their children's survival in the very competitive environments existing in those schools. As Attewell has noted, some "star" public high schools "have developed winner-take-all characteristics" that end up stratifying their students (2001, 1). Along those lines, Alberta reported that the workload at Brooklyn Technical High was more intense than anything she had ever experienced. In some ways, she felt unprepared. It was also then that Alberta started working an afterschool job and met the "wrong people," ethnic Chinese from Vietnam, who had dropped out of high school and "hung out" in Chinatown. Alberta, soon a pool-hall regular, started cutting classes, and failing classes, including her entire junior year. She was able to make up the credits in night classes held at another high school and in summer school, but due to a bureaucratic mix-up, she still ended up staying back a year. Somehow, though, Alberta was able to keep most of this a secret from her parents, whom she says had little knowledge of what was going on.

The College Application Process

Beyond having an impact on how my respondents experienced elementary through high school on an everyday level, limited family resources played a crucial role in that key rite of adolescence—the college application process. Family college visits, a summer staple in middle-class families, were simply not an option. The parents of my Hunter respondents, while encouraging them to go on to college and even providing the names of some target schools, could not take the time off from work to accompany their children on school visits. Nor were they able to help with the essay process, or simply with filling out the applications. Consequently, many of my respondents reported that the application process seemed to occur in a void. Not only were parents absent from the process, but teachers and counselors were also minimally helpful since my respondents typically attended large, urban schools where attention to student needs was sparse. *peg kuu*

By the time some of my respondents had figured out the application process, not to mention the complicated financial aid forms, they had missed many of the deadlines, and suddenly there were few options left. Even for those who were on time with their applications, happenstance more than a deep understanding of the school marked their decisions on where to apply. Quite a number said they had made their college decisions based on which ones "looked nice in the brochures" (and understandably, they had often regretted their decision afterward). Others might have heard about a college from friends or relatives who thought they might like it, but once they enrolled and got to campus, they found that they hated it. Still others were unprepared for living in a small town or city and the responsibilities that came with being on their own. It should not surprise us, then, that some took a circuitous path to the bachelor's degree, with stops along the way for stints at different institutions, and for exits from the educational system altogether to reflect and work.

Money as Deciding Factor

The role of financial pressures, even for families who had a middle-class status in the enclave, cannot be underestimated in why my respondents chose to attend Hunter, a public commuter school. Despite their parents' hope that they would end up at an elite, private university, many of the parents would have been unable to pay the steep tuitions at such institutions unless the child won a scholarship. Robert Ong was one example. His older brother had to leave New York University after a semester because, even with financial aid, the tuition had been just too much for his parents, a retired chef and a nurse's aide supervisor, to manage. Robert did not even bother applying to NYU, despite his own interest in the school. He was fortunate, however, in that he applied for and was awarded a fellowship from a national funding agency, which covered his tuition and research costs at Hunter.

The need to help out the family financially was another issue. In some cases, my respondents were already working part-time. Lan Jong and her brother, for example, had to schedule their classes around the shifts they worked at their father's restaurant business. Others were trying to complete their undergraduate degrees quickly so as to contribute to the family on a full-time basis (Kwong 1987; Hune 1998). Bonnie Tai, for example, had started off as an accounting major at Pace, a private university. By her third semester, she wanted to switch fields but was fearful of taking longer to graduate (and consequently of paying more tuition than she had originally anticipated). The pressures were intensified because, as the oldest child she was expected to graduate "as soon as possible" and to financially assist her parents. She eventually decided to transfer into the CUNY system because it was cheaper.

Barbara Zhu, a Hunter junior with hopes of attending law school, was wrestling with a dilemma of her own. With her mother, a seamstress, out of work, the family could not subsist on the father's income as a restaurant worker. To support the family, Barbara's older sister had settled for an associate's degree and had started working full-time. The assumption was that she would return to school once Barbara had graduated from Hunter and started working. Barbara did not even know how to bring up the possibility of her going to law school:

> I haven't really talked to [my sister] about the fact that I'm thinking of grad school. If I go to grad school, that's at least a couple of years more. So I don't know what's going to happen. I don't want her to stop [school]. She deserves to go to school just as much as I do, and she has already sacrificed. And I really don't know.

Money was the chief reason why Hunter respondents ended up there. First, they wanted to stay in the city (mainly because they could not afford to go away for school); second, they knew of CUNY's cheaper price tag in general, and of Hunter's reputation as one of the best CUNY schools; and third, they wanted a school conveniently located on a subway line that ran by their home. Barbara Zhu, for instance, turned down the chance to attend the State University of New York at Buffalo because her family did not have a car and she realized traveling to and from school would have meant an eight-hour bus ride. The drawback to CUNY schools was that, while they were cheaper than private and state universities, classes were often overbooked and it sometimes took more than four years to graduate. And while tuition and fees at Hunter may have been relatively inexpensive ($1,600 per semester for full-time students who were city residents), they were expensive enough for students already on tight budgets to schedule in additional work time to pay for school. Mary Sing's schedule was not atypical: she worked twenty hours a week at an interior design firm, interned sixteen hours at a media conglomerate because it would further her goal of a career in public relations, and took a full load of five classes at Hunter, somehow maintaining a 3.0 average out of a possible 4.0.

This chapter has been about the resolution of an apparent paradox. While my Hunter respondents identified the Asian family as a strong motivating force in children's education, they also cited the importance of structural constraints that could presumably challenge the ethnic culture explanation. Instead, the structural constraints were ultimately subsumed to this idea of culture. Consistent with Clifford Geertz's insight that individuals are called upon to provide a rationale for exceptions to cultural norms if their "received ideas of the 'normal and the natural' are to be kept intact" (1975, 14), my Hunter respondents still subscribed to the idea of an ethnic advantage, as mediated by parents. The key difference was that they believed their parents were somehow lacking, deviating from the "standard." For this reason, they believed that the rule did not hold up in their case.

In this way, my Hunter respondents were able to resolve what might have been a serious challenge to their own beliefs. Despite their eloquent reflections on how structural factors had influenced their own road to college, these respondents nevertheless ended up supporting the cultural script. The class explanations that they provided did not actually shake their belief that the Asian immigrant family is the key to the educational success of Asian Americans. The irony is telling, as my Hunter respondents ended up continuing to support a script that cast them as failures, or at the very least, as outliers.

Chapter 6

A PLACE AT COLUMBIA

How did my Columbia respondents understand their path to college? In the case of those students from middle-class, white suburbia, the majority of my Columbia sample, the path to college was a straightforward one. Their accounts emphasized the role of parents, specifically the high level of parental involvement in their education.

This is consistent with the research showing that parental involvement acts as a powerful mediating variable in the relationship between family background and educational attainment (Baker and Stevenson 1986; Lareau 1987; Useem 1992). In Lareau's (1987) study, for example, working- and middle-class white families both valued education but promoted educational success in different ways. Working-class parents turned over their children's education to the teacher, while their middle-class counterparts were more likely to view the teacher as a partner in their children's schooling and to devote "time, money and other material resources in the home" to reinforce and add to what their children learned in school.

The puzzle for researchers is that even when socioeconomic background is controlled, Asian students outperform their peers, persuading some to argue that an "Asian effect" exists; in other words, Asian parents are distinct in the ways in which they use their resources to enhance their children's educational achievement (Fejgin 1995). For example, Kao (1995) finds little difference in the average incomes of white and Asian families in her study; what is different is the "greater commitment of resources for education" on the part of Asian families. Asians are more likely to save money for college, to provide their children with a place to study, to have a personal computer in the home, to restrict the number of hours spent watching television, and to "enroll their children in art, music, ethnic history, and computer classes." Whites, on the other hand, are more likely to give their children a room of their own, and to monitor the types of television programs that their children can watch, as opposed to the number of hours. Thus, Kao attributes the higher grades earned by Asian eighth graders to family socioeconomic status, parental levels of education, and to the decisions of Asian parents to invest more in educational resources, which she argues is a cultural difference.

Similar to Kao, Sun (1998) finds that the typical East Asian family invests most of its resources in such strategies as saving a portion of the annual family income for the children's college education and providing a computer at home for educational purposes, as well as cultural classes and activities for their children, all of which promotes their academic success in math and science. Or, as Sun writes, "If parents of other races adopt a more aggressive investment strategy in these resources, the Asian effect [will] be much smaller" (1998, 452).

It should be noted, however, that the Asian American families in the National Educational Longitudinal Study (NELS), a data set commonly used by educational researchers, tend to have high incomes (e.g., in Kao's study, the mean family income of Asians was $48,676, as compared to $46,964 for whites) and high educational attainment (e.g., in Sun's study, 49 percent of the East Asian parents had a four-year college degree or higher, compared to 30 percent for whites, 13 percent for African Americans, and 12 percent for Hispanics). It seems likely, then, that these strategies are more commonly adopted by middle-class Asian parents.

In this chapter, I demonstrate that such strategies were indeed crucial to how my middle-class, suburban respondents understood how they came to Columbia. As evidenced in Chapter 3, while feeling very much at home in suburbia, my suburban respondents nevertheless believed that they could claim an ethnic advantage over their white peers. That their parents were more highly involved than other suburban parents and that they participated in a wider array of afterschool lessons and summer programs led them to believe that their path to Columbia was logical. The feelings of commonality that they experienced among fellow Asian American students at Columbia only reinforced this idea. Those respondents who came from the urban enclaves, about a fifth of my Columbia sample, had had a decidedly different experience, one grounded in class constraints and thus closer to that of my Hunter respondents.

Parental Involvement

K–12 Years

We saw in Chapter 5 that my Hunter respondents' parents were very concerned about the particular schools their children attended, a task complicated by the fact that they lived in urban areas with poor or mediocre schools and by their own limited financial resources. Along similar lines, my suburban Columbia respondents reported that their parents were quite consumed with the search for the right school, which became a dominant feature of their childhood and adolescent years. As one would expect, these parents had many more options to choose from. For example, some children attended elite private schools, including the boarding school Phillips Academy in Andover, Massachusetts, and day schools like Mirman in Los Angeles and the Trinity and Dalton schools in Manhattan. Other options were well-funded suburban public schools, and in a few cases, urban public schools with magnet programs. What the schools shared was their high performance. It was through their own research and talking to teachers and administrators that these parents learned of such schools.

For example, in advance of their move to Los Angeles from Alaska, the Fans asked their daughter's teacher whether she knew of any good schools in Los Angeles. Although their daughter Ava was attending a gifted program at an Alaska public elementary school, her teacher suggested Mirman, an exclusive private day school in Los Angeles. Mrs. Fan related that she had at first considered the Los Angeles Unified School District and its gifted program, only to be disheartened by the response she received from public school officials:

We found out that she would have to go to the regular school and then wait a year, basically waste a year. And then the next year she'd be placed in the highly gifted program. Actually, a principal of L.A. Unified told me, "If financially you're capable, if she were my child, I would send her to Mirman." So that was a decision that was made for us.

After graduating from Mirman, their daughter continued on to a private high school. Returning to public school was always an option, but it just never seemed the right thing to do. In Mrs. Fan's words, "Private school just offered so much more in terms of the school environment, in terms of curriculum, in terms of what's being taught and their approach."

For other parents, who could not afford private schools, the next best option was to seek out the best public school districts, often going to considerable lengths to do so. Diana Chin's parents are illustrative of this option. When they moved to Boston, Diana was four years old and the Chins' immediate concern was where she would attend school, with a long-term view of what the school would provide vis-à-vis college placement rates, highly motivated peers, and high-quality teaching. The decision was between Boston, which had more affordable housing, and Brookline, an upscale suburb where they could only afford to buy a small condominium. In the end, the choice was easy—the best school district won out. Mr. Chin:

> I knew that if I live in Boston and the greater Boston area, our daughter Diana will have to be bussed. She will go to a school that she may not like. So I decided that the best thing for me to do is to buy an apartment in Brookline. Because Brookline High School, it's what other people say is a neighborhood school. It's like a private high school, except that it's a public high school. . . . She got a very good crowd in Brookline. She mixed up with the right people. And most of her classmates in Brookline, from grade one, kindergarten on, they're all honor students. They're all merit scholars like her. She got a prize in biology and her friend got a prize in something else, they walk to school together. They go from our apartment to her house. They walk to school together. And she went to Harvard and Diana went to Columbia. . . . That is how I made my choice for my daughter.

The Chins did not think twice about their choice, especially given the fact that parents from neighboring towns were willing to pay $8,000 a year to send their children to Brookline High School. Following Diana's high school graduation, though, the Chins moved to a house in Framingham, a less prestigious address, to be sure, but one that came with more space.

Two of my respondents' mothers were forced to leave the suburbs follow-ing their divorces and were thus faced with the unpleasant prospect of send-ing their children to urban schools with fewer resources. Mrs. Wu is an ex-ample. She moved to New York City, where she eventually confronted a dilemma: the local elementary schools were fine, but the local public middle school was not highly ranked. Yet she could neither afford to pay for private school nor return to the suburbs. As an alternative, Mrs. Wu concentrated her energies on locating urban public middle schools with magnet programs that would allow them to accept students living outside their designated bound-aries. Finding these schools was a task that involved delving into the bureau-cracy of New York City public schools, a daunting prospect even for native-born parents, let alone for immigrants. According to Mrs. Wu, persistence was the key: "I ask. I ask. And then the magnet school, we got the informa-tion from her elementary school. We read from newspaper, or journal some-times have some information."

Melinda, her daughter, had more striking memories of how she ended up at Intermediate School 194. Describing the school she had been zoned for as "crappy," she distinctly remembered not wanting to go there and her mother's role in trying to get her someplace else:

> I had been saying, "I don't want to go there." And the kids were really kind of scary looking, at least the ones I saw. I'm stereotyping. But just the kids that I saw in the schoolyard, at least the ones that tended to still be there at 12 midnight or something like that. It was very intimidating. But she definitely helped make the decision, she didn't want me to go there either.

> And she was actually very, very, very very not only encouraging about the process, but actually a big driving force. For example, to insure that I got into the magnet school, she told me to write letters to the person in charge of choosing on the Board of Education. And also to get recom-mendations from a couple of teachers. I think I'm the only one that did that in the school because most kids in elementary school didn't do that.

The strategy of writing to the Board of Education and of soliciting teachers' recommendation letters might not have ensured Melinda's admittance into the school, but it did instill in her more confidence about the process. The ex-perience underscored a key lesson for Melinda: school was important, and getting into a good school was something she should fight for. In the forefront, waging her own campaign while keeping a watchful eye on her daughter, was her mother.

Learning Outside of School: The Role of Parents

Another key theme voiced by my suburban Columbia respondents in support of the ethnic culture narrative was how involved their parents had been with their schooling. It was the kind of involvement that my Hunter respondents thought was so lacking in their own families. According to my suburban students, their families did not rely solely on schools. It was equally important to them that the learning process extend well beyond what could be gained in a school setting. In this they proved similar to middle-class white and Asian American parents (Baker and Stevenson 1986; Lareau 1987; Kao 1995; Chiang 2000). These parents monitored their children's free time (in one case, installing locks to the TV room), assigned supplementary homework, and offered help in math and science; for those subjects, the fact that they were not native English speakers did not pose an obstacle. Judy Lai, the daughter of shoe import/exporters, recalled her mother's taking part in her schooling:

> My mother was very rigid in terms of my schoolwork when I was younger. She didn't think the school system was giving me enough in terms of how much I was studying, so she gave me supplementary homework often, and when I had tests or exams, she always expected 100s. So she would stay up with me studying and doing spelling, all that stuff.

Another common parental strategy was enrolling children in afterschool activities; unlike white middle-class parents, however, these activities typically had an academic component to them and thus were unlikely to be sports or arts and crafts. In the few cases where the children pursued sports, it was likely to be tennis (Chiang 2000). Instead, the parents paid for private instrument lessons (piano and violin were quite popular), summer school programs, and academic tutoring programs. Brenda Hsieh, for example, remembered having a teenage interest in acting and dancing but never mustering the courage to ask her parents to send her to those classes (although she was already taking piano) because she feared they would think it a "stupid" investment.

Classical music, in particular, emerged as a key element in the childhood and adolescence of my suburban respondents. Mrs. Chang reported on why she encouraged her children to pursue music, an interest that later took them to Julliard, the famed school of music in Manhattan. In her account, the homeland figures as the frame of reference:

> I come from Taiwan. Usually, we spend a lot of time studying with first or second grade. Always have lots, lots of homework, you know. We don't have time for ourselves. But here they don't have anything to do, right. After school, they can finish your homework in twenty, thirty minutes and nothing to do, right. So I think they have too much free time and I hate to see kids waste their time. You know, I don't think that life should be like that, you know, waste time. So then I heard some other friends, their children are learning music. And so I think it's good that they can learn music.

Many of the suburban mothers worked only part-time, if at all; if they did have full-time jobs, the mothers would leave the children in the care of a babysitter or nanny, or with close relatives, and hire a housekeeper to free them from chores, arrangements allowing them more feedback on their children and time to be with them. Because these parents came from higher socioeconomic backgrounds, were literate both in their native language and in English, and were knowledgeable about the American school system, they were more likely to speak with school faculty, attend the PTA, and, in general, become involved in their children's schooling according to conventional measures (Siu 1996, 33; Chiang 2000).

Mrs. Chang, for example, had been a stay-at-home mother while her children were growing up, with the better part of her days spent monitoring their progress in school. A typical school day back then started off with Bible reading for her son and daughter, followed by some time to have them plan their day. Later, when they returned from school, Mrs. Chang sat with them throughout their homework exercises; she made a point of scheduling regular meetings with her children's teachers. Mrs. Chang took a particularly active role with her son, since he had more problems in school. One measure of her involvement was the daily discussions she had with his teacher about his classroom behavior, a strategy that has been identified with middle-class white parents (Lareau 1987). In Mrs. Chang's words:

> For my son kind of involved because he's naughty. He usually gives the teacher a hard time, like make faces or something like, not organized. So

I manage to communicate with the teacher. We had a notebook. I write notes to the teacher and the teacher writes back to me. And I have to make sure what kind of homework we have, you know. Like, what did you do wrong today? And I also write to my son almost everyday or every other day, "Make sure you have a good day or something like that. I love you very much." I still keep that book. Or sometimes I will highlight with red pens, "This is very important today. You just have to remember to bring your science book home." Or, "You just have to remember to hang your coat up," you know. Because when they go to school right, younger age, they just pick up the coat and throw it on the floor in the classroom. So the teacher says that he is not organized. I always mention the same thing. "Remember, remember." So I'm very involved in that.

The College Application Process

This kind of parental involvement extended well beyond the early years of schooling into the college application process. My suburban Columbia respondents remembered their parents' engagement with all facets of the college application process: preparing the list of schools, campus visits, essay writing, and overall strategizing. My interviews with a few parents spoke to this high level of engagement, as parents relayed vivid memories of how some schools were chosen and how others were discarded. In some cases, the recollections were more detailed than their children's. For example, Mrs. Leong remembered how her daughter Sandra had her heart set on attending Cooper Union in New York City, sight unseen. Cooper Union was initially Sandra's top choice both because it was an art school and because it charged no tuition. The Leongs, though they lived in an upscale suburb of Boston, were already in debt from putting Sandra's older sister through Brown University. Still, Mrs. Leong encouraged Sandra to make an informed choice, free of financial worries, rather than rely on word of mouth or the schools' official information:

> We said, first of all, there's no guarantee you can get in. Second, you might not like the environment there. I insist, you should go to the open house. Even when you look at pictures, it's something different. The last open house, she went. We said, even if you apply to the school, would you please take a look at the campus? I said, if you make a trip there, why don't you go to NYU and Columbia?

According to Mrs. Leong, the visit changed Sandra's mind about Cooper Union, and she ended up at Columbia.

The Chins delighted in providing a detailed narrative about how their daughter Diana had decided on Columbia after a series of college visits. Mrs. Chin:

> Diana made a list herself. At that time, Johns Hopkins was number one on the list. And the University of Virginia was also somewhere up there. So, we did all the way down, but as we went down [from Boston], we had to pass New York. I think we had to go in. So her daddy said, "Since we are here, we might as well have a look." And we did look. And then we rushed to UPenn, and then we rushed to, and so on and so on. . . . When she went to Georgetown, she fell in love with the whole town. She absolutely fell in love with it. And she liked Georgetown. It was not on her list.

Added Mr. Chin:

> It's between Georgetown and Columbia. And finally, she chose Columbia. And that's basically because, first of all, it's an Ivy League college. It's a smaller college. It's something she wants. She wants an urban university with a lot of multicultural people, diversity. And also, she's got a very active social life. She wants to know a lot more people. And she found that the Georgetown crowd, although they're very good, Georgetown is very good, but the students, they were more like yuppies. So she went to Columbia. And one of her reasons was that they have a real good core curriculum. The core curriculum basically gives her a broad liberal education without making her into a professional.

In speaking of the rich resources that suburban parents drew on for their children, I certainly do not wish to imply that money was not a factor in these families' educational strategies, both in the K–12 years and with regard to college. It was quite clear that some of the families, like the Leongs, found it a strain on their budgets to send a child through private school and/or private college. In Frances Ma's family of four daughters, her father took to working two jobs—as a hospital administrator by day and as a laboratory technician by night—to fund the children's music lessons and private college tuitions. Her mother, meanwhile, started to work as a nurse to help support the household. Yet even those for whom the stretch was the greatest discovered alternative ways to send their children to the schools they considered the better choice. So Sandra Leong turned down a scholarship to New York University in favor of Columbia, which did not offer nearly as attractive a financial aid package. Mrs. Leong explained why she supported and even encouraged this decision:

> Well, at that time, I know Sandra probably would like to go to Columbia. Another thing is, we wanted to be fair. I do not know what to do. The piano teacher said, the school is important. People saying, do you know how many people want to get into that school, if your kid gets accepted, you should see them through. That's the only thing I know. I should see them through. So I see them through. But I don't know if I did it right and wrong.

In sum, my suburban Columbia respondents found ample support of the ethnic culture narrative within their own family experiences with education. They reported that their parents had used their resources, notably, financial resources, and their English-language facility, to learn and make use of the best school options for their children. This knowledge came in part from their interactions with school administrators and teachers, whom the parents made a point of getting to know as they monitored their children's progress. Opportunities for their children to learn outside of school also proved to be important for these parents. Thus, we can see how these parents, nearly all with some form of higher education and a substantial number with graduate degrees, were able to pass on their educational and material advantages to their children in direct and indirect ways (Useem 1992).

Sources of Reinforcement

The Model Minority? Not Such a Bad Thing

Two things further reinforced the ethnic culture explanation for my suburban Columbia respondents by showing them that it was not only their parents who were so involved with education. As with the Hunter respondents, but to different effect, the model-minority stereotype was one of these, in that it held up a prescribed image for my suburban respondents to fulfill. We have seen how the Hunter respondents, growing up as they did with strong ties to ethnic enclaves, rejected the model-minority stereotype because it did not fit their lives or what they saw around them. The model minority referred to someone else's experience. It was not their parents who were living in the suburbs, and they were not attending Harvard, Yale, or Columbia.

Understandably, the middle-class children who lived in the suburbs and whose parents were professionals felt that the model-minority stereotype was more relevant to their lives. As such, it lent additional support to how they liked to imagine their parents and themselves, specifically with respect to the strong bond between them concerning educational goals. In other words, the model-minority thesis provided a more benign entity to these students. As Becky Wang remarked: "I think a lot of people think like Asians are nerds, or all they do is like study, which isn't bad." The suburban students did not embrace the image in its entirety, and they were careful to point out that it depicted only a fraction of reality. But it was a reality that they certainly knew about.

Melinda Wu, for instance, was inclined to support some of the claims of the model-minority stereotype, at least the ones centered on education:

> I think that the stereotype that Asians are good in math is true. Okay, I actually think that. It's not that I think their brains function better in math, but I think that it has to do with their kind of family background. I think if you don't understand a math problem, it's really easy for you to ask your parents. And most Asian parents I know are pretty good, even ones that only graduated from high school, you know, the high school level of math in Asian countries is much higher than that in the United States.

Sandra Leong, though, had a less than positive view of such stereotypes, at least when they were applied directly to her (as opposed to the stereotypes about parental involvement with children's schooling, which she did endorse). In her conversations with other people, she tended to bring up—and then quash—stereotypes of Asians as "nerdy, unathletic, socially inept, and quiet." By taking the lead, Sandra felt in control over the situation and less resentful at being expected to conform to a certain image:

> I think, in high school, I was very conscious of the stereotype of Asian Americans, and I tried very hard not to fit into it. Like I can be really harsh. Like I shock people by saying things like, joking, "Oh, you're just saying that stuff because I'm Asian right?" I'm just joking, but they'll be

like really defensive, "Oh, oh, I didn't mean that." The way I deal with it is making fun of it, making it not a big deal. By like joking about it.

At the same time, the story underscored how racial stereotypes were a part of Sandra's everyday life, so much so that she had actively thought about ways to counter them.

Collegiate Encounters with Ethnicity

The notion that Asian parents are somehow distinct was further buttressed by the encounters with ethnicity that my suburban Columbia respondents had in college. Consistent with what Kibria (2002) and others have found, the college years marked both an ethnic and pan-ethnic awakening among many of my respondents, who embraced becoming Chinese for the first time and also intuited bonds with other Asian ethnics (Louie 2003). Some continued to believe that they were like everyone else, thus downplaying their ethnicity. For all, however, a central feature of the college experience was the relevance of the Asian American concept to their lives. No matter how they self-identified, they nevertheless were surrounded by the Asian American concept in the university's ethnic studies programs and ethnic student organizations. Even more ubiquitous was the presence of Asian American students, who made up 17 percent of the Columbia undergraduate student body during my year in the field. All my suburban Columbia respondents had at least a few Asian American friends, in many cases, for the very first time. All of this meant that the abstract quality attached to the term "Asian American" that had characterized their youth had given way to an immediacy that they needed to situate themselves in relation to.

One cause and consequence of increased ethnic and pan-ethnic friendship circles was my respondents' tendency to see commonality in how Asian parents came to the United States and raised children, especially with regard to schooling. This was something that transcended ethnicity and ethnic language, as my respondents found themselves sharing things in common with students from Korean, Indian, and Filipino backgrounds. The following respondents, for instance, described the commonality along the lines of shared values that set them apart from other Americans. This was clear in Frances Ma's reflections on ethnic identity:

I: Do you identify as being Asian American? More or less, compared to Chinese American, or is it the same thing to you?

A: I find myself saying Asian American more. When someone asks, "What are you?" I'll say Asian American. And when they say, "Well, which?" I'll say, "Chinese." I don't know why. I'm specifically Chinese American, but I think politically, and in a larger sense, I am Asian American because I feel I have more in common with someone who is South Asian than someone who is Irish American because there are similar values upheld, and also there are similar reasons why our parents got to come here. Like one of my friend's father is a researcher, you know. And my father came here because he was a science person because during that time, there was the Brain Drain. . . .

I: What do you think are the shared values?

A: Oh, what are the shared values, I think education. I think it's just idiosyncratic, also, I guess it's kind of funny, our friends all came over to dinner, and we have like a plastic sheet over our tablecloth, and my friend, who is Indian, said, "My mother did the same thing." Or the way that we talk to our parents, the same way when we're not home by a certain time: "You should be studying," "Are you studying?" Like, "Why aren't you studying?" Or the way they value money, or just the different things.

When asked why her closest friends were largely Chinese and Taiwanese, Melinda Wu provided a similar explanation:

I think that a lot of it has to do with the fact that I think I have the same kind of upbringing they have. Just stuff like, me and my friend both get S's on a report card. And I would say to her, "I'm going to go home and my Mom is going to be upset about that." Satisfactory for S. And I know that she would understand because her mother would be upset about that. Whereas my Caucasian friends would be, "What's wrong with an S?" And their parents aren't like mine. I guess that just blankets with, it has a lot to do with upbringing.

Central to such friendships was how easily other Asian ethnics grasped the unique features of their growing up as 1.5 and second-generation Chinese in suburbia. That is, even if my respondents grew up thinking of themselves as being like their white peers, they also understood that their parents had raised them with different rules and were often stricter. It was these things that Asian ethnics seemed to "get" and that friends from other racial and ethnic groups did not. Noted Sandra Leong:

> Oh, you know, Chinese parents are very demanding and strict. They didn't let us do this. They didn't let us do that. They cooked this weird food. Really quirky things that Chinese Americans would know. I think a lot of Asian Americans have gone through what I have. There are a lot of them who have grown up in predominately white communities like that. They experience the same things.

Two themes characterized these responses. First, they were consistent with what Kibria has described as "ethnic pan-Asianism," which is seen in "broadly ethnic terms as a community of shared culture and life experiences" (2002, 108). Rather than articulating the ideology of "official pan-Asianism," which, as I noted in Chapter 3, is centered on issues of racial politics, these suburban respondents talked about "shared personal histories and outlooks produced by race" (121).

Second, the life experiences underlying these seemingly complementary ethnic and pan-ethnic identities were specific to being 1.5 and second generation, middle class, and from predominately white suburbs. With a few exceptions, such as Sandra Leong, most of these students gave sparse attention to the class dimension of their newly emergent ethnic identities. Overall, ethnicity was the salient feature they spoke of, one that centered on and thereby reinforced a shared narrative about Asian immigrant families and education.

The Enclave Students at Columbia

Class Is Important

About a fifth of my Columbia sample were students who came from the urban enclaves, and they had substantially different views about how they had gotten to Columbia. Essentially, they saw themselves as the lucky ones who made it, while not everyone else did. Ivory Miao, the Barnard student whose family started off living in Chinatown and owned a jewelry business there, reported on the different educational experiences of her younger brother. After much frustration on the part of her parents, who tried to force him to study and do well and, finally, just stay in school, Ivory's brother had nevertheless dropped out of high school at the age of sixteen.

Jannelle Chao was another example. Drawing from her observations of the children of family friends, she was highly critical of the model-minority stereotype:

> Sure, I can say that Asian Americans are the model minority. But it is seriously not true. I have sort of, you know, a close family friend—he's fourteen now, right, and he's in trouble with the law. He's been robbing people. Like he knew those two people who killed a cabdriver a month ago. He's been taken to police stations. There really is no Asian character or anything. To say Asian American parents are really caring about their kids, I don't think that's true, I mean, a lot of Asian American parents aren't like that. Like this kid, his parents didn't really pay that much attention to him. His dad was a cabdriver. They are like family friends of ours. The mom's sort of a housewife, but she was probably busy with other stuff.

To varying degrees, the enclave Columbia respondents highlighted the influence of social-class background, especially differences in class status within the enclave, in explaining why they had been able to get to Columbia. Jade Soo, a Barnard sophomore and a graduate of the elite Bronx Science High School, discussed at length the disparities in her own extended family. All the adult members of Jade's extended family worked in the ethnic economy in Chinatown, but that did not mean they were all on the same financial footing. The most telling difference between Jade's father and her aunts and uncles was that her father managed a noodle factory and her aunts and uncles performed such manual labor as waiters and seamstresses and brought home significantly less income. Occupying a middle-class status in the ethnic economy, Jade's parents could invest in their children's education in ways that her aunts and uncles could not. Jade pointed to her parents' enrollment of her brother in the ethnically run academic preparatory schools that have been the focus of much media and scholarly attention as one example:

> My parents are like crazy believers in "You must be going to school. And you must excel academically." But the rest of my family, my uncles and my aunts, there's not that much of an emphasis for them for their kids. I think it's because my parents make more money. So they have the leisure

of saying, "Yes, this is what you can do." Because they spend a lot of money for my brother to go to tutorials. They're, let's see, probably $800 for like a month and a half. It adds up. And he used to go like continuously. To cram for exams, or just to get ready for school. Like the year before, he'll learn the stuff that he's going to do next year. And my aunts and my uncles just aren't willing to put the money into this. Because, first of all, they just don't have it. They don't have that leisure.

This is not to say that parents like Jade's can provide the types of advantages available to her suburban Columbia classmates. Since both her parents still worked long hours, they could not closely supervise their children's progress; nor did they have the necessary language skills and educational background (they were high school graduates) to help with their children's homework. It is my intention only to point out, as she did, that her family came from a more privileged Chinatown strata, which had an impact on her educational experiences as compared to other children.

For instance, Jade compared herself to some friends from less privileged backgrounds who were unable to engage with school. By doing well in school, Jade was able to meet peers from other socioeconomic, racial, and ethnic backgrounds and family histories and to enter different parts of the city and state that had once seemed far removed; in essence, doing well in school served as her passport to the world beyond Chinatown. In contrast, her friends had stayed behind in Chinatown, a world where life was often precarious:

> When we were kids, there was gang warfare. And I lived right there. Yeah. Because the gangs were on Pell, and there was the gang on Confucius. And they fought. And I remember so many times when we had to run home because somebody was shooting. Or somebody had committed suicide, or something that had happened. But you definitely see it there. Even with friends, you see them, like, getting caught, sort of, in the system.

As Jade explained, the key was that her friends dropped out of high school or college; after that happened, their world became increasingly smaller, until it was limited almost exclusively to Chinatown or the other Chinese enclaves:

> Because a lot of my friends aren't going to school anymore and they're just stuck in Chinatown. They don't move out of there. They hang out. They try working on and off, odd jobs in Chinatown. But, otherwise,

like, unless they were going out to see a movie or going to shoot pool, it's always in Chinatown or the Chinatown in Brooklyn. I think it has something to do with not doing well in school. Then, after a while, they think it's pointless and they don't want to continue school, because it's just a waste of time and they don't want to do homework anyway. And so they don't see a point in going to school anymore.

While their peer circles were also predominately Asian, my enclave students at Columbia did not experience an ethnic awakening at Columbia. They came not only knowing they were Chinese but working-class Chinese. Hence, their Asian friends tended to be of similar class backgrounds, who thought it was a luxury that they were at an Ivy League college, not necessarily a foregone conclusion. As Janelle told me, for working-class Asians, money matters, whereas their middle-class counterparts "just throw away money." She went on to say of her friends:

> It just seems like we sort of have a common view in life or something. We're more serious about our careers. And we don't do like crazy things, like you know, smoke pot, stuff like that. We like Chinese things. We like the singers. We might come from the same background socially, or economically, socioeconomically.

For some, Columbia, with its history of privilege, was a bit alienating. Many of these enclave respondents, in fact, went home on the weekends, if they could, to return to a world more familiar to them. Nonetheless, for all the importance they attached to class, my enclave respondents, much like their Hunter counterparts, never openly challenged the ethnic culture narrative. Even Jannelle Chao, who clearly saw life in a "socioeconomic light," as she put it, subscribed to the narrative of hard work and high educational expectations among Asian immigrant parents, one that makes them ethnically distinctive. Thus, Jannelle had this to say of her parents: "I think they do have some of that 'Asian parents thing.'" It is to the parent–child relationship, as it is experienced by the second generation, that we turn to next.

PART THREE

The Second-Generation Experience

Chapter 7

PARENTAL SACRIFICE
AND THE OBLIGATIONS OF CHILDREN

The immigrant experience is traumatic, bringing as it does loss in any number of dimensions, from language and status, to social and kin networks, or, in short, an internal map of the way the world works. For immigrant families, the consequences are profound, as parents must learn the "new rules of engagement" of the receiving country (C. Suarez-Orozco M. Suarez-Orozco 2001), and their children become both witnesses and participants in the migration process (Chen and Lan 1998). Perhaps not surprisingly, then, a powerful sense of obligation emerges on the part of second-generation children in response to their parents' losses and trials (Portes and Rumbaut 2001a, 192).

My respondents' internalization of the educational message relayed by parents derived from their own takes on the immigrant experience and ensuing notions of family sacrifice and, relatedly, children's obligations. Instead of passively absorbing expectations transmitted by parents, my respondents actively interpreted the validity and implications of such expectations and the supposed link between achievement and mobility. They quickly discerned that trying to do well in school (whether one ended up doing so was another matter) was certainly an effective way of making up for the losses incurred by their immigrant parents. At the same time, they understood the educational message to be valid in the context of their parents' struggles in the United States as immigrants. This reinforced the notion that education was crucial to one's mobility.

Migration, family sacrifice, and children's obligations characterized another part of my respondents' educational experience, namely, the process of choosing what to study in school and what careers to pursue. Parents expected their children to pursue a narrow set of utilitarian, technical fields that offered big payoffs in the labor market. My respondents described these as the "Asian fields," and they believed this parental tendency had been embedded by the immigrant experience.

Understanding the Educational Message: The Migration Context

Parental Losses

The general pattern that I encountered among my respondents was the notion that parents bore steep costs in coming to the United States. Mrs. Wu, a mother whom I interviewed, lent support to this narrative. She explained that American life offered benefits for her children but not necessarily for herself. Formerly a teacher in Taiwan, she was now a computer programmer in the United States. This simple statement of her occupational history fails to capture in all its complexity the obstacles she had faced in getting from one point to the other. It was all too clear to Mrs. Wu what she had gone through:

> I: Do you think you would have been better off staying in Taiwan?
> A: I would think so, yes. Because all my friends, they are doing so well in Taiwan. For myself, yes. But for my children, I don't think so. I think America still has better opportunity for them. Because I was born in Taiwan, I was raised up in Taiwan, so my personal will be better if I stay in Taiwan. But for my children, I am glad I have my children here.
> I: So what kinds of things are your friends doing in Taiwan?
> A: Oh, they are the chief editor of the newspaper, or the magazine. Or they, some of them marry a real, real rich people so they don't have work. And even they just teach at school like I used to be, they have a very smooth life because teaching job, you have three months off, they can travel a lot. It doesn't cost much if you have to have self-help travel. So they have a very easy life there.

Instead of the life of leisure enjoyed by her friends, Mrs. Wu's early years in the United States were marked by marital difficulties and frequent moves around the country, in addition to the complexities of adapting to a new culture. As I briefly mentioned in Chapter 1, Mrs. Wu's former husband was never able to make the transition to an American culture that prized the strategy of "self-presentation" along with the prestige of one's educational background. In Taiwan, her former husband would have been able to land a high-profile job on the basis of his educational credentials alone, as he was a graduate of one of the nation's top universities. In the United States, he found that he had to go through job interviews and present his ideas as well as his "fit" for the job, a process he found wholly alien. Following their divorce, Mrs. Wu tried to collect child support without success, and although she could not yet speak English well enough, she now had to support two children on one income. Mrs. Wu, herself a graduate of a top-notch Taiwanese university, took to waitressing to pay the bills.

It never occurred to her to return to Taiwan under such circumstances, which she could only see as shameful. Mrs. Wu: "You really have no face to go back. Because you have no job, you have no green card, you have two young children, no marriage, no husband. Why do you want to go home?" If the United States was to be her home and she was to move up in it, Mrs. Wu knew she had to learn English. Armed with a captioning machine and a dictionary, she took to watching historical epic films like *Gone with the Wind* and *Dr. Zhivago* in the hope of picking up the cadence and vocabulary of the language. Eventually, she became fluent enough to enroll in a community college, where she learned enough computer programming to get a job.

Such sacrifices were not lost upon her daughter Melinda. When asked to name the things that her parents had given up in coming to the United States, Melinda answered:

> Everything, working, having to work harder. I said to my mom after she divorced my father, "Why didn't you move us back to Taiwan?" Because I would have done that if I was my mother. I would have been like, "I'm going back to my country then." I'm sure if she hadn't had any kids, she might have gone back. So I'm sure it was for the future. Now she really loves it. Now she would never go back, she loves the U.S. But the sacrifices just in terms of time and money.

As we saw in Chapter 3, Melinda articulated the notion that Asian immigrant parents are distinctive in how they motivate a strong work ethic in their children. She did not think that the kinds of sacrifices her mother went through, however, were specific to Asians as much as they were grounded in the immigrant experience: "I don't know if it's such an Asian thing. I think that it's just what all immigrants have to do, all parents have to do, and especially immigrants."

Children Trying to Give Back

From the time they were young, my respondents realized there was little they could do about the confounding, and at times demeaning, dictates of their parents' lives outside the home. One thing that they could do was to make sure that the interior world of the family accorded with their parents' expectations. And they learned that one way to accomplish that goal was to perform well in school. This need to "give back something" through doing well in school proved to be uniform; class and gender did not matter much here. The task gained particular urgency if the "better life" sought by immigrant parents fell far short of their expectations.

Jannelle Chao's story is illustrative. As I mentioned in Chapter 2, Jannelle's parents divorced in the United States, largely due to the financial and emotional pressures of migration. Her father, who had been in the Taiwanese army, now worked as a car service driver, and her mother, formerly a bank teller, owned a small deli that she largely ran by herself. Neither was very happy with how life had turned out for them in America.

The one part of their journey that did work out as intended was their children's schooling and careers. Jannelle and her siblings ended up faring well in the American educational system; her brother had graduated from the Leonard N. Stern School of Business at New York University and was working in finance; her sister had received an engineering degree and was working on a Master's degree. Jannelle was a junior at Columbia and looking ahead toward law school. Jannelle and her siblings had already gone further in school than their father, who did not finish college in Taiwan, and their mother, who had only completed high school. When I asked whether her parents derived satisfaction from their children's achievements, she responded:

Yeah, I think that's what keeps them going. You know, we're working in school, and my brother has a good living, and my sister is going to have her living. You know, I don't talk to my parents that much, but I still feel really close to them. You know, because we've been through the same thing.

Joseph Pang provides another example of how my respondents experienced this intergenerational dynamic of sacrifice and obligation. Joseph's parents had left behind a comfortable home and living in Hong Kong in 1972 because they feared that the government of mainland China would overtake the island. The family settled in New York City, where Joseph's father was able to obtain a bachelor's degree from Pace University and eventually found work as a laboratory technician. For a time, Joseph's mother had her own grocery store in Chinatown, but after the store failed, she found work in a garment factory. By many standards, the family had done well: they owned a two-family house in a solid working- and middle-class neighborhood in Kew Gardens, Queens, and they rented out one floor to help pay for the mortgage; Joseph was applying to medical schools; and his older brother was already a physician. Yet Joseph's parents' existence in the United States represented the sum total of toil, or what sociologists would refer to as downward mobility. In Joseph's words:

> My dad was really well off in Hong Kong and so was my mom then after she met him. And he basically threw everything away; he fled the Communists, basically. That's why they came over. My dad threw all that away, came here, started at the bottom of the totem pole, and didn't have much money, and they just had to kind of work their way up to where they are now. So my parents actually sacrificed almost everything for myself and my brother. I think that's one of the reasons why I feel that I kind of owe a lot to them. So I try to respect them, and do what they say, and work my butt off in school, and not party all the time. Make something of my life just to say thank you to them.

Downward mobility also emerged in Jonathan Kong's account of his family's migration to the United States, at least at first. He described their experiences in slightly hyperbolic terms:

> Like, my mother and father, when they came here, they didn't have any money really. They were like working as waiters, and they paid like $7 for rent because they lived in the worst area of the Bronx, you know. They were like listening to gunshots every night.

Although Jonathan's parents, both college graduates from Taiwan, managed to achieve upward mobility, at one time living in a Long Island house on a three-acre lot, the cycle of hardships continued after his father left the family. His mother was left to raise Jonathan and his brother in public housing in Flushing. The second generation, Jonathan pointed out, does not have to make such sacrifices of time and effort.

Although many family fortunes did improve with immigration, upward mobility did not lessen the feeling of obligation among children. Rather, children considered it their duty to make use of the material opportunities and basic freedoms available to them in the United States (the specter of discrimination notwithstanding), if only because those very opportunities had not been available to their parents in the homeland. Joan Jung, who was from one of the more upwardly mobile enclave families, related a story that speaks to this:

> Recently, while we were renovating the apartment, it got really late at night and we were still laying down the new kitchen floor. And my mother started talking about how lucky my sister and I are, because in America we never had to consider being separated, whereas in China life was touch-and-go all the time, and she would have to be separated from her mother and brothers, and she was never sure when they would all meet again. And it was very lonely. The chief distinction my parents draw is that we're very comfortable in America. We've always been in America, there's always been enough to eat. We don't know what it means to suffer.

Through achieving in school, these children sought to compensate their parents for the struggles they had endured both in the homeland and in their adopted country.

Reinforcing the Lesson about Education

As they witnessed their parents' often painful adaptation to a new country, my respondents not only found themselves hoping to make up for these losses but also agreeing with what their parents told them—education *was* crucial. Put another way, the processes of migration put flesh on the bones of parental messages about education. My enclave respondents had only to look at their parents' lives to know what a future without higher education looked like.

Even Joan Jung, whom as I mentioned came from one of the better-positioned enclave families, spoke to this. She understood her father's limited income potential in relation to his few years of formal schooling: "I know my dad, he's a smart man. But he doesn't have an education, so he is going to spend the rest of his working life probably as a garment presser. And I don't think it's his fault." She went on to contrast her father's grade-school education and low earnings to her mother's higher salary. The key difference was that Joan's mother had been able to take English and business classes in night school after arriving in New York City; education gave her access to a wider set of job opportunities, including her present post doing accounting work for a non-Chinese-owned firm in midtown Manhattan.

Even children whose parents had high levels of education and financial resources understood their migration as having been fraught with struggle and, consequently, thought of education as a way to avoid those kinds of obstacles. Judy Lai spoke at length of her parents' attempts to expand their family's import-export shoe business to the United States after they immigrated in 1978. Although both her mother and father had college degrees in their native Taiwan, they came to the United States for better economic opportunities. Here, though, their academic training was not readily transferable, and that, along with their lack of English fluency and unfamiliarity with a new country, put them at an initial disadvantage. Their climb up the mobility ladder was a slow one: from peddling shoes at flea markets, to opening a small office, and, finally, adding on a warehouse. With each improvement in their business fortunes came a better quality of life, culminating in the family's move to an exclusive, gated community. The family's initial hardships had nevertheless stayed with Judy, who viewed her education as a path to a life with more certain outcomes. Through her training in operations management, Judy felt that she was developing a global set of skills that could serve her anywhere. That meant she would never have to start over again somewhere new, as her parents had done:

> I watched my parents work when I was still young, and how they kind of built up their income until now. They were kind of starting from ground zero, and they were able to get where they are through hard work. And I don't know, I don't think I could be that brave. So I would rather just have the stability.

Choosing College Majors: The Asian Fields

Migration, family sacrifice, and children's obligations characterized another part of my respondents' educational experience, namely, the process of choosing what to study in school and what to pursue as a career. In the popular imagination, Asian Americans are not only academic achievers, but they are achievers in particular fields, namely, medicine, engineering, computer science, and increasingly, law. This claim has an empirical basis. In 1991, when Asian Americans represented about 3 percent of the total U.S. population, they earned nearly 7 percent of the bachelor's degrees awarded in science and made up 7 percent of the nation's scientific and engineering workforce and 9 percent of medical school faculty (Tang and Smith 1996; Elliot et al. 1996; Espiritu 1997). In 1994, Asians garnered nearly 10 percent of all science and engineering bachelor's degrees awarded, compared with 1 percent of the B.A.'s in English (*Chronicle of Higher Education* 2000). In studies measuring career interests, Asian Americans consistently prefer careers stressing logic skills (such as engineering) rather than verbal and interpersonal skills (such as sales) (Sue and Frank 1973; Leung 1994).

While many of these trends can be attributed to the brain drain that has drawn highly trained foreign-born adults, particularly in the technical fields, to the United States, there is also evidence that these trends are salient for the children of immigrants, who receive most if not all of their schooling in the United States (Leung 1994; Wong 1995a, 1995b). Current scholarship on such ethnic-specific career decisions highlights parental aspirations. Asian Americans tend to take their parents' opinions into consideration and thus view the career decision-making process as more of a collective enterprise rather than an individualistic matter (Tang 1999; Leong 1990; Gordon 2000). For example, Chinese parents, perceiving structural constraints to their children's future mobility, encourage them to pursue "safe" careers that rely less on face-to-face contact, subjective judgments, and language skills, and more on objective data and licensing, such as the law, engineering, math, medicine, and the physical and biological sciences (Sue 1973; Lyman 1974; Kwong 1987; Hsia 1988; Schneider and Lee 1990; Lee 1996). The literature, however, has not paid much attention to how the children of immigrants make sense of these expectations and respond to them, particularly in the context of immigration, and that is what we turn to next.

"The Asian State of Mind": A Utilitarian View of Education Embedded in Migration

While ethnic-specific data on fields of study at Hunter and Columbia were scarce, the available data for Asian Americans corresponded to national trends, highlighting the group's disproportionate representation in technical fields (Jacobs 1996). Asian and Pacific Islanders at Hunter were thus underrepresented in the Humanities and over-represented in the sciences and mathematics. In 1996–97, nearly 60 percent of the Asian American Hunter graduates earned degrees in only three fields—the sciences, math, and nursing. Data were scarcer at Columbia, but it was readily known, for instance, that Asian Americans comprised 41 percent of the student body at the engineering school.

In fact, that Asian American students were concentrated in a narrow band of majors was common knowledge among my respondents. To illustrate his point about the "Asian fields," Benny Sen, a Hunter junior, offered to take me to Hunter's "Asian" wing. That turned out to be the Departments of Physics, Chemistry, and Biology, where, in Benny's words, we would find "research assistants, and researchers and students, 70 percent to 80 percent of them Asian." A few miles away at Columbia, the scene was little different. This is what Joseph Pang, a premedical concentrator in history,[1] had to say:

> People that meet me at Columbia, they actually say, "Oh, are you an engineer?" or "Are you premed?" Computer science, engineering, premed, those are the big ones. If I tell them I'm premed, they assume that I'm a bio major. But, yeah, I think even at Columbia, for whatever reason, there's certain majors that a lot of Asian students go into.

My respondents understood the Asian fields in the context of the hardships that their parents faced with migration. As I outlined in Chapters 1 and 2, the families of my respondents had left behind homelands dominated by political, economic, or social instability. It was not surprising, then, that despite having lived for some time in the United States, many of them still viewed life as a deeply uncertain proposition, and they transmitted the need for "stability" to their children when it came to education. Thus, they conveyed a utilitarian view of education to their children, one that put emphasis on the financial rewards that were to come from one's degree. This is how Deborah

Ow, the daughter of a chef and garment worker, described her parents' cues about school: "The objective is to have a job at the end of the academic experience. It's just to strive for success to get a good job." Daniel Fong, the son of an entrepreneur with multiple graduate degrees, expressed a similar outlook on the part of his parents: "Education is a means to an end. It is not an education in itself. It's more like, get your education so you can make money. That's sort of the bottom line."

According to my respondents, parents believed that only a small number of fields would lead to this financial stability. Different though my respondents' parents were on many indicators (educational level, occupation, and place of residence), they shared a singularly narrow view of which majors were "good" for their children. Even highly educated parents who had received their graduate degrees in the United States did not perceive the relevance of fields like archaeology or East Asian Languages and Civilizations. This is how Laura Toy described her parents' reaction to her decision to major in anthropology: "They don't get it. You can do an anthro major, but you have to have a good job. And you can quote this, they always say, 'You can't live in the dirt forever.'" Fields like psychology were described by parents as "a dead end." More to the point, my respondents reported that parents did not see the practicality of those fields, with practicality understood to mean the potential to attract high-income jobs.

On one level, this finding seems counterintuitive. It would make sense for the enclave Chinese, especially manual workers, to stress financial security because they probably rely on their children's financial contribution to the household (Kwong 1987; Hune 1998). At the same time, it would seem reasonable to expect that suburban, middle-class parents would come to define their children's education as a quest for knowledge rather than as preparation for a particular career or primarily in economic terms, and thus they would be expected to encourage their children to partake of the academic curriculum (Siu 1995; Hune 1998). My interviews, however, showed a remarkable convergence across class. Just as my respondents reported that their parents expected them to go on to at least a four-year college, they remembered that their parents had similar ideals as to the kinds of careers they should pursue, ideals that were born of a similar social logic of the world.

It was along these lines that Mr. Chin, himself a lawyer who had immigrated from Malaysia, described why he wanted his daughter to become a doctor. As we can see, the deprivations of coming of age in war-torn East Asia had given Mr. Chin to understand that a good education was one that instilled a body of knowledge that could be taken anywhere and easily used to find gainful employment.

> To me, security is very important, you know. When I was young, we went into a terrible war. The Japanese were on us. They were killing a lot of Chinese in Asia. And having gone through the war, my father suffered a lot. My mother suffered a lot. So we didn't have a lot. First thing I did when I finish high school, when I had this university exam all done away with, was to get a job. The hospital job, the administrator job is very secure. I had a government house. I got paid my salary on time. I don't have to work that hard. I have a lot of security in government, in working in the hospital. So I have a bias. And I know doctors. I know that doctors would never, never worry about not having a job. Always a job, always have security, always get paid. And always would have people needing their services.

Another important factor in shaping parental expectations was the conditions that immigrant parents faced in the United States. As we have seen, many of the immigrant parents perceived a racialized social structure in their adopted country. In response, they stressed not only higher education to their children but also technical and licensed professions that they believed might offer some protection from possible discrimination. Winston Woo put it well: "In Chinese thinking, it's like get a good job, one that pays well, that doesn't discriminate against Chinese, one that you can easily get a job in."

Victoria Chang remembered the caution underlying her mother's career advice, specifically, to become a doctor like Victoria's father:

> Because this is a white man's world. That was basically it. And I think it also has to do with the whole doctor thing. Because she does want me to succeed in what I do. But she also wants me to be prepared and, you know, face reality instead of thinking that I can do anything, which I'm pretty sure I can do. But she has prepared me so that I would never fall flat on my face and be like, you know, completely crushed. And that also had to do with why she wants me to be a doctor, because it's something that obviously Asian Americans have been established in instead of forging into unknown territory.

Secondary Fields in Enclave Families

Whether parents actually believed their children would actually become doctors, lawyers, and engineers is another story, one that reveals clear class differences. My interviews indicated that the suburban Chinese definitely expected their children to pursue these professions. This was reasonable, since many of these parents were already in such fields. The enclave Chinese who attended Columbia also reported similar expectations. Since their children had already made it to one of the nation's elite private universities, these parents were willing to believe that they could also successfully compete at the elite level of occupations.

For the rest of the enclave Chinese, it was a more complex story. While maintaining the same ideals, the parents nevertheless realized that some professions might be unattainable for their children. Instead, they pushed a secondary tier of professions that would provide a solid income but that would not necessarily require several years of graduate school along with a substantial financial investment, and thus were more within reach for their children. From this vantage point, medicine might lie outside the realm of possibility, but pharmacy would still be very doable as would computer science or accounting.

These enclave parents came to such conclusions by utilizing the same dense web of ethnic networks that informed their knowledge of the New York City public educational system. That these networks provided parents information about which occupations to steer their children into is evident from this exchange between Lily Gong and Grace Li, Hunter classmates. Both their mothers worked in garment factories, Grace's as a seamstress and Lily's as an owner.

> Grace Li: One thing funny is that my mom, they always like to follow trends. Like if one person's daughter is a pharmacist, that was the "in" thing this year. Being a pharmacist. She would always bring it up. Oh, you know, pharmacists make good money.
>
> Lily Gong: What other people say, they listen. It's like, the whole workplace is saying, my kids are into botany or something, and they'll come home and say, "Why don't you go do botany?" It's always a trend.

What their children ended up pursuing was a further reflection of their parents' status within these ethnic networks. As Lily observed: "They want to be proud to say, 'Oh, my son or daughter is a doctor, or a lawyer, doing very well.' They can't really explain what geography is, or a history major, or anything they consider lower."

Children's Responses

How did these kinds of parental pressures affect the academic decision-making of my respondents? In the course of my interviews, I identified three groups of students—two of the groups had chosen what we might call broadly the "Asian fields," often for different reasons, and the third had selected non-Asian fields. A common thread in all groups was an internalization of the parental message about the "practical" fields to study. What was different was how they had responded. With each step away from the Asian fields, the sense of obligation, guilt, and anxiety had increased on the part of my respondents.

Following the Family Example

The first category of students had gravitated toward the "Asian fields" primarily because they wanted to follow the example of family members. For obvious reasons, this scenario occurred mainly in the suburban, middle-class families, where the parents were already established in the mainstream economy as professionals. Most of the enclave Chinese did not see their parents' jobs in the restaurant and garment industries as anything to aspire to; rather, they viewed education as a way out of these jobs. In the suburban families, however, the experiences of kin provided a useful lens through which respondents could view their own occupational choices. Chloe Gao reported that it was natural for her to consider engineering as a potential career since all her uncles were already in the field. Interestingly, one of her uncles pointed to himself as a cautionary tale that making one's choice based on what was familiar was not necessarily the best approach:

He always says, "Just make sure you're happy with whatever you're doing." I think I agree with his views the most. He explained to me how he got into engineering because the family convinced him that, you know, that it was the best thing to do financially. He's still working as an engineer, but I think he's going through like a life change, you know, trying to find something that makes him happier.

Jackie Lee, whose late father and older sister were both physicians, reported on the family example, too. Breaking from family tradition when she was at Phillips Academy, Jackie had decided to pursue art history. Yet even while she majored in art history at Columbia, landing some exciting internships at museums and galleries, Jackie never quite shut the door to a medical career. Since she already knew what was involved, she took the premedical classes "just in case, just kind of a fallback plan." As things turned out, she made the right decision. When Jackie decided that the art world was too rarefied for her tastes, she was still able, academically speaking, to apply to medical school right away.

Choosing What Is Practical

The second group of students who gravitated toward the "Asian fields" did so because it was "natural" and "normal" for them to think about which fields were secure and which were not. It was difficult to determine where internalization of the parental message had ended and where the students' genuine interest had begun. As a young woman at Columbia observed: "Asian parents kind of restrict the fields, like, you know, they probably wouldn't be happy if you majored in art or music, therefore you grow up with the pressure of limiting your own fields, eventually you take on those values."

Margaret Wang, a student at Columbia's School of Engineering, exemplified this type of decision-making. She had come to Columbia thinking that she would pursue biomedical engineering but had quickly realized, after one class, that her talents did not lie there. In thinking through her options, Margaret never lost sight of the crucial issue: "What else would be a practical thing for me?" The answer in her case turned out to be operational research, a field that would allow her to pursue a business career.

It was clear that some of these students had considered other fields that their parents might have viewed as "dangerous." In fact, some had excelled in the Humanities, receiving their best grades in fields that seemed to better reflect their true interests. Nonetheless, they continued on in engineering, computer science, or economics since they had already invested so much time in those endeavors or they thought these fields would be more likely to lead to a high-paying job. Paul Chen's story is illustrative. A junior at Hunter, he was majoring in economics and accounting, despite his absorption in philosophy and history, disciplines that he believed gave him a nuanced way of understanding human life. He described his reasoning:

> I don't really like economics, believe it or not. I mean, if I had my choice, I would major in philosophy and minor in history (voice brightens). *But*, I don't see a future in being a philosophy major. I really don't, so I chose something more practical, a little more practical, so economics is what I chose.

As can be seen from Paul's comments, the idea of choice was more restricted in the lives of the less mobile enclave Chinese. If education was to be Paul's ticket to a life outside of his family's cramped apartment in Chinatown, then education had to lead to a viable job and career. Seen in this context, economics made perfect sense and philosophy made no sense at all. In his mind, he really had no choice. His family's financial situation had already made the choice for him.

Another example is Jonathan Kong, a history major at Columbia who planned to apply to law school even though he had scant interest in the law. He was doing this because he wanted to help out his mother, who had struggled financially after his father left the family. While Jonathan dreaded going to law school, he nevertheless saw this path as necessary and not as a sacrifice along the lines of what his mother had gone through in trying to make a life in the United States: "We second-gens, we definitely have it easy. Honestly speaking, I think the second-gens are, the sacrifices we make are sort of like, okay, I don't want to be a lawyer, but I will be. Compared to the things that my mom went through, they're nothing."

Reluctant Rebels: Venturing Outside the "Asian" Fields

A third group of students followed their interests in fields that lay outside the boundaries sanctioned by their parents. Asked what he liked about his major,

Robert Ong, a psychology and sociology major at Hunter, replied, "None of the Asians are doing it, one." He did not say this because of any embarrassment he felt with his ethnicity. Robert was very proud of being Chinese and most of his close friends were Chinese American. Still, he was proud that his choice of a major ran counter to the expectations of Chinese-immigrant parents, his own, in particular: "You keep on pushing me, I go the other way." He was also cheered by his younger brother's fledgling stand of independence from their parents: "He's having doubts about (being a pharmacy major), which is kind of good in the sense of, come on, it's about time you got out of Mom's wings and start to think for yourself. Mom says this, he'll do it. Maybe mumble a word or two."

In this group, Robert was an exception, because most of the other students spoke of wrestling with feelings of obligation and their own sense of trepidation at venturing into the unknown, a dilemma they often described in ethnic terms. Joan Jung thus viewed her decision to major in archaeology as a deeply "American" one, insofar as it was rooted in individual choice. Rather than factoring in her parents' wishes, she put faith in her own counsel. At the same time, Joan believed that she was taking a risk:

> I'm thinking, this is my life, and I'm going to do what I want with it. I'm going to pick my major. I'm going to pick my job. Yeah, I've got to do what makes me happy, whereas I could have said, I'm going to be premed because it makes me and my parents happy. That's more of a Chinese decision. I feel guilty when I'm with more traditional Chinese Americans. Guilty because I'm not being practical. I'm not doing the sure thing.

Sandra Leong's account further highlights the dilemma faced by most of these students. Sandra had a strong interest in art that, like Jackie Lew's, had developed at Phillips Academy, in this case, during its summer program. But unlike the Lews, Sandra's parents were having a tougher time financing their daughter's private university education. As a high school senior Sandra had wanted to apply to Cooper Union, both because it was free and because she had wanted to study art; she eventually decided against specializing at such an early age. Instead, Sandra chose Columbia, a school with a core curriculum designed to familiarize students with various areas of knowledge. But when she began her sophomore year and it was time to pick a major, Sandra found herself conflicted once more, and she mulled over what seemed like dozens of choices before finally settling on visual arts. Sandra began our interview by reflecting on this dilemma:

> My parents are kind of like, not for visual arts, and I can see why visual arts may not be the best major. Since I was in a liberal arts college, I finally decided I might as well major in something I really enjoy, and I convinced them. I wanted something I really wanted to major in. Even if I major in something like East Asian Studies, what can I do afterwards? If you want to find a job afterwards, that has nothing to do with the major you're in, and I told them I wanted to do something with the Internet. That's something good I can get into. And I think, my dad, he's in computers. I don't know. I could still do a double major, double concentration something like English, sociology. But even then, what would that do? It would give me no edge. . . . I really give my parents a lot of credit for not pressuring me, making me, because I know a lot of [Asian] kids who are in the same situation as me who are forced to, you know, you really have to be a doctor or a lawyer.

Despite all this reflection, Sandra obviously remained uncertain. She was still looking for ways to make her decision more palatable, not only to her parents and relatives but also to her parents' Chinese friends, none of whom seemed to know how to react when she told them her major was "visual arts." Sandra understood this reaction as a phenomenon specific to being Asian American. As she tells it, people of other racial and ethnic backgrounds simply did not see what all the fuss was about: "It's funny because I didn't really grow up with friends of the same [racial and ethnic] background, and they were like, well, 'Why don't you go to art school, whatever?'" Given that Sandra came from a background with a different set of sensibilities, it is easy to understand her preoccupation with trying to pair visual arts with a more "legitimate" intellectual field of inquiry, one that would garner the approval of her family.

What Sandra did not voice was that she was quite possibly still looking for a way to justify the decision to herself. Somewhere along the line, she had internalized her parents' views about majors and financial stability, even as she was making a decision very contrary to those views: "My parents worry about it, but I try to counter that fear. 'No, I can still get it together if I do that. I can still do something with it. I'm not going to be the starving artist on the street.'" Not knowing how to break the news to her parents, Sandra let her parents read it for themselves in an annual progress report that she had to write for her arts scholarship:

After I handed in the letter, I was like, this is what I'm really doing. They were like, really, so you weren't just saying that. I'm like, yeah. It was really weird. Then I had to package it. Well, I'm going to be majoring in visual arts, and I'm going to be taking digital media classes. I'm going to be interning at an interactive advertising place. I'm going to be hopefully doing something either in graphic design or design on the Internet. That's definitely something good for the future. (laughs) I don't know, my mom was kind of like, so what else are you majoring in? And my dad was like, you know, okay, that makes sense, cause he is really into the Web. They're just really concerned that I'm going to be cornering myself, but that's not how it works at Columbia.

As far as Mrs. Leong was concerned, it remained to be seen how her children's forays into "unsafe" fields would turn out. In addition to Sandra, the Leongs' eldest daughter, a Brown University graduate, had decided to become an elementary school teacher, another choice they had had trouble accepting. So their initial reaction to Sandra's decision to major in visual arts was not positive. Mrs. Leong:

Of course, we told them, your family, we are not a well-off family. We won't be able to support you when you pursue your art, or we won't be able to give you an exhibition so that people can buy up your artwork. And then we are trying so hard to pay you through college. Actually, we are in debt because of that. Hopefully, you will be able to earn your living. But if you go art, you will go hungry. We know that. A few lucky ones, you'll hit, when you're dead. (laughs) When you're dead. We won't be able to support you.

But after a year, Mrs. Leong said, she and her husband had come to accept Sandra's decision. She noted with a wry laugh:

As much as we want them to do what we want, we also understand, they are the ones that have to study, they have to like what they study. We already told them, you are going into a dangerous field, you might not make a living, but that's only so much we can do. We don't believe in pushing them. I don't know whether we do it right or wrong. We are still questioning, me and my husband, should we push our kids or force them to take certain courses or whatever? Some kids will turn out okay that way, but there's also others that resent, and even if parents pushed them, the kids still did not do what they learned. They follow their own heart.

Laura Toy's experiences document the self-imposed boundaries with making these types of choices. In our interview it became clear that while Laura enjoyed majoring in anthropology (much to her parents' chagrin), she had her best experiences in visual arts, which she thought were the best classes she had taken at Columbia and which she eventually decided to make her minor. Yet for all her positive interactions with the visual arts department, it never occurred to Laura to major in the field. When asked why she did not consider it, Laura could not really say, except to remark: "That's not why I came to college, to major in something."

The decision to go against her parents' wishes was a painful one for Elizabeth Wong, a Hunter student. She was aware of her parents' efforts to support the family—her father worked two jobs (as a city bus driver and an airport employee), and her mother routinely put in overtime at her post office job. Elizabeth, however, found that she could not meet her father's expectations when it came to choosing a major, and she keenly felt that she was letting him down:

> He would say, you know, being an education major, I guess, because my aunt was a teacher, but she was down in Florida and she got laid off and everything. So, he was saying that, "Oh, teacher's salaries are not so high." If you are one of the new teachers, your tendency of getting laid off is higher than, you know, the tenured teachers. So he was telling me all that, "Oh, why don't you go into business or accounting." And then so I took my first accounting course here, I did pretty good, but I don't know, I didn't have the interest or motivation to do numbers for the rest of my life, you know. I like working with kids. I didn't care about the money, you know.

To appease her father (and perhaps assuage her guilt), Elizabeth promised she would somehow make her way to business school, at the same time that she was privately hoping that her father would forget about the MBA as the years went on. In trying to explain why her father felt so strongly that she should not pursue education as a career, Elizabeth pointed to his own experiences growing up in Taiwan as the eldest child of seven in a family that did not have the resources to send him through college: "That's why he had all that pent-up ambition, you know, he doesn't want us to choose the wrong major, and end up regretting it or suffering later on, that's why."

For this group of students, the role of mentors proved crucial. Dean

Chang, for example, learned of Hunter's highly regarded School of Social Work from a social worker who had provided service to his family. Later on, he worked for a counselor with a Master's in social work, who showed Dean its everyday dimensions and advised him about which Master's programs to apply to. In the same vein, following her own interests in archaeology became easier for Joan Jung once she was able to rely on mentors to show her how to make her way through the field. She met the mentors, all women, through classes she took at Columbia and other local colleges and institutions. The women introduced her to the world of archaeology, pointing her toward research opportunities and possible career paths. On one level, the benefits were personal and made Joan feel more confident about her ability to succeed in a field in which she would essentially be a groundbreaker. But the benefits of mentorship also allowed her to make a stronger case for archaeology to her parents, who became persuaded of the seriousness of her intent: "My parents know they can't change my mind, and now they see that I've taken an actual effort to go to archaeology lab sessions, to go to digs, to talk to people. They're becoming more reconciled to it, as long as they can see I'm serious."

Mai Liao is another example. She entered Columbia on the HEOP program for economically disadvantaged students with the idea that "college was just to get an education for a career." She took an internship in asset management with an investment banking firm, but quickly realized that her interests did not lie in finance. With the help of a mentor assigned by the HEOP program, Mai decided to go with her natural bent toward English literature. But she did not necessarily view her major as leading her to a set career path, since her goal is to obtain a law degree. Mai's decision to major in literature was not exactly what her parents had hoped for. It was her father's dream for her to become a doctor, and he still did not understand how literature would eventually lead her to a career in law. Meanwhile, her mother continued to hope that Mai would do "something practical," without specifying what that might be.

Gender

While the general pattern was for parents to have similar career aspirations for their sons and daughters, there were a few notable gender distinctions, mainly along class lines. A few of the enclave parents, for example, encouraged their daughters to pursue what one respondent described as "the traditional feminine fields." However, these families proved the exception rather than the norm. This is surprising, given that most of the enclave Chinese strove to mold their daughters into "proper" women, as we saw in Chapter 4. Perhaps not surprisingly, in those families that did differentiate along the lines of gender, the theme of "appropriateness" came up often. Peggy Teng thus recalled her mother's thoughts on women's abilities and occupational choices:

> I think she has a certain idea of what women can do, and what men can do. What do women do? They work in banks, you know. They become secretaries, blah, blah. Obviously, that didn't appeal to me. I didn't like her thinking that either because I think that she was pretty intelligent, and that if she had schooling, [she could be something].

Benny Sun spoke thoughtfully about such gender-based expectations. His parents had made it clear that the most Benny's sisters could hope for were jobs as clerical workers, a nurse perhaps, or a flight attendant. Professional jobs were the province of men, not women. The longer they spent in the United States, however, the more their attitudes changed. What spurred the transformation was their understanding that things were done differently in America, a point that was made concrete when their daughter decided to join the police force (most definitely not a woman's job). When asked how his parents reacted to his older sister's career choice, Benny replied:

> They reacted. They tried to stop her, but she was persistent, she wanted to do it, show the world what a female Asian can do. She persisted. They couldn't stop her. There were a lot of arguments, my parents tried to ridicule her in trying to stop her. "How can you, little Asian woman?" And she was like, "No, I'll take karate classes, I'll work out." She started to work out a lot, so she won't embarrass herself, Asians or females. So she made sure she could do her job pretty well. And now she's been there for four years. Doing a fine job, and my parents are pretty much resigned, they've accepted it.

Much of the parents' initial disapproval stemmed from the danger inherent to police work, regardless of gender, or, as Benny observed, "Every morning, after you have breakfast and leave the house, you don't know if you will have another meal, you don't know if you will see your parents or siblings again. So that was definitely a major one, no matter what sex you are, so that was a big concern." Gender, however, did factor into the picture. According to Benny, his parents held the "Asian view of women: for example, that women shouldn't be a cop, that they shouldn't be in a profession that is traditionally male, for males, and being assertive publicly." But just as the migration process transformed views of women and higher education among most of the enclave Chinese, it contributed to the Sens' eventual acceptance of their daughter's career choice. This is evident in the following reflection by Benny:

> I mean, it's America, they can't discriminate. For a while, my parents were very traditionally minded. But then they realized, that's counterproductive to be that way in America. But they figured, you know, there's only a certain amount of time you can hold on to those beliefs in America. I guess they figured, why fight it? And the way my twenty-seven-year-old sister had a hard time in deciding and being what she wanted to be, with all the opposition from my parents, so why fight it, do whatever you want.

It is important to bear in mind that these daughters did not follow their parents' wishes in this regard, nor did they experience much anxiety or guilt about not following their parents' wishes, as they did when they pursued fields of study that their parents disapproved of for *both* daughters and sons.

The suburban Chinese, on the other hand, expected both sons and daughters to have high career aspirations. Still, the effects of gender were not entirely absent. A few of my respondents reported that their parents had cautioned them about what Arlie Hochschild (1989) has called the double shift—that is, the burdens working women face with balancing paid employment and family duties. Since this was a burden that only affected women, parents encouraged their daughters to have enough flexibility in their careers so that they could raise a family (Kim 1993). Sons did not receive this message.

Mrs. Chang is one such example. She advised her daughter Victoria to pursue medicine in part because she saw it as a convenient way for her to combine a fulfilling career with motherhood. The key was that Victoria could work at the clinic founded by her parents and thus set her own hours, a luxury she would not otherwise have:

> We think if she can be a doctor, right, she can just work with her dad. And we always say, "You can just work part time." Because she said, "No.

I'm not going to be a doctor because Dad has been working too much, too long hours." And I said, my husband also said, "But if you became a doctor, probably you won't have to work like more than twenty or thirty hours. You don't have to work as much because we started with nothing."

Victoria, however, had her own plans that were not necessarily consistent with her parents' ideas. She did not want to follow either her father's path to medicine or her mother's decision to forego a possible career in international affairs to be a stay-at-home mom. In Victoria's words:

> Sometimes I wonder, my mom gave up a lot, she could have had some-what of a career in journalism or maybe even one at the U.N. She did give it up for us, which I'm very grateful for. But then I think some-times, and I'm like, I wonder if I ever did that, would I regret it? I'm sure she doesn't. Because it worked out pretty well for her. But I think I couldn't be like her. At least at this point in my life. I'm personally of the opinion that I'm not going to become a housewife, and I'm going to have a career equal of my husband, and I definitely want to have some-thing before I have a family.

In sum, the narrative of family sacrifice born of migration instilled in children a powerful sense of obligation to make up for those losses through the one thing that seemed to matter most to parents—their children doing well in school. My respondents further felt the need to follow their parents' wishes by pursuing a narrow set of fields of study; but more were willing to forge their own path here, despite the ensuing guilt and fear of treading into the unknown.

Yet, as important as matters of opportunity, education, and mobility were to my respondents and their parents, they were not the only concerns. Often, they were not even the most salient concerns in the lives of the second generation. Like so many adults of their age group, my respondents were in the midst of dating choices, leisure activities, and religious and political partici-pation. It is to these aspects of their lives that we turn next.

Chapter 8

SECOND-GENERATION IDENTITIES

The generation gap that is so typical of parents and children is only magni-
fied for second-generation immigrant children, as they must navigate the
American world-at-large and parental expectations that do not always seem
to fit well in this context. For them, the process of growing up becomes a negotiation with parents across language, culture, and national context. In this
chapter, I explore such dynamics in the dating choices that my respondents
make (or, in the cases of those young adults not yet dating, their views on the
subject), the kinds of leisure pursuits they are engaged in, and to a lesser extent, the religious and political activities they find meaningful.

As we shall see, my respondents seek sources of meaning in diverse ways,
certainly more diverse than the common image of academic propensity as-
cribed to young Asian Americans, which one respondent laughingly described in this way: "They walk around, big load of books in their school bag,
and heavy, thick glasses. First one in the classroom, last one out. You know."
This description was voiced by Linda Eng, a young woman who clearly does
not fit the stereotype. She showed up for our interview in an all-black out-
fit, spiky neck choker, multiple ear piercings, capped by a carmine shade of
lipstick and dramatically drawn-in eyebrows—looking, as she said with a
laugh, appropriately "Downtown." As Linda told me, this was her everyday
wardrobe—much to her mother's dismay. In fact, academics and career
prospects were only one part of my respondents' identities. And, like Linda,

my respondents' choices did not always meet the expectations of their parents, who were forced to grapple with the processes of Americanization in their own children, in some cases, becoming more American along the way, and in others, actively resisting. As with the other parts of my respondents' lives, class and gender often served as lines of difference.

Dating Choices

Perhaps not surprisingly, choices related to dating and marriage resonated with many of my respondents. Dating and courtship assume central importance in understanding immigrant children's changing identities. Census data have given us a good sense of who the U.S.-born generations are marrying. For example, we know that, nationally, in 1990, the out-marriage rate for U.S.-born Chinese men and women was 44.5 percent and 48.2 percent, respectively. Across groups, more than 60 percent of Asian Americans who out-married typically married a non-Hispanic, white partner; however, interethnic marriages (e.g., partners of different Asian ethnicities) have been on the rise, nearly doubling from 11 percent in 1980 to 21 percent in 1990 (Lee and Fernandez 1998). The distinction is important, as out-marriages with whites might signal assimilation into the mainstream majority, whereas interethnic marriages might speak to a pan-ethnic identity that transcends ethnic lines (Lee and Fernandez 1998; Kibria 2002).

Intermarriage trends with other racial minorities are also telling. In 1990, only 2 percent of out-married Asians were with black partners, in keeping with the color line that still exists, a color line demarcated by low rates of black–white marriages. In contrast, Asian–Hispanic marriages have gone up, from 3 percent in 1980 to 11 percent in 1990, perhaps because the "immigrant experience" is a common bond and, more practically speaking, because these two groups live in the same or nearby neighborhoods (Lee and Fernandez 1998, 329).

It should be noted that a good many of my respondents at both schools (about 25 percent overall) had not yet begun dating, and this may have been a function of their relatively young age as a group. For those who had a dating history, there were interesting racial, ethnic, and class dimensions to their choices. My middle-class suburban respondents at Columbia typically had dated only whites, or whites and other Asians (Chinese and Koreans). A very few also reported dating Hispanics and African Americans. The dating patterns of my urban students were different. More than a third reported dating interracially, but the range was much wider—with the majority of dating partners being blacks and Latinos and the rest whites. About two-thirds dated only Chinese partners, with a few also dating Koreans. It was mainly in the case of dating whites that my urban respondents crossed class lines, as the whites tended to be from the middle class. Non-white dating partners tended to come from similar social classes, which is consistent with the fact that most of my urban respondents lived in neighborhoods made up of diverse minority groups of similar socioeconomic backgrounds.

Given that dating and marriage are often symbolic of racial and ethnic group identity (Espiritu 2001), did the parents give their children explicit cues about dating and marital choices? How did the children respond to these cues? Relatedly, how did the parents react when their children did something different? We turn to those topics in the following sections.

"Conservative" Urban Families: Marry Chinese

The parents in urban families explicitly made their expectations known to their children: date Chinese, marry Chinese. In his laid-back manner, Greg Zhang said he understood such parental expectations, since common cultural ground might increase the odds of making a marriage work. This proved to be the typical explanation given by my respondents: that their parents wanted them to marry people who shared the same ideas about life, and that those people happened to be Chinese. In many of the urban families, however, this common-sense approach imparted to the children was often accompanied by pressure or a warning to, in fact, *marry Chinese*. Perhaps suspecting that it would be relatively easy for their children to interact with people of other racial and ethnic groups (certainly easier than for the parents themselves), the urban parents threatened severe sanctions if their children dated outside the group. Mary Soo remembered that her father had warned her: "My father said if you date anyone other than Chinese, that you'd be disowned or something of that nature. Something really terrible like that." Other parents did not explicitly name the "something terrible," only hinting at negative repercussions for their children.

It should be noted here that some of the urban parents explicitly warned their children not to bring home or marry anyone black. My respondents often felt uncomfortable discussing this, even as they themselves raised the subject. A few did point out that their parents held racist attitudes toward blacks; but for the most part, my respondents were reluctant to voice why their parents had such strong feelings against intermarriage with blacks. Tellingly, parents did not mention any other out-group (e.g., whites or Latinos); a singular—and negative—emphasis was attached only to out-marriage with blacks. This suggests that the immigrant parents have been absorbed into the prevailing American racial hierarchy that continues to stigmatize blacks. In other words, the process of becoming American for these immigrant families also meant a social distancing from black Americans (Waters 1999).[1]

Dating Interracially

Another interesting dynamic is how a good number of the urban respondents rejected their parents' cues outright. As I mentioned earlier, of those who did date, more than a third were involved in interracial relationships, quite often with Hispanics and the blacks that their parents explicitly told them not to date. One group of these respondents kept their interracial relationships a secret from their parents. This was not difficult because, as I mentioned in Chapter 2, many of the urban respondents experienced a generational disconnect from their parents, who were often at work or who seemed to come from a different part of urban-enclave America entirely. Communication between parents and children around emotional issues was uncommon.

Ivory Miao, for example, was able to keep the fact that she was engaged to a Puerto Rican man from her parents for four years. Ivory attributed her engagement in part to a desire to escape the constant "pushing" by her parents to embrace their values.

> A: Pushing their kids to the point where they can't, they don't even identify with your values. I always grew up hearing my father saying, marry somebody Chinese, marry somebody Chinese, marry somebody Chinese. I mean, that's why when I was engaged for that period of four years, I didn't tell them.
> I: You didn't tell them you were engaged?
> A: He was Puerto Rican, that's why.

In the end, the relationship ended without Ivory ever having to tell her parents, which, as she admitted, was a "relief."

A second group of respondents openly dated interracially, negotiating their parents' displeasure as best they could. For example, when Lois first brought home her Jewish boyfriend, now fiancé, her parents did not hesitate to voice their unhappiness. Her father labeled the young man a "gangster" because he wore a leather jacket, and her mother muttered, "Again, you're not dating a Chinese person." Approval was gradual and grudgingly won as her parents began to see the young man's virtues.

> But like as we went on, [my mother] realized he would walk me to the door. He would make sure that everything's okay. If I drove home by myself, he'd call and make sure I'm home okay. He always treats my parents with utmost respect no matter how it hurts him. But my father, I think, is coming around. He now says my fiancé's name without grunting.

Victor Lim is another example. His longest relationship had been with a Jewish woman, whom he dated for several years. While Victor's father was polite to the woman, he would often take his son aside and suggest the idea of finding him a Chinese wife from abroad. "He sort of brought up, oh, when we go to Hong Kong, you know, I'll introduce you. You know, we'll find you a wife. Even while I was dating her, he would bring this up."

Among those respondents who dated blacks, Ling Choy was one of the few who actually told her parents. She made no attempt to hide her relationship with the West Indian young man from her parents, despite their evident disapproval.

> A: They don't like it. They deny it.
> I: But they've met him?
> A: They've met him. (laughter from Ling Choy and interviewer) He comes over, you know. They're not that strict. They won't throw him out. But there's a lot of tension.

With the exception of Deborah Ow, whose husband is Chinese American, all of my urban respondents were still single. Thus, it remained to be seen how much longer those who were dating interracially could keep it a secret from their parents, how their parents would eventually react, and the implications for the children's relationships.

Dating Chinese for Second-Generation Reasons

Other respondents did indeed prefer to date Chinese Americans, but for reasons that spoke to their second-generation status. So while immigrant parents might refer to a common Chinese culture as a reason for dating other Chinese, their children had a distinctly American take on this. Robert Ong, for instance, agreed with his parents (with whom he did not agree on much else) that a shared culture between husband and wife was important. But his definition of a shared culture included what he called "a similar history of oppression" along racial lines. Thus, while Robert had only dated Chinese Americans, he could see himself dating someone who was black or Latino but not someone who was white. According to Robert, the discrimination experienced by American minority groups was a part of his identity in a way that whites could not understand.

> The history of, oh, we oppress you, yes, now let's forget it and move on, you know. The dominant society doesn't like to tell people what they did wrong. In other words, we did wrong, we apologize, let's move on. But they really don't understand how much of that remains a part of our identity.

For some of these respondents, it was the perception of a shared class and social outlook grounded in race and ethnicity that underlay their perspectives on interracial dating. Deborah Ow, for example, had a cousin in Utah who married someone "Caucasian," and whenever she visited, she could not help but remark to herself on how different her in-law's culture seemed: "It's sort of like they have their own little jokes and their own way of talking. But that's how I feel, it's sort of like a life that I'm not in and I can't just immerse myself." And yet when Deborah spoke of her own husband, and what they shared in common, she highlighted both the racial and class dimensions along the lines of struggle:

> Just growing up in a working-class family. We understand how hard it is. We understand the struggles our parents went through. We clearly communicate. We can clearly understand what we're going to impart to our children. I think that's the key thing, that we're totally in agreement that, you know, we have to teach that life is not easy, that, you know, it's hard. Being Asian American is hard, that not everything is fair.

The complexities of race and class are also evident in Paul Chen's thoughts on the subject. When I asked him whether it was important for Chinese to marry other people who were Chinese, he initially replied: "It's 50/50. I don't really care about that. Depends. Sometimes, I see this person married, or with a white guy, black guy, or Puerto Rican guy, I don't really care."

However, Paul's nonchalance quickly turned into fervor as he recast the issue of intermarriage along the lines of race *and* class. As the exchange below indicates, it was when a white, well-to-do "outsider" who was not from the surrounding Chinatown area came in and started dating a Chinese American woman that he felt a profound sense of violation. This is not difficult to understand, given how marginalized Paul felt as a second-generation Chinese American born and raised in Chinatown; as I have noted elsewhere, he referred to Chinatown as a ghetto. Notice how he depicts this *particular kind* of interracial dating as a symbolic and literal theft from the Chinatown community. Such incidents bothered Paul so much because they signaled to him once again how he and the folk in Chinatown were so cut off from mainstream, middle-class America, a place that always seemed distinctly out of reach:

> A: Yeah, I don't really care. But sometimes, I see this white guy who is so cocky looking, he's wearing a suit, driving a nice car, nice hair, you can't help but want to throw a brick at him. There's just something that's there.
>
> I: Why?
>
> A: I mean, the people in my neighborhood, they know what's, they respect us, sometimes they have the same experiences. I don't care if they go out together, it's just like no big deal.
>
> I: You mean white people who grew up in the neighborhood?
>
> A: Yeah, Puerto Ricans, blacks, I have no problem with that. Then I see some white guy coming from a suburb, who probably grew up with a silver spoon in his mouth, and he takes, it's like, essentially robs from us, that's what it means. It's like you want to throw up at that. I see it more of a class thing, not a race thing. It's like the rich versus the poor, or the middle class versus the poor. That's how I see it as.

"Liberal" Suburban Families:
Race Does Not Matter

In the suburban families, the parents were more relaxed about dating, and
also more accepting of interracial dating. At least, that was the initial view
expressed by my respondents. In actuality, the dynamics were more complex.
Becky Wang is one example. Becky's initial take on this subject was that her
parents were "very liberal," even though they would most prefer that their
children marry Chinese or, even more particularly, Taiwanese; practically
speaking, though, they would welcome anyone into the family. A less open
perspective was conveyed, however, when Becky started to talk about her sister's experiences dating a Dominican man whom she nearly married; it became clear that her parents did not embrace all non-Chinese groups to the
same degree. Some were more welcome, others less so, and race had a lot to
do with it.

> My parents were really against it, actually, because they said their kids
> would have a lot of problems being like half-Asian, half-Dominican be-
> cause he's really dark-skinned and things like that. And my sister was
> like, "What are you talking about?" But, I mean, he didn't have a lot of
> ambition, so she ended up breaking up with him anyway. But now she's
> with a Jewish guy, and they're probably going to get married. And my
> parents love him. Because he's very ambitious, he works hard, and he
> treats her well. And I think that's what important. I don't really think it
> matters like what race you are.

Interestingly enough, even as Becky belies the influence of race in dating
and marriage choices, her take on her sister's experiences can be read as a
racial and ethnic script. The very way Becky contrasts the two men, the Jew
as an ambitious hard worker and the Dominican as unambitious, and by im-
plication, not a hard worker, maps onto common stereotypes about the two
groups. This is not to deny the validity of Becky's take on the two men, but
it does highlight how difficult it sometimes can be to disentangle racial and
ethnic stereotypes from our everyday understandings, even among young
people seeking to be free of such labeling.

Interracial Means Asian/White

In fact, the parental acceptance of interracial dating that my suburban respondents spoke of often meant dating between Asians and whites, which
was the dominant interracial pattern among them. In a few cases, grandparents voiced their disapproval of such out-group practices, but often to no
avail. Luisa Kao's grandmother, for example, would advise the young girl to
"marry someone that is Asian, or who is Chinese." As a young adult, however, this was not an issue for Luisa, who did what felt right to her (e.g., dating Asians and Hispanics).

The possibility of grandmotherly disapproval also came up in Veronica
Hsu's account. When her mother asked Veronica for a recent photograph to
send to a grandmother in Malaysia, the young woman could only find pho-
tos of herself with her (white) boyfriend. The mom sent the photograph anyway, aware that the grandmother would ask who the young man was. The incident became an inside joke between Veronica and her mother.

On the whole, the suburban immigrant parents themselves did not have a
problem with Asian–white partnerships. According to Veronica, the fact that
she had only dated white men was never even a topic of conversation in her
family. Of course, as she pointed out, she had no way of knowing whether
the silence stemmed from her parents' neutrality on her choices, tacit approval, or reluctant acceptance: "I don't think it's an issue with my parents,
and I don't know if it's because it's not an issue or they have resigned themselves to the thought that this is just how I am."

Melinda Wu is another example. She reported that her mother, who was
herself engaged to a British man, wanted her children to "marry Asian or
white," no one else. Reflecting on this, Melinda believed she had come to in-
ternalize her mother's values and that was why she could only see herself with
someone Asian or white; her only dating partners were young men from
those two groups. As her comments indicate, however, Melinda did not feel
altogether comfortable about this. Nonetheless, she really did think that there
were racially based cultural barriers that would be too difficult for her to
bridge if she, for example, were to marry someone who was black or Hispanic (Waters 1990).

A: And I know it's really bad because that's just being racist. It's not
that I don't like individual boys I meet that are black or Hispanic or

something, it's not that I don't like them. It's that, in terms of marriage, I believe that when you marry someone, you're marrying their culture and their friends. I don't know if I feel really comfortable in a group of African Americans. And I don't think I would feel comfortable being married into one.

I: Is there any particular reason why you don't feel comfortable with them?

A: I don't know, the wall might come more from me. It might be really knowing that I'm different, and therefore they think I'm different. Sometimes I'm not really sure if it's like they're treating me like an outsider, or I think I'm an outsider and I'm perceiving that I'm treated like an outsider. It hasn't come from any personal bad experiences or anything.

Chinese Might Be Best

Even someone as committed to issues of diversity as Frances Ma found herself thinking that it was important for her to marry someone Chinese. Frances, a native of a predominately white neighborhood, developed friendships with members of other minority groups for the first time when she came to Columbia. These ties grew out of several activities, as she worked with black and Latino students on student and faculty minority recruitment efforts, engaged in activism with other students (Frances was one of a group of students who in 1996 took over an administrative building as part of a call for the creation of an Ethnic Studies Department), and tutored black schoolchildren in the Morningside Heights area.

Yet, despite these interracial friendships and her older sister's marriage to an American of Irish descent, Frances wanted to marry someone who was Chinese American. Her sister had successfully blended both the Chinese and Irish cultures—the birth of her son, for example, was heralded in traditional Chinese fashion with a celebration when he turned a month old, but Frances's nephew also had an Irish name and would be raised knowing both cultures. Frances knew all this, but for her, the choice had a lot to do with language. She had made a conscious decision to study Chinese in college as a way of reconnecting with her roots, and more immediately, of connecting to the histories of her grandparents, who could only speak Chinese. It was not something she wanted to lose.

I think, for me, it's very important. I'd like to marry someone who's Chinese, and not just Asian. And what's important for me is language. I really want my kids to learn Chinese because I feel it has added a lot to my life, not being able to speak and then being able to speak it, being able to read the newspaper, or any of the texts in Chinese. It's very important.

A few of the suburban parents expressed a preference that their children marry other Chinese. Daniel Fong's parents were at the far end of this spectrum in that they wanted him to marry a Chinese woman born and raised in Asia. Similar to Melinda's account, the purported issue was more one of culture than race. In their desire for their son to marry someone raised abroad and thus "old school," Daniel's parents were seeking to retain the ethnic values that they themselves had grown up with in the Chinese diasporic community in the Philippines rather than yield to Americanization. As immigration researchers have noted, whether the ethnic values that Daniel's parents remember still exist is open to debate, as immigrants may end up keeping alive customs and social practices that are no longer followed so closely back in the home country. At the time I met Daniel, none of this was an issue since he had never dated; he had agreed to a trip on the infamous "Love Boat," a summer tourism program subsidized by the Taiwanese government to introduce Chinese youth to their cultural roots, more for the chance to travel than for any notions of romance.

While there was no evidence of the "secret dating" that I found among the urban respondents, a few of the daughters in suburban families expressed dissatisfaction with their parents' conservative attitudes toward sexual behavior and possible impropriety. The difference was that they felt able to discuss such issues with their parents (even if they did not always agree). Brenda Hsieh brought up this subject as something I should raise with other respondents, framing it as a generational gap issue. Note her surprise at what she perceived to be the sudden tightening of her parents' otherwise fairly liberal attitudes (in contrast to the urban respondents, who would have been unlikely to engage in such an exchange with their parents, since they took the conservatism of their parents as a given):

Like, for instance, my parents are, I mean, they are pretty cool, I can't complain. But like I know, my mother, I don't know why, I know my mother is really conservative about guys. I remember telling her I was going up to Boston one weekend to visit my friends, and she was like,

"Who are you staying with?" I was like, "When I am at BU, I will be staying with Janie. When I am at Boston College, I'll be staying with either Tom or Fred, both of which are guys." And she was like, "You can't do that." I'm like, "What are you talking about?" She was like, "No, you can go to Boston, but you can't stay in a guy's room." I was like, "Why?" She was like, "You never know, you know, you never know what they're really like." I'm like, okay, I don't know where that came from. I was like, "Okay, what if I were to visit my best friend in California?" Like, our families are friends, she knows his parents and everything, and she's like, "No, you can't stay with him, either." And that was really the last straw because she like knows him so well. She just has very, very conservative views on, like, my dad also, on propriety when we are talking about relationships, guy-girl relationships.

This dynamic was interesting, given that these same parents had socialized their children in gender-neutral ways when it came to education and social roles within and outside the home, as I discussed in Chapter 4. In these families, sexuality was an area where gender continued to matter.

Leisure

Unlike dating, leisure pursuits were an area where my respondents did not experience much tension with their parents. As I noted in Chapter 6, a large part of the childhood and adolescence of my suburban respondents had been spent playing musical instruments like the piano, violin, cello, and learning the repertoire of classical music. Most remembered enjoying these lessons rather than being pushed into them by parents against their will; for a few, however, there was a degree of parental negotiation when children found themselves compelled to pursue classical musical training. Milly Lin had this to say about her seven years of piano lessons:

Piano was their idea. But eventually we had a compromise. End of the classical music after the fourth year. And then I played like three years anything I wanted, like theme songs like *Aladdin* and *Forrest Gump* and all those scores. That was fun. The first horrible years weren't fun. They were very miserable.

As Milly told me, her parents continued to insist on the lessons because it was something they had never had the chance to experience as children.

As my suburban respondents became adults, they branched out beyond what parents thought was good for them to learn (e.g., classical music) into a diverse set of interests, including dance (ballet, hula dancing), singing, sports (crew, cross-country running, hiking, tennis), sororities, and art (painting and photography). As I mentioned in Chapter 7, parents generally did not take issue with such leisure interests as long as they remained a pastime. Mrs. Wu, for example, was very supportive of her daughter Melinda's desire to tutor young children and of her son's participation in a high school Shakespearean acting troupe. Mrs. Wu herself was an "amateur writer" and professional computer programmer. It was only when Melinda considered teaching as a career, or her son thought of becoming a professional actor, that her views changed. Mrs. Wu's ambition was for Melinda to pursue the law and for her son to become a stockbroker. Consistent with other parts of her interview, it was Mrs. Wu's struggles as a single mother in the United States that had led to this point of view. A literature major in university, Mrs. Wu had firsthand experience that enjoyable pastimes did not easily translate into bankable skills.

> And then when I divorced, I couldn't make living by literature. So I took a class in computer programming, that's why I can bring the bread home to feed my children. And that's why I have freedom to stay single if I don't want to [get married again]. And I don't want Melinda to do the same thing.

Melinda's account generally agreed with her mother's, and she acknowledged that her mother would have a tougher time with her brother: "The problem with this is that whereas I want to be a lawyer, he doesn't want to be a stockbroker. He hates economics altogether. It's been more of a friction between them because his career is so off."

For Margaret Wang, it was more that her parents were so uninterested in her extracurricular activities as to make them nearly invisible, when she would have welcomed their support. In high school and in her freshman year of college, Margaret was a cheerleader. The enjoyment that she derived came in part from going against the grain, dispelling stereotypes having to do with race, ethnicity, and gender—the first Asian American cheerleader in her high school class in a predominately white suburb of Maryland, the only cheerleader who got straight A's, a cheerleader who was also an engineering major, one of the most challenging fields of study. To Margaret, her parents never grasped what cheerleading was and why it was so important to her. She recounted the one time they came to see her perform in high school:

> Once, I was like, "Mom and Dad, why don't you come to one of my games?" So they did. Then they realized they had to pay to come in. So my mom didn't want to pay. So, you know, they brought a video camera. So what happened was, she picked my little brother to go and to use the video camera. And like it ran out of batteries. It was just really funny, though. It's just the way my parents are. I mean, I really don't expect them to understand a lot (about my life).

Jonathan Kong described a similar dynamic with his parents, who never understood his fascination with Japan. Majoring in East Asian Languages and Cultures, Jonathan specialized in Japan, gaining fluency in the language, spending a summer in the country, joining the Japan Club at Columbia, and becoming an aficionado of anime, a form of Japanese animation. Given the history of discord between Japan and his parents' native China and Taiwan, Jonathan's fascination made him stand out in the family.

> A: Like my parents were always on my case about it.
> I: Oh, they didn't like it?
> A: Well, they were always like, "Why are you so interested in Japan?" I mean, like, definitely Japan and China have not had the best history. And my aunts and uncles are always like, "This is the weird Japanese kid." So I really see myself as Chinese American, and at the same time, as Japanese, which is something most people wouldn't accept. And I don't really care.

Another shared element among the suburban respondents was doing volunteer work for Community Impact, Columbia's umbrella community service organization on campus. My respondents had engaged in a wide range of activities, from leading tours of New York City for school-aged children, to tutoring GED students and high school students on the SAT, to teaching English and basic literacy to adults, to visiting the elderly in their homes, to serving as rape crisis advocates, and to helping out at a shelter for victims of domestic violence. For some of the respondents, the volunteer work had brought them out of the suburban world they knew at home and the more diverse but still rarefied world of Columbia to interact with people of different racial, ethnic, and class backgrounds. As Audrey Hong noted:

I just think it's a personal thing. There are no like far-reaching goals I have in mind or anything like that. It's good also in some sense when you go to Columbia and you tend to forget, not that there's a real world out there, but that there's other people out there and other things that happen to people that's kind of outside the bubble that we live in.

For the urban respondents, the parental role in their leisure activities was even less visible. As I have mentioned elsewhere, the key concern of parents was that their children steer clear of the Asian gangs and not become delinquents. Once that goal was met, the children were free to pursue what they wished. The generational disconnect was such that, to a greater degree than with the suburban respondents, my urban respondents did not believe that their parents really grasped the things they did for fun. It is worth pointing out that the urban parents were also working intense schedules, and leisure of any kind—their own or their children's—was not a top priority. If anything, the children would try to reach out to their parents occasionally by joining in on one of the parents' pastimes, such as watching a Chinese serial on video.

This did not mean, of course, that the urban respondents had any lack of leisure activities. While they did have more intense schedules than their suburban counterparts, in terms of commuting and working part-time jobs outside of school (which generally paid more), they also tried to find time for a life outside of family, school, and job. Again, the activities were varied: karaoke, ballroom dancing, writing, student government, sports (archery, weightlifting, martial arts), and film.

Religion

Observers have noted the rise of evangelicalism among Asian American college students and, in particular, the increase in the number of Chinese Christian churches in the United States (Busto 1996; Yang 1999). Consistent with this, more than a few of my respondents pointed to the rise in second-generation Chinese and Korean Americans joining Christian churches, especially campus ministries. Michael How mentioned this topic as a "dissertation waiting to happen," and I assured him that researchers were on it. However, in contrast to the dominant pattern found by other researchers (Chai, forthcoming), the religious participation of my respondents tended not to exhibit any break in family tradition (e.g., a child of Buddhist parents embracing Christianity) but rather showed a continuation of the family example. Thus, even those who were Christian had found their way to Christianity via a family member, for example, a parent, an aunt, a cousin, or a distant relative. This was the case for both the urban and suburban respondents. The few instances in which one of my respondents had embraced a faith different from that of their family at large became a cause of tension.

Winston Woo's road to evangelical Christianity, for example, fits the pattern found by Chai (forthcoming), who discovered that "Christian identity takes [second-generation Chinese Americans] further away from their families." Ironically enough, it was Winston's mother who had set him on the evangelical path. Concerned that her young son, then a junior high school student, was not socializing enough, she had decided to send him to sleep-away camp. Winston had agreed, his only specification being that it be a Chinese camp because he feared getting "beat up" by non–Chinese American children. In a Chinese language newspaper, Mrs. Woo found what she thought was the perfect choice—a camp sponsored by a Chinese church. It was there that Winston said he found the Lord. The more Winston became immersed in Christianity, always in ethnic settings, the more concerned his mother became that he was retreating from the world rather than being part of the world. According to Winston, his mother's worries only intensified after the death of his father, which effectively left him as the "man of the house." It did not help matters that Mrs. Woo herself was not Christian. The fact that she followed traditional Chinese customs of ancestor worship left her unable to relate to her son's religiosity and vice-versa.

Robert Ong experienced a similar dynamic, although his religious shift was the opposite of his classmates'. The church had been an integral part of Robert's childhood. His mother, a convert to the Jehovah's Witnesses, would take both her sons to church twice a week. When he was in junior high school, Robert rebelled. Rejecting both the faith of his mother and the "superstitious Chinese practices" of his father, Robert fashioned a faith of his own from reading Buddhist texts and from his martial arts training.

Political Participation

Politically speaking, there was a noticeable lack of engagement among my respondents. My respondents, in fact, described non-political participation as a
common pattern among Chinese and Asian Americans, from their peers to
their parents. To a certain extent, this claim is borne out by the existing evidence. While rates of naturalization have been very high for Asian immigrants, the group's rates of voter registration have been decidedly low when
compared to rates for white and black citizens (Lien, Collet, and Wong 2001).
Voter registration, however, may be increasing among Asians in response to recent campaigns to limit immigrant rights (*Village Voice*, 30 May–5 June 2001,
Citystate Section). The chief concern for my respondents, however, was not
voting in elections. Rather, they complained that Chinese and Asian Americans did not "care about the issues" or "just did not have an opinion" on anything. Beyond the matter of political participation, it was a lack of curiosity
about the issues they objected to. In this fashion, my respondents were speaking of politics in a broad sense, more along the lines of issues-oriented mobilization, whether it had to do with school-wide admissions, tuition hikes and
faculty recruitment, community matters such as developing a local political
voice for an ethnic enclave like Chinatown or Flushing, or national debates
such as affirmative action or bilingual education.

Frances Ma, who had taken part in the 1996 student protests that called
for an Ethnic Studies Department at Columbia and an active member of a
number of campus-based social movements, noted the lack of mobilization of
Asian Americans around these kinds of issues. She acknowledged that the explanation might be partly economic: already coming from a relatively higher
economic strata, some of her Asian American classmates perhaps were unable
to see the relevance of issues having to do with equitable representation. Yet
she also felt that the actual practice of political protest was of no interest to
her Asian American peers, regardless of the issue at hand: "The idea of writing, protesting, that kind of political extremism is just foreign to a lot of Asian
Americans."

Other students voiced a range of explanations for this apathy: the belief
that responsibility lay with other people, or, in other words, it was someone
else's fight; the immigrant need to manage economic survival; or the all-con-
suming aspirations of the second generation to join the upwardly mobile. For
some, the frustration was keen. Judy Lai did not consider herself an activist,

by any means, but she was concerned enough about affirmative action, for example, to try to learn more about it. She had a difficult time getting any of her Asian American friends engaged in similar pursuits, as she made clear in her answer to a question about the worst traits of Asian Americans:

> It bothers me that most of my friends are not politically conscious. That they don't care about any issues or anything like that, it's just what's going on in their lives right now. And I can't get people to go with me to any purely like, discussion forums on race relations or political issues involving Asians or not involving Asians because they just don't have an opinion and they don't really care about the issue at all.

Only a handful of my respondents were politically engaged, whether as occasional attendees of political forums or active participants in social movements, on or off campus. Among these politically engaged respondents, Ling Choy was the only one who reported parental conflicts about her activities. Unlike Frances Ma, who was organizing around issues of racial and ethnic solidarity, which brought her into conflict with other Columbia students but not necessarily her family, Ling was organizing around issues at the heart of the urban, ethnic-enclave community. Ling was fighting for workers' rights in the restaurant and garment industries, the twin economic engines of New York City's urban-ethnic enclaves. Her primary affiliations were with the National Mobilization Against Sweat Shops and the Chinatown Staff and Workers' Association. On one level, Ling believed herself to be fighting for the cause of her immigrant relatives, all of whom were involved in this line of work. Instead of supporting Ling, however, her relatives were openly cynical about the groups she was involved in. Her own father told her, "If they don't pay you, don't help them. Or, you should be locked up anyway." This is consistent, on the one hand, with Kwong's (1987) depiction of Chinatown as a polarized community comprised of a small, elite class engaged in internal exploitation of working-class co-ethnics and limiting mobility, and on the other, with the idea that workers, whether from a belief in co-ethnic ties, fear, or suspicion, are sometimes wary of the very people, Chinese American or not, who are seeking to improve their labor conditions (*Village Voice*, 30 May–5 June 2001, Citystate Section).[2]

While my respondents generally did not feel much connection to political organizing around the issues of race and ethnicity, their personal views on this subject were diverse and deeply felt, as we shall see in the next chapter.

LOOKING TOWARD THE FUTURE:
A RACELESS WORLD OR A WORLD
DIVIDED BY RACE?

In Chapter 3 I suggested that Chinese immigrant parents from all types of socioeconomic backgrounds and educational levels understood they were entering a racialized social hierachy that privileged whites as the "real Americans." Thus, they stressed education to their children as a defensive strategy to offset the effects of perceived discrimination. Now I turn to the views of the 1.5 and second-generation children on this subject. How did my respondents situate the role of race and ethnicity in their lives and, in particular, in how others saw them? Did they believe they could claim the American label for themselves?

Relatedly, how did they situate the role of ethnicity and race with respect to mobility? My respondents were busy acquiring the educational credentials they thought would be necessary to attain a middle-class life: Did they think they would have the same opportunities as everyone else? Or did they feel they would have to do more to get less, as their parents argued? This chapter looks at those questions and at what the answers to them tell us about assimilation into the American social fabric.

Assimilation Theories

In the study of racial and ethnic identities in the United States, the experiences of the South-Central-Eastern European immigrants who arrived here in the late nineteenth and early twentieth centuries have set the standard. Indeed, a central concern of early American sociologists was whether these new immigrant groups would be incorporated into America given their different cultures, limited skills, and low levels of literacy (Lieberson 1980; Waters 1990). Beyond their own disadvantages, the immigrants were received in a manner that did not seem to bode well for their adaptation and assimilation. Discrimination forced them into low-level jobs and ethnic slums and was accompanied by an intense xenophobia that culminated in the end of large-scale immigration by the 1920s. Still, as we all know, the story of white ethnics is one of success. Subsequent generations eventually became incorporated into the nation's social fabric by virtue of their social mobility. Groups that were once viewed as distinct races unto themselves are now seen racially as part of the dominant white group and are understood to be American (Steinberg 1982; Brodkin 1998).

Yet, contrary to this classic assimilation paradigm, ethnicity persists among white ethnics (Alba 1990; Waters 1990). The key distinction is that it exists on their terms. White ethnics lay claim to a "voluntary symbolic ethnicity": they select particular strands from their ancestry or ancestries (if they are multiethnic) to highlight, and they choose "when and if voluntarily to enjoy the traditions of that ancestry" (Waters 1990, 137). Based on their own experiences, white ethnics believe that ethnic heritage is optional and without social costs for everyone. But, as Waters suggests, that is not necessarily the case in a racially stratified nation like our own.

Tuan (1998), for example, finds that third- and later-generation Chinese and Japanese Americans, while middle-class, continue to have experiences common to a "racialized ethnic group," one "for whom racial and ethnic concerns are salient"; as such, classic assimilation theories derived from the model of white European immigrants prove inadequate for understanding the constrained ethnic options among Asians. Tuan argues that as long as whiteness continues to be the norm and the unspoken basis for American identity, being an Asian ethnic somehow means being less American, regardless of one's degree of assimilation.

Another take on this subject is Claire Kim's concept of racial ordering, which she sees as operating on two axes, "superior/inferior and insider/foreigner." According to Kim (2000), the mid-1800s, which saw the first arrivals of substantial numbers of Asian immigrants, gave rise to a racial order that had blacks and whites as the major anchors (at the bottom and at the top, respectively) and put Asians into a triangulated position that reinforced white dominance over both Asian and African Americans. In this way, Asians were seen as superior to blacks, but at the same time, as foreign and unassimilable when compared to whites. Kim's argument is that even in the post–civil rights era, the racial order privileging whites over blacks—and the triangulation of Asian Americans that supports this order—has survived as "a shared cognitive map," one with real consequences for how members of all three groups fare in the opportunity structure, from residential segregation to labor market outcomes.

As I discussed in Chapter 3, in contrast to their parents, who typically immigrated as adults and thus had dual frames of reference, my respondents' frame rests exclusively in the United States. As the generation born and/or raised in the United States, my respondents did not have to confront the language and cultural struggles that their parents faced. For instance, even as my respondents sought meaning across a range of interests that at times overlapped and at other times departed from mainstream American youth culture, they were, at the very least, conversant with its particulars, as expressed in popular TV, music, and fashion. This was a facility that they interpreted as distinctive to growing up American. In light of these experiences, they had certain expectations that they would be accepted as American. Yet, as we shall see, they were also well aware that they could be marked as un-American simply by virtue of their physical appearance, although they interpreted this differently, depending upon their own social class background.

Asian Americans as Forever Foreigners

"It's true, we are all seen as outsiders":
Enclave Chinese

This idea of Asian Americans as foreigners was especially troubling to my enclave respondents, who spoke of the common assumptions that they spoke only Chinese, must live in Chinatown, and were steeped in Chinese traditions. In fact, it was a common assumption on the part of others that anyone who was Asian was most likely Chinese (American Attitudes towards Chinese Americans and Asian Americans 2001). As many of my enclave respondents told me, it was one thing for them to see similarities (and differences) among Asians, and quite another to be told that all Asians were the same. They found the meanings conveyed by others to be clear—they were foreigners, quite indistinguishable, and somehow inauthentically American all at the same time (Kibria 2000; Tuan 1998). As Lily Gong observed, there is a tendency for some to identify Asian Americans with premodern traditions: "They always think, ohh, Asian, mystical, some sort of mystical powers that we have. I get [white] people coming up to me and bowing to me. It's like, what is this? We don't do this. Maybe back then, a *long* time ago."

Within this context, Mary Sing made note of an incident that stood out because of its rarity:

> Q: Do you think other people consider you to be an American?
>
> A: It depends on what people I speak with. If they're educated, they'll say I'm American. My boss did. Because I was complaining to her about my Chinese skills. About me like, not doing well on my final. She was like, "It's very hard to learn another language." I'm like, "But I'm Chinese. I should, you know, be able to learn it better." She's like, "You're American." She said that to me. I was shocked. She was like the only person that ever said [that] to me. Like she's white, so that was kind of nice.

While nearly all my enclave respondents praised New York City for its cosmopolitan aura and widespread acceptance of diversity, they nevertheless had encountered their share of racially and ethnically charged incidents from childhood onward that underscored their foreignness. Comments ranged from the innocuous—"Why do you have eyes like that, are you Chinese?" "Where is China?" "Do you know Kung Fu?"—to the more hostile— "Asians can't drive," "Asians are so pushy," "Ching chong, chink," "Go back to where you came from." Such comments were elicited in everyday encounters with fellow New Yorkers, on subway platforms, on school buses, in a museum where one student was interning. Male respondents, in particular, remembered being physically harassed when they had visited parts of the country where there were few non-whites, like upstate New York and Baltimore, or even when they had ventured into other New York City neighborhoods where there were few Asian Americans.

Ivory Miao was not physically harassed when her family moved to a predominately white neighborhood in Marine Park, Brooklyn, in the early 1980s. Growing up, however, she had been verbally harassed on a daily basis. And paradoxically enough, the cumulative effect was that Ivory had taken refuge in the model-minority stereotype, despite her deeply felt disavowal of it.

> I just hated being Chinese. 'Cause it was different. It was not something anybody could understand. I mean, I didn't have friends because of it. People always stereotyped me, and I got really angry in high school whenever somebody said anything racist, I hate when people say something racist to me. Like, "You Ching Chong Wong." Anything to that caliber. It happened in my neighborhood, and then I'll perpetuate the stereotypes, like, well, "There's a reason why we're the smartest people in the world because we speak the most complicated language, and it's obviously too simple for you to understand." And I'll actually perpetuate that stereotype. I hate that about myself.

Another example is Elizabeth Wong. She remembered an incident involving her younger brother that signaled to her that Asian Americans were somehow not quite the same as everyone else, even in cosmopolitan New York City. For her, a citywide celebration in honor of a World Series victory by the Yankees became an ugly reminder that there was a racial gradation defining who was more accepted than others:

> They went to the Yankees' parade, and people were throwing toilet paper, and the cop, he was Caucasian, the police officer went up to my brother and said, "You, stop throwing the toilet paper." My brother says, "We didn't throw anything, we didn't have no toilet paper on us." The police officer answers, "I saw you, you throw it one more time, and I'm going to arrest your ass." So what happened was that my brother said, "We don't have anything." The cop goes, "That's it, I'm going to arrest your ass," like that. And then my brother's Caucasian friends went, "Yeah, man, chill, we don't have anything, you know." Like to say, "This Asian kid's with me, he's my buddy." He wasn't doing anything, and the cop didn't believe him. But when his Caucasian friends spoke out, the cop was, "Okay, fine." Like my brother's word wasn't enough.

The community of Flushing, which went from largely white to predominately Asian during the 1980s, provides yet another window into these kinds of racial tensions. Many of the white residents who had initially welcomed the revitalization of Flushing's downtown commercial district and the rise in real estate prices that accompanied the immigrants later came to see them as overly dominant, bringing too strong a foreign influence in Asian languages, businesses, and foodstuffs.[1] Jannelle Chao pointed out these tensions during our interview, which was conducted at a McDonald's in the heart of Flushing:

> Around here a lot of the native Caucasians are like unhappy with what we've done to Flushing. You know, it's like we conquered this place or buying up properties, or you know, making Asian businesses. There was a time in college when I was back for the weekend, and I was like at Genovese, waiting for someone. There were two older Caucasian women walking. I think they saw me standing there, so when they passed by, they said in a loud voice: "And these are all Korean stores now." And they were staring at me. First of all, I'm not Korean.

Such tensions framed Jannelle's account of her parents' run-ins with a group of unruly white teenagers in the first few months after they had moved into the neighborhood and bought a deli business. Although she acknowledged these teenagers would have probably harassed any new business owner or any new family on the block, she believed that race could not be easily discounted:

> [The teenagers] just caused a lot of trouble. Like one July 4th, we were in Maryland visiting our cousins. On the Fourth of July, they threw these firecrackers into the mail slot. It's a really traditional store, so we got a mail slot even though we had a gate. So it caught fire, the papers and stuff, and it like destroyed the interior of my parents' store. I think those teenagers, they were just bad people. They would do that to, I don't know, Italian people, but there was something added, definitely.

It was against this backdrop that my enclave respondents formed their understandings of what it meant to be American. They all had different takes on what being American meant to them, but many believed that regardless of what they thought, others saw them as Asian first and American later, if at all. Just as Tuan (1998) and others (Espiritu 2001; Lee 1996) have found, whiteness became the yardstick against which to judge whether one was American or not. Grace Li observed: "When people say American, they automatically think of the white race. They wouldn't consider Filipinos or Vietnamese, 'Oh yeah, they're Americans,' because they're still considered foreigners." It was something that Peggy Teng took issue with: "I don't like it when people say, blah, blah, Americans, as in whites. As meaning whites. I'm American, you know. So if they mean whites, they should say whites."

In light of this racialization attached to being American, most of my enclave respondents felt they could not logically claim the American identity as their own. The template of identities available to them was narrow: they could be either whiz kids, prostitutes, gangsters, and/or foreigners. As Paul Chen observed, it is seemingly impossible for Asian Americans to be seen as normal people having everyday interests and concerns. Paul was especially critical of the role of the media in disseminating images of Asian Americans as exotic Others:

> It's true, we are all seen as outsiders. The only time you see an Asian movie star, it's either a Kung Fu star kicking some guy or some sort of hoodlum. I'd like to see one day a *Seinfeld*, sort of like a *Seinfeld*, like four Asian people sitting in a café, doing nothing and talking about nothing. I mean, we don't see that. It's totally different. I don't remember ever seeing myself as just a lonely American. I never ever see myself as just a plain old regular average Joe American. I see myself as Asian American, that's how it is.

Deborah Ow gives us further insight into the role of the media in reinforcing the idea that Asian Americans are not like everyone else. Just as Paul talked about the iconic series *Seinfeld*, Deborah brought up the popular television show *Ally McBeal*. On the one hand, Deborah was impressed that the show featured an Asian American female cast member, a feat in and of itself, but more importantly, the character was portrayed as an aggressive attorney rather than as being stereotypically passive. On the other hand, Deborah was keenly disappointed by an episode in which a Chinese restaurant chef fries up someone's pet frog and serves it to several cast members, who unknowingly eat the dish and are quite disgusted afterwards. The episode reminded Deborah of all the misperceptions that she has had to deal with in her interactions with non–Asian Americans; according to Deborah, eating strange foods that would revolt the average American is just one example of the barbaric customs attributed to Asians in the United States (Tchen 1999):

> And I just found it interesting that you know, like we're still at that point, you know, we have governors right, Governor Locke [of Washington State]. I mean there are people who have lived here for so many generations, they are totally American, they are so American that you know, my

cousins were born here and they live in Utah. I truly believe they believe they're Americans, there's no question about it. But with these images of how Asian Americans are and associating them with this food thing, it just brings us all back to this, "Oh, they're still eating dogs," it's like that I take issue with, I'm very offended by it. My father was in the war [World War II] and fought for this country as an American, so, and we're here. I don't imagine myself going anywhere else, but it's like a fight. It's not an automatic though. It's something if I can say I'm an American, but I'm conscious of the fact that I'm Chinese American.

Beyond unpacking the common perception of Asian Americans as exotic Others, some of my urban respondents attended to the complex nature of the American racial hierarchy, pointing to a triangulation of Asian Americans along the superior/inferior and insider/foreigner axes that Kim (2000) outlined. The general understanding was that Asian Americans are more socially accepted by whites than blacks, who are often thought of in mainstream society as ignorant and as willfully speaking their own dialect of English. As Paul Chen noted, "I think there's a perception that Asians tend to be more civilized. There's that perception. Let's see, and you do good in school, it's more acceptable. Sometimes we speak better English. We don't speak Ebonics and stuff like that. That's how it is."

The other side of the story is that African Americans are unquestionably seen as American. It is not only whites who think of Asian Americans as exotic Others; my respondents specified that whites, blacks, and Latinos, notably Puerto Ricans in New York City, uniformly interacted with them as if they were foreign and thus inauthentically American. Even the group's purported academic prowess did not provide a refuge. Observers have noted that the academic achievements of Asian Americans are not always welcome. Kibria writes: "Anxieties about an 'Asian takeover' are reflected in the appearance, in informal student cultures, of such phrases as 'Made in Taiwan' to refer to MIT, and 'University of Caucasians living among Asians' to refer to UCLA" (1999, 32). Along these lines, Winston Woo reported on the unsettling insults that marred his friend's graduation from a New York City public high school. He recalled: "It was like Edward Murrow [High School], and there were certain awards, and all the Chinese people, their names were being called, and all these people were screaming out 'Pork fried rice,' and it was like, 'What's up with that?' That was really bad." This incident is reminiscent of Stacey

Lee's (1996) fieldwork experiences at an East Coast special-admit high school; according to Lee, when the names of the first large group of Asian American students were announced at graduation, they were met with hisses and boos from the audience.

As these accounts indicate, it is not an ethnic identity that intrudes upon the enclave respondents' sense of being American. Rather, it is quite the other way around. It is other people's misperceptions about them that make them feel distinctly un-American and that reinforce their Chinese ethnic identity. Deborah's comments bring home what is a key issue for this group of respondents: What will it take to be considered an American if you are of Asian descent? How many generations do you have to be in the United States? How many things do you have to do before others can see past physical markers such as the color of your skin? What is unarticulated are any issues of power that might underlie such conceptions of Asian Americans as foreigners, and the ways in which they might be used to maintain institutional mechanisms of inequality.

Even the few enclave respondents who did view themselves as American were deeply aware that others did not see them in the same way. This is Annette Tai's take on the subject:

> In a lot of ways, I do consider myself American, but I don't think I consider myself as American as someone who's Caucasian would. I guess it's also the way people treat you. I mean, I don't think people think I'm an American, either. Just because of the way I look. I don't think you can get away from that. I think it's more when you open your mouth, and you start speaking, and they're like, "Oh, wow, you know." They kind of just don't expect you to speak English fluently. I mean it's not most people, but still, I think you get that once in a while, and it sort of reminds you that, "Okay, I am Chinese first, and an American."

Equally telling, some who self-identified as Americans and thought that others did as well would later contradict themselves by referring to Americans as "whites, blacks, non-Asians." In other words, at some level, they bought into the idea that being American could not mean being Asian.

A Matter of Time and Education:
Suburban Chinese

Given the comfort level that came from their backgrounds, self-identifying as American was generally an uncomplicated issue for suburban respondents. The question of whether *others* identified them as American was quite a different matter. My suburban respondents were still mindful that their physical characteristics might mark them as foreign. However, it is worth pointing out that they were not as distressed about this as my enclave respondents because they felt, to some degree, that they did fit in. Consequently, their responses tended to be more optimistic. While acknowledging that others might initially regard them as foreigners, based on physical characteristics alone, my suburban respondents were confident that these same people would quickly change their minds once their shared experiences in education, class background, and cultural tastes became known. Thus, when asked whether she believed others considered her to be American, Victoria Chang answered: "Not from physical appearances, but when people get to know me."

Frances Ma was inclined to think that it was her responsibility to break down barriers through personal encounters. Similar to my other suburban respondents, Frances grew up believing that little distinguished her from her Italian and Irish classmates. She was also cognizant, however, that others outside of her close circle of friends would probably not think of her as an American. Realizing that she would have to earn that designation, she nonetheless bore no resentment. Frances was never in doubt about what the actual outcome would be—once other people gave her the chance to show them how American she was:

> Like non-Asians will look at me and be like, you're American? Someone is always going to ask me where I'm from. So in that way, yeah, I feel like, on the one hand, it's a limitation because some people were surprised, I don't know, that I had gone through certain experiences, like I know all the words to *The Sound of Music*, I know all the words to *Guys and Dolls*, and I've seen *The Wizard of Oz* a million times, like how that's weird to them because that's an American thing. So I think, at first, people will look at me automatically with a certain list of assumptions, and I may have to break them down, instead of just looking at me, and thinking, ah, she can be anything.

Veronica Hsu's optimism rested with her belief that the more educated and worldly people were, the more likely they were to consider her an American. In other words, racial hostility was a matter of ignorance borne of isolation and lack of higher education, whether it was situated in an urban or rural community. Consider her response:

> I think it depends on the person and the circumstances. I think in general at Columbia, yes, it's a different setting. If I were like to go into the Bronx, maybe not. But at Columbia, it's very different. I think it's educational level. I do think it's something you learn by being more exposed to the world, than like a little community in the middle of North Dakota. I think being at an Ivy League school or any major university, you have a different perspective.

Race and Mobility

Race Matters Now

When it came to the subject of race and ethnicity in the mobility process, my respondents generally concluded that education was a neutral institution where hard work mattered and race and ethnicity did not prove detrimental to their outcomes. In contrast, the next step after higher education—the workplace—provoked anxiety among more than three-quarters of my respondents, who agreed with the prevailing view expressed by parents: that race did matter in the workplace. As my respondents were on the cusp of entering the work world with the benefit of their college degrees, they were wondering what the payoff would be, both short-term in the kinds of first jobs they would land, and long-term in the kinds of careers they would have. One could argue that it made sense for my enclave respondents to perceive a more difficult route to success in the mainstream economy, given that they had grown up in largely working-class and immigrant neighborhoods and that their parents worked in working-class jobs. But that my suburban respondents shared these views was unexpected. After all, they were the ones who had grown up in white, suburban communities thinking "they were like everyone else." They had attended highly ranked schools, had enjoyed privileges like private music lessons and summer programs, and had ended up at one of the most exclusive universities in the nation. Why would they agree with the idea that race matters at all?

Yet the prevailing view on this subject echoed the one I described in Chapter 3 as set forth by parents to their children: American institutions, particularly corporate America, are not race-neutral. Race is definitely a factor. Said Becky Wang: "I think there's like this whole racial hierarchy. I think like there are more opportunities for whites and that's the way it is." Laura Toy put it even more simply: "Whites have it easier."

Such assessments, however, were not merely a replication of the parental viewpoint. As I mentioned in Chapter 3, in the case of the twice-marginalized parents, their perspective derived in part from their previous experiences with exclusion. There were other disjunctures between the sources of children's and parents' perspectives. The urban-enclave parents, for example, were mostly unable to draw from their own workplace experiences to discuss racial barriers. Even in the case of suburban parents, who did have plenty of professional experiences, their children were hard-pressed to discuss more than the commonsense knowledge passed on by parents that race actually mattered in outcomes. I acquired a deeper perspective from my interviews with suburban parents, in which they provided more specifics, but even here, they generally did not like to speak of particular incidents in their work lives but more along the lines of common knowledge.

Rather, the parental viewpoint was only one—albeit crucial—source of data about race for my respondents, as it was experienced in the work world. Also informing my respondents' perspectives were the things they themselves had seen on the job, or had heard from fellow classmates (also on the job), or had read in newspapers and magazines. Ironically enough, the model-minority stereotype also informed their largely pessimistic views of race in mobility. Drawing from all those sources, my respondents discerned a troubling gap between the highly touted picture of Asian American academic success and the hard and anecdotal evidence that showed only a marginal Asian American presence within the power elite. Their question was simple: If higher education is the key to mobility, and Asian Americans are so well educated, then why are they so absent in the top professional ranks? Or as Margaret Wang put it, Why are the "ratios so skewed"? Margaret, for example, was hard put to understand the ratio at the Fortune 500 company where she interned: "You have a meeting, and there are thirty males and maybe three females, and you know, I'm an intern and the others aren't even brokers. And there are only two Asians in the room."

When asked why he thought Asian Americans were absent in the upper echelons of corporate America, William Jen drew on similar experiences of working at a Fortune 500 firm and of interviewing at several others:

> Like just working in the financial field, I was the only Asian intern, even Asian worker. And especially through a lot of interviews I've gone to in finance companies. You can go visit offices, and you pretty much survey the people around. They were pretty much all Caucasian.

In answering this question, the explanation that my respondents came up with was simple: closed opportunities. Certain jobs, mainly the plum management positions, were available only to whites. Asian Americans could have the other, less choice jobs. Thus, William Jen reported: "Although they may say they're an equal opportunity employer or they won't discriminate against anyone, you get a feeling that there definitely will be [discrimination] just because you are different."

Daniel Fong, who had just landed a job with a top-flight financial services firm, was even more explicit:

> I think there's a glass ceiling. Like you know, every CEO out there is white, basically, you know. Depends on how far you can go. Like a senior VP, sure, you make it, but past that, no. Within corporate America, I don't know if you can realistically expect to go any higher.

Such views, ranging from the sense that people tend to hire and help those who are like them to the idea that the opportunity structure is inherently unfair, characterized the sentiments of the majority of my respondents. There was divergence, however, in how these respondents saw the salience of race in their own futures.

And Race Will Matter in My Future

About three out of every four respondents who believe that race matters in the present thought the issue would have a bearing on their own mobility. These respondents did not necessarily believe that a four-year degree or more would be sufficient protection against possible racial discrimination in the workplace. The effects of race might be mitigated, insofar as they would at least get a look by potential employers, but it did not mean that they would be hired, or if they were, that they would be promoted. It was clear that these respondents believed that, at some point, the mere fact that they were Asian American might hurt their chances. It might not have happened *yet*, because they had not entered the workforce full-time, but the specter of race would always be there. Their responses on this subject ranged along a spectrum of pessimism. Some, like Diana Chin, thought that race-based barriers could be overcome if Asian Americans developed their own professional networks, in other words, if they were to find a way to leverage the very racialized ethnicity that kept them shut out of certain positions. Others, like Chloe Gao, who brought up the glass ceiling, were decidedly less hopeful, saying that institutional obstacles might be "difficult if not close to impossible to overcome."

As a way of explaining how race might be an issue, An-Huei Hum drew a simple comparison between herself and a hypothetical Italian American being considered for the same job. An-Huei had always felt herself to be an American, but she realized that in the workplace it mattered little what she thought about herself. It was how others perceived her that mattered, and her racial characteristics could not be discounted. Thus, in comparing herself to an Italian American job applicant, An-Huei's comments speak to Tuan's (1998) argument that Asian Americans do not enjoy the same kinds of ethnic options as white ethnics; their racialized ethnicity will always be something imposed on them, regardless of how assimilated they feel themselves to be.

> A: Like let's say we are applying for the same job, and he or she would get it over me, I would wonder to myself, maybe I didn't get it because I was Asian American, because I was Chinese American. I mean, that would be in the back of my mind.
>
> I: Why would you think you might not have gotten it?
>
> A: Because I was Chinese. Because, let's say, it was a job selling knives door to door. They might think that a white person would sell more knives than a Chinese person, that they would have a better chance of it, you know, something like that. I do think that like race comes into play, in terms of like just dealing with people, especially in a business.
>
> I: Why do you think that?

> A: I mean, you don't see it as much in New York because it's so global. But like, even in Long Island, I must say, people are just miseducated about like ethnicities, and they still have prejudices or stereotypes that remain with them that might affect their decisions about someone.

Based on several years spent working at technology firms before deciding to complete his bachelor's degree, Victor Lim believed the issue lay less with hiring than with promotion structures. Asians might get into a company, but where they went afterward was another matter. Zweigenhaft and Domhoff (1998) have argued that professional Asian Americans assume a middle-man minority role, that is, they are often middle managers who take orders from white supervisors and who directly supervise, as well as fire, African American and Hispanic employees. Consistent with this, Victor maintained that Asian Americans could not legitimately aspire to go any higher.

> If what I wanted to do was get into a big company and move up towards a higher management level, that would be problematic. I think that when I was working at the software company, I mean I would say that a good percentage, a majority of the employees were Asian. Most of the management was white, the upper management was all white. I was sort of a middle manager. Again, it was a small company, too, but the people [who] were getting paid the most, I would definitely say, were definitely not Asian. They were all white.

That such pessimism bears certain costs was sometimes obvious. Margaret Wang contrasted the naive optimism she had had as a youth to the more resigned perspective she had as a young adult. She observed: "I think when I was little, I was more idealistic and I used to think, 'Oh, you know, this is America. I can do anything I want.' I think as I grew older, I just kind of realized, 'Well, you know, it's not necessarily everything you want, you get.'" Another source of her pessimism was the idea that even a Columbia degree, good grades, and high test scores might not be enough when it came to applying to graduate school, especially in a field with an increasing number of Asian Americans. Margaret Wang learned this from a friend, who worked in admissions at a top-rated business school:

> She was saying that they make comments about all the applications. And on one of the applications, they wrote, "Another Chinese engineer. Another Asian American engineer." And so, at first I didn't recognize it. I

recognize it now, I certainly do. Because people actually, it's a known fact. I mean, they actually do place these confinements and draw these lines between people. So now I do, I do realize that there are limitations.

Benny Sen gave a thoughtful account of how, although American-born, he lacked a key passport to moving upward in the power structure in the United States—namely, a Western European background that mirrored that of the majority of existing power brokers. As for his own prospects, Benny tried to downsize them to fit what he thought society would let him achieve. So he made the distinction between "fantasy" jobs and jobs that he would be allowed to do. Notice here that Benny did not necessarily think he lacked the ability for the "fantasy" jobs, although that might have been the case; what he did think was that he would never get the opportunity to display this ability even if he had it.

> A: Well, sometimes I fantasize about, I can be a guitar hero, a guitar hero as in a rock star or maybe a race car driver, definitely a race car driver. So during those times, I think maybe it would help if I were a white American. But when I think about job aspirations, my jobs in the future, I think about me being a Chinese American, because that's what I have to deal with, the fact that I'm Chinese, which doesn't mean I don't have to worry about my qualifications. So for fantasy jobs, or being a CEO, I think about being an American. But when I think realistically, when I think about my real job aspirations, it's a lot safer to think of myself as Chinese American.
>
> I: What you mean by safer, in what sense?
>
> A: Safer in that I won't be, I won't kid myself into thinking I can become this great, uh, political leader or CEO, which is not the most positive way of thinking, I realize that.
>
> I: Do you think Chinese Americans generally can't attain those positions of power?
>
> A: I know some of them have, like NBC has this guy in California, I think No. 3 guy at NBC. I think in principle they can. But when I see myself, I just don't think so.

Another subject that some of my respondents had strong views on was affirmative action. This was not a question I posed in the formal interview instrument, but it was one that was on the minds of some. The role of Asian Americans in affirmative action is highly complex. On one level, as Ancheta notes, their inclusion or exclusion in affirmative action policies depends on what one thinks of as the goals of affirmative action, which can include "remedying the present effects of past discrimination, preventing ongoing and future discrimination, or encouraging inclusiveness and diversity within an institution" (1998, 158). On another level, the multifaceted role of Asian Americans in these debates speaks to the complexity of race relations. As Takagi (1998) outlines, charges of possible discrimination voiced by Asian Americans during the 1980s centered on the lower rates of admission for Asian American applicants to elite public and private universities as compared to whites. Such claims met with several responses. University officials shifted the discourse from one of Asian Americans as stunning academic achievers to one of Asian Americans as not quite well-rounded enough, particularly when it came to such criteria as creativity, academic interests, and extracurricular activities. Ironically, university officials were drawing on a discourse that had been used once before to great effect—to exclude American Jews from elite institutions of higher education at the start of the twentieth century. In fact, this emphasis on well-roundedness and other such admissions criteria has its roots in these earlier attempts to retain higher education as the province of affluent Protestants, who had traditionally been its core student body (Steinberg 1982).

Neoconservatives, meanwhile, rearticulated their concerns about affirmative action by turning away from the depiction of whites as the "victims" of affirmative action policies and highlighting Asian Americans as the group that lost out in an admissions process that favored blacks (Takagi 1998). Ironically, the role of whites in these debates, either as "victims" compared to blacks, as voiced by neoconservatives, or as "beneficiaries" compared to Asian Americans, as expressed by Asian Americans, disappears from view.

The views of my respondents toward affirmative action were largely grounded in concerns about the ongoing and future discrimination they might face and in the inclusiveness and diversity within an institution (Ancheta 1998). A few believed that Asian Americans were included in affirmative-action policies and were pleased that such policies thus offered a way around possible race-based barriers. The majority, however, believed that Asian Americans were singularly absent in discussions of race and diversity, a subject that elicited a mixture of views. The common thread in reactions that ranged from disapproval of affirmative-action policies at one extreme to full support at the other, with a host of views in between, was sheer frustration at being invisible. Many expressed shock at their first realization that affirmative-action policies typically did not include Asian Americans, and they were thus left wondering about their place in a racial hierarchy which seems to be cast as a black–white dyad (Okihiro 1994). The question they often asked me was the following: If whites did prefer "their own," and if affirmative-action policies applied only to blacks and Hispanics, then on what grounds could Asian Americans be chosen?

Grace Li, for instance, had long thought that affirmative-action policies would open doors that would otherwise have been closed to her because she was Asian American. Then she discovered that Asian Americans are not considered racial minorities in most cases and thus she would not be eligible for affirmative action. Her account captures the keen disappointment and bafflement of most of my respondents to this policy:

> I know there are places and schools that will hire you because they want a minority population, that might help. But as I found out, Asians are not really minorities. I was like, what the hell, what happened there? We're not considered minorities because you have to be black and Hispanic. But then what are we? We're not the majority. So we're stuck nowhere.

This is not to say that my respondents believed that affirmative-action policies should not exist for blacks and Hispanics. In fact, about a fifth voiced the idea that blacks and Hispanics had it worse in American society than Asian Americans. There was a clear sense that blacks and Hispanics were less welcome in "white" schools, neighborhoods, and workplaces, and were penalized more heavily for their race. This was usually accompanied by a sense of unease rather than the feeling that Asian Americans deserved a more privileged position.

Even those most vocal in their opposition to affirmative-action policies believed that de facto racial-based barriers continue to exist. Rather, they were opposed on the grounds that such policies deny that racial-based barriers exist for Asian Americans as well. These policies left them feeling displaced on a symbolic and practical level—it told them that they had the same opportunities as whites, a claim that was at odds with what many saw and felt. Thus, when asked if he felt limited because he was Chinese, Joseph Pang answered:

> I think in some respects, yeah. Affirmative action, actually, I'm not very for affirmative action just basically because it works against Asians. In terms of the job market, I guess, most people would probably be more comfortable hiring white workers. I think in some respects [affirmative action] definitely works, it might work against me.

Frances Ma represented the other side of the divide. Acknowledging that Asians might not benefit as much from affirmative action, she nevertheless still believed in its merits. She had a particularly insightful view on the subject because she worked as a student recruiter for the Columbia Admissions Office:

> I think Asians are not given as much through affirmative action as Latino or black students because a lot of the programs are income-based and if you have low test scores. They'd rather take a black student over an Asian. I recruit for minorities. One of my friends really couldn't understand it, she was like, "That's really sick that you would give help to other people just because they're black, or because they're whatever." And I was like, "It's not as if they got this because it's a corrective. It's because so much has been done against them." Yeah, my friends who don't understand why there should be ethnic studies, or why there should be special treatment of those minorities.

Hank Chiang, who put himself through school by copying and delivering documents at a top-notch financial services firm, was of the mind that both African Americans and Asian Americans had been marginalized by affirmative action. Neither group had gained as much as was popularly imagined, and pitting the two groups against one another had obscured what he felt was the real issue: the advantage whites held in the labor market (Takagi 1998):

> You know in this company I work for, you know how they deal with affirmative action. Okay, you know, all they say is like we need a certain percentage of minorities. Okay, all the traders who make six figures are mostly white, okay. All the minorities are the research assistants who help out the traders. That's how they deal with affirmative action.

Thus, students like Frances and Hank tended to believe that the racialized social structure hurt all minority groups in similar ways, though in varying degrees.

And Race Will Not Matter in My Future

About 27 percent of my respondents who viewed race as a matter of conse-quence in mobility were decidedly more optimistic about their eventual out-comes. I call their optimism contradictory because it was expressed in the face of their own acknowledgment of race-based barriers—in other words, in the face of much evidence that they themselves had cited to the contrary. Most were consciously choosing to believe in the American Dream, a meri-tocracy where faith in oneself, ability, and hard work would be the key to success, and where things like race, ethnicity, class, and nativity status were not supposed to matter, even as they recognized the possible naiveté of their optimism. Daniel Fong, who gave a rather bleak assessment of the labor mar-ket as structured along racial lines used a sports analogy that drew on the viewpoint of a well-known black player in the National Basketball Associa-tion: "I sort of cling to a very idealistic view, like Charles Barkley, I don't care if I'm black. If I'm good enough to make it, I'll make it."

Julia Lau, who worked part-time as an administrative assistant while putting herself through college, was another example. When asked if she had had the same opportunities as everyone else, she responded:

> A: I may be naive, but yeah, I think I do have the same opportunities.
> I: Why do you say you may be naive?
> A: I mean a lot of people used to say, oh, you know, because you're different, and because you don't fit the frame of a Fortune 500 company, that you probably would not be hired. But if I had the same skills as somebody who would fit that physical frame or whatever, then maybe I would get it, but maybe I wouldn't, so.
> I: Who tells you these kinds of things?
> A: People from my job that encounter people like that in the workplace.
> I: So, you mean people that are minorities at your job?
> L: Yeah. Yeah, I guess they had that experience before. So, they are telling me because of that.

Similar to many of the enclave respondents, Peggy Teng highlighted the idea that race was only one pivot of inequality; another central one was class. Thus, Peggy provided a detailed account of how socioeconomic status and neighborhood can play a part in where people end up by influencing the kinds of schools children have access to and how teachers respond to their students. She remarked: "I think that even though I went to public school, we had a lot of great reinforcement. Teachers really cared about us. As a class, we really liked learning, and they really encouraged that." At the same time, Peggy made explicit the idea that "Asians have a harder time than whites, definitely," as they are left to fight for the same spots (since Asian Americans are not viewed as minorities and thus not considered along with blacks and Hispanics for affirmative action). Notwithstanding such strong views, Peggy preferred to think that race would not play a role in the workplace: "I want to be optimistic. I want to say, you know, they're going to pick whoever they pick. Like whoever they feel has the best vibes. I mean, if the two people are equally qualified, it's the vibes."

Another common sentiment was that the passage of time would diminish the impact of race. Linda Eng was a proponent of the passage-of-time argument, although even she acknowledged the contradictions in what she was saying since she did not back away from assertions of the centrality of race:

A: There's absolutely no restriction against [American freedom]. It's very limited as well. But I'm just saying, when I'm here in 1982, and now it's 1998, it has been a big, big progress. So, I'm sure, one day.

I: There'll be more progress?

A: Every day is progress, I feel. You're hearing more Asian voices out there. You're like seeing a lot more faces, hearing a lot more voices.

I: Do you think you have the same opportunities as everyone else, then?

A: Same opportunity? If given by the right connection. But I believe so. But not everyone believes so. And that's where the restriction comes in.

I: But you don't think people in power believe that?

A: Not all. And that's when the restrictions come in.

Race Does Not Matter: Assimilating Into the Mainstream

Despite the popular perception of Asian Americans as "honorary whites" (Tuan 1998), only a handful of my respondents subscribed to the idea that racial barriers do not exist and that they are assimilating into the mainstream of the American social fabric in an unproblematic manner. Some of those who did feel this way used the language of ethnic options that observers (Alba 1990; Waters 1990) have found with white ethnics. In fact, they brought up their similarities to white ethnics in this regard (Kibria 2002). Veronica Hsu, for example, believed that Asians and Jews had been more willing to assimilate into the American mainstream, as contrasted with blacks and Hispanics, who do not try to "fit in." Jackie Lew drew a pointed comparison between immigrants who come to the United States in search of the "American Dream" that, as she says, "instills in these people a drive to succeed." Racial dissimilarities across immigrant groups, she believed, were subsumed by this shared vision.

Comparisons

Intragroup

It is important to note that the picture offered here is distinctive to Chinese Americans. While not a representative sample, my respondents nonetheless belonged to two worlds within today's Chinese American community. Their experiences, however, do not speak to that of Asian Americans generally. There are certainly shared elements among Asian ethnics, particularly with regard to the high educational aspirations of Asian-immigrant parents across ethnicity and to the view of education as possibly the only avenue for social mobility.

However, there are also key lines of difference that would likely shape different views and outcomes. Korean Americans, for example, are similar to the Chinese in that they also draw upon ethnic networks, but the group's class bifurcation, while present, is not as strong. The contrast with Southeast Asian Americans is even clearer, as they are newcomers to the United States, comparatively speaking. Groups like the Vietnamese, the Cambodians, Hmong, and Thai were virtually nonexistent in the United States before the 1960s (Portes and Rumbaut 1980); and a substantial number of Southeast Asians arrived as refugees with low levels of human capital, particularly the Hmong and Lao. Consequently, their patterns of settlement have been very different, not only from the Chinese but from non-refugee Asian ethnics as well (Chan 1994; Portes and Rumbaut 2001). Future studies will provide a deeper understanding of how such issues play out in segments of the Asian American population other than Chinese Americans.

Between-Group Comparisons

What of comparisons to other immigrant, racial, and ethnic groups in the United States? I found, for example, that the family dynamics for my urban-enclave respondents is quite similar to what researchers have found in working-class Mexican immigrant families, where the parents are typically laborers with low levels of formal schooling. Thus, Mexican parents transmitted to their children an emphasis on schooling and an ethic of hard work, though this is expressed in more general life terms rather than specifically with regard to academic achievement. Indeed, the importance of school was underscored in similar ways, with the common refrain that education was a means for children to avoid the manual-labor jobs of their parents (Gandara 1995; López 2001; Stanton-Salazar 2001). Similar to the parents of my urban-enclave respondents, Mexican parents also find themselves constrained by their immigrant status, their lack of English language facility and education, and their limited resources.

The need to conduct comparative research that will carefully disentangle immigrant status, race and ethnicity, and socioeconomic status in views on and experiences of education and mobility has been much noted. Several studies have yielded interesting insights, and there are a number of ongoing research projects that promise to shed additional light on this important question (Zhou and Bankston 2000; Zhou 2002; Settersten, Furstenberg, and Rumbaut 2004; C. Suárez-Orozco and M. Suárez-Orozco, forthcoming; Swartz, forthcoming). Subjective views on success, for example, can vary between immigrant and native-born groups in New York City in ways that reflect "their different class origins as well as the collective experiences of their group in New York and of their parents in the sending countries" (Mollenkopf et al., forthcoming).

Situating Contradictory Narratives about Ethnicity and Race

Comparative work also needs to be done on the two major themes that have been at the heart of this book: the ethnic-culture argument that my respondents strongly endorse and the belief that race and ethnicity are major barriers in contemporary American society. Unlike other groups, Asian Americans have been characterized in mainstream society as having superior ethnic cultural resources, which lends an immediacy to this argument for my respondents. Accordingly, my respondents articulated both themes, embracing ethnic culture as an explanation for group and individual mobility and yet believing that racial discrimination would limit their own chances for advancement, no matter what their educational credentials.

On one level, this seeming contradiction speaks to the fact that race continues to matter in the contemporary United States as a line of divisiveness and stratification. We know this has occurred in especially powerful ways for blacks. In spite of the gains of the civil rights movement, there is a continuing black–white gap in wealth (Oliver and Shapiro 1995; Conley 1999), and the black population itself has polarized into an urban underclass and a middle class (Wilson 1980, 1987, 1997). Moreover, contrary to the assimilation narrative, race continues to be highly relevant to the lives of the black middle class (Feagin and Sikes 1994; Lawrence Lightfoot 1994; Zweigenhaft and Domhoff 1998; Patillo-McCoy 1999; Steele 1999). Even the experiences of West Indian immigrants and their children, a group that has been held up as a black model minority to African Americans, reveal the force of continuing racial inequality, as West Indians find their immigrant optimism undermined by the structural realities of American race relations (Waters 1999).

What was most salient to my respondents are the barriers particular to their own racialized status as Asian Americans (although many were certainly aware of the barriers against blacks), a group that is neither black nor white. The ethnic-cultural narrative carries so much weight because it offers my respondents a way to reconcile themselves to the effects of racial discrimination against Chinese and Asian Americans that they have been warned about, have witnessed, and have often experienced. Although they acknowledge that such barriers exist, to them, the supposed distinctiveness of the Asian immigrant ethos which privileges hard work and, above all, a respect and keen desire for education should be of some utility in offsetting these obstacles. Even those of my respondents who had a history of disengagement from school placed the responsibility on their families, never unpacking the logic behind the cultural and structural factors they themselves cited. The weight of ethnic expectation, the all-pervasive image of the Asian American over-achiever, not to mention the empirical evidence of at least some Asian Amer-ican overachievers, especially those in the enclave, left the ethnic-culture narrative as the most compelling explanation, regardless of individual back-ground or actual experience with school. Consequently, my respondents did not fully articulate the larger structural mechanisms underlying mobility. Ul-timately, their narratives lead back to the family and to the individual.

This is in keeping with the post–civil rights context that my respondents have encountered. They live in a world that is far removed from pre-1960s America, where it was perfectly acceptable and legal to exclude by race, eth-nicity, and gender. Theirs is a world where equality of opportunity is more visible than ever before. The persistent racial inequalities observed and ex-perienced by my respondents and their families highlight the elusiveness of equality of condition, but at the same time, equality of opportunity offers the possibility of real hope.

It is at this intersection of fear and hope, pessimism and optimism, that the ethnic-cultural narrative assumes importance. By making primary the eth-nic-cultural narrative, my respondents are in effect choosing hope over fear. It is a hope, however, that comes with real costs. By prizing individual effort over institutional factors, the ethnic-cultural narrative makes it difficult for my respondents to problematize institutional mechanisms of inequality and, relatedly, to identify with members of other groups who confront similar kinds of barriers. As I was giving a talk at Hunter College a few years ago on the findings from this study, someone noted how strongly felt the views on discrimination were and asked: "But do your respondents go the next step and see themselves as part of a larger community of likeminded individuals that can and should strive for social change?" The answer is, "No." Some, of course, critiqued the model-minority thesis and a small number did join broad-based coalitions for social change. Whether this will change over time as my respondents transition to adulthood remains to be seen. At the time we met, the ethnic-cultural narrative provided most with a symbolic safe space from the injuries of race. The idea that the immigrant Chinese or Asian family is the ticket to mobility makes systemic change seem less of a pressing issue. To borrow from one of my respondent's comments about political apathy among Asian Americans, it becomes someone else's fight.

The irony is that by not participating in this struggle, Asian Americans only end up maintaining a status quo that continues to marginalize them. Nor should the responsibility be placed on any one group. The task of problematizing institutional barriers to mobility falls to all groups, immigrant and native-born, as we turn our collective gaze to the question of whether the post-1965 strides will actually lead to equality of condition or create new inequalities.

One of the many things I enjoy about research is that you are never sure of what you will find—there is always the unexpected. This book is a case in point: the story I have just told is not the one I anticipated telling. Similarly, the particular challenges that I encountered in the field were wholly unexpected and yet spoke to the themes expressed by my respondents.

The Gender Narrative

My original goal with this project was to look at the effects of gender. More specifically, I was interested in the role of gender and class in the educational preferences of immigrant parents and in the ways their daughters and sons responded to these preferences. Drawing from the social science literature, I expected to find working-class parents encouraging their daughters (and not sons) to postpone further studies so as to help out with family obligations and to be working in the paid labor force to help support the household. I also expected to find that parents, regardless of class, encouraged their daughters to pursue "softer" fields of study rather than math, science, or economics— the fields commonly associated with Asian American students. Other ways that I thought gender might matter was that immigrant parents would fear that education would bring about too much independence for women, too much exposure to American culture, and a decline in marriage opportunities (Kibria 1993; Wolf 1997; Hune 1998; Espiritu 2001).

Indeed, that would have been a great story, except for one thing—that is not what my 1.5 and second-generation Chinese American respondents told me. After a number of interviews, I realized that the striking theme emerging from them was gender egalitarianism on the part of parents, particularly in education. This is not to say that gender considerations were absent. As I have shown in the preceding pages, gender was a key theme—it just played out in ways that I did not anticipate.

The Class Narrative

In addition to gender, the class dimension of my respondents' experiences also proved surprising to me on many levels, underlying my dynamics in the field, particularly the process of recruiting interview subjects. In 1998, I obtained permission from Columbia and Hunter to conduct my work at both sites. However, given that I was not able to get access to the names and addresses of all of the Asian American or Chinese American students enrolled at each school, I was unable to obtain a representative sample. (At Columbia, the former dean of students kindly wrote a letter in the summer of 1998 in which he explained the project to Asian American undergraduates and asked them to contact me if they were interested in participating. As a result, more than a dozen students did contact me and come to participate in the study.) Although I realized that it would not be possible to have a representative sample, I still aimed for a diverse pool of respondents. Toward that end, I recruited from a wide range of courses and student clubs, both ethnic and non-ethnic. The former involved contacting the professor and getting permission to make an initial pitch to students in the classroom, during which time I circulated a sign-up sheet so that interested students could provide their contact information. The latter involved contacting students at the various clubs and following very much the same procedure.

In making my pitch to students, I thought it would be useful to draw upon my role as an insider: this was the advice I was given by experienced ethnographers and by how-to ethnography texts. Along these lines, I highlighted the fact that I was second-generation Chinese American when asking fellow second-generation Chinese Americans and 1.5ers to participate in the study. I underscored that they would be contributing to much-needed research on immigration, race and ethnicity, and higher education.

What I did not expect was the different effects my role as an interviewer and observer would have at both field sites. My experiences in recruiting students to participate became a key source of note-taking and insight. The particulars of my experience notwithstanding, the overall issues of insider/outsider and relationship to one's subjects are ones that all qualitative researchers have to face on some level.

Us versus Them: Challenges at Hunter

I found recruiting to be a very complicated process at Hunter. Since the student clubs generally did not have email lists, I took to my feet and periodically checked in at the club offices, trying to run into a student leader and make my pitch right then and there. In one case, I visited a student club office every few weeks for months, leaving notes in the makeshift mail slots in an attempt to catch up with two students (my efforts eventually paid off). Where I encountered the most resistance was in trying to recruit Hunter students from classes that were not in Sociology or Asian American Studies. (And even in those classes, there was not ample interest, as only a few students out of many signed up at any one time.)

I sensed an unspoken unease among Chinese American students at Hunter about what I was doing, what I was asking about in the first place, and why I needed their help. This may be because Hunter students were not as familiar with the research process and the need for human subjects as the Columbia students were. (At Hunter, I saw few signs calling for participation in research experiments.) After I became familiar with the rhythms of the school, I also understood that Hunter students already had tight schedules crammed with commuting, jobs, classes, and family obligations. In short, they were hard-pressed to find time to talk to some stranger about anything so nebulous as their educational experiences. They were just trying to *get* their education.

And yet, I sensed something else at play as well, something besides time and work commitments. Something having to do with me. I first realized this when Hispanic and black students, who were no less burdened with personal responsibilities, would offer to show me around the school; when after yet another fruitless presentation in class that netted no participants, Hispanic and black students would come up to me and offer a kind word (one student said, "It's a damn shame"), or, thinking that I was studying other groups besides the Chinese, would volunteer themselves.

The problem came into focus after I had completed my first few interviews with Hunter students: in short, I represented the kind of student that Asian Americans were *supposed* to be. As a student at an Ivy League university, I was somehow emblematic of the model minority, an image my Hunter respondents felt to be at odds with their own lives. None of the respondents told me this directly. Rather, they told me how strange it was to see this image of Asian Americans in the media as super-achievers, nerdy, and wealthy, given that it did not reflect their own reality. As one student noted, "It was just another standard to uphold." The closest that I got to a direct answer was one that came from Paul Chen. After our interview, when I asked him for suggestions on how to get people interested in the project, he told me that the mere mention of schools like Harvard and Yale was just a real "turn-off" to the Hunter students I was trying to recruit, but he could not tell me why.

My next strategy was to overcome this distance by bringing up elements of my personal history that intersected with the Hunter students'—that I had been born in Chinatown, that my mother was a garment factory worker, that my relatives had attended CUNY schools, and that I still had ties to the Chinatown community. Then I ran into another problem, one related to the ethnic networks that informed the lives of my Hunter respondents. By highlighting that I was from a similar background, I was also calling attention to the fact that I had managed to enter the ranks of an elite institution—and they had not. In some ways, I could have been another example cited by their parents of so-and-so's daughter or son, from an enclave background, who had gone to an elite school, one more frame of comparison that would inevitably make the Hunter students feel lacking.

Let me say, however, that after the initial unease passed, my Hunter respondents were incredibly generous with their time, thoughtful, and very insightful. Their reactions taught me two things: the constraints of class background, in general, in persuading people to participate in projects like this one that rely on individuals sharing their stories; and the power of the model-minority stereotype and ethnic networks in shaping how urban-enclave Chinese American students saw themselves, and how they saw me.

One of Us: A Straightforward Process
at Columbia

Columbia proved an easier place to recruit students. Judging from the posters I saw all over campus, soliciting the assistance of students in research projects, the idea of participating in an experiment or a survey was quite common-place. The ethnic extracurricular organizations also maintained extensive email membership lists (numbering a few hundred), and that also made my job a lot easier.

My Columbia respondents were, on the whole, very eager to speak with me and needed little prompting to open up about their experiences. While my family background was very different from theirs and there might have been barriers because of my age and educational background (my being a Ph.D. student), my Columbia respondents were more inclined to see our similarities in having attended Ivy League institutions. After the interview, they often asked what Yale was like, sought out my advice about careers and graduate school, or underscored our similarity by simply prefacing their comments with, "But you must know how it is, being at Yale," or, "Things must be the same at Yale."

The particular ways in which students responded to me in the field had meaning on several levels. First, it spoke to the respondents' individual reflections on the subjects of race, ethnicity, and class, as revealed in the transcripts from their recorded interviews; my field notes on our interactions prior and after the interview provided another lens through which to understand what they told me in the interview itself. Later, as I was tracing the narrative arc from all the many transcripts and field notes, I realized that these early reactions to me in the field presaged the larger themes that I was seeing— namely, how the Hunter students saw themselves as failures for having "ended up" at Hunter, and how natural it was for the Columbia students to see themselves at an Ivy League college.

The Family Interviews

Hunter and Columbia students also had very different reactions as to whether I could contact their parents for an interview. I later realized that their reactions spoke to the contrasting types of relationships they had with their families. Many of the Columbia students were enthusiastic about the idea, provided that, of course, I refrain from revealing to their parents any confidences they may have shared with me. I was able to compile a list of about a dozen parents of Columbia respondents and ended up interviewing seven parents and one adult sibling. However, this idea was met with considerably less enthusiasm or, in some cases, outright suspicion from Hunter students. Part of this reaction may have been that, in most cases, the Hunter students did not enjoy particularly close relationships to their parents to begin with and they were not sure how their parents would react to my request. So as not to jeopardize the relationship I had painstakingly formed with my Hunter respondents, I acceded to their wishes and did not push the point. I interviewed only one adult sibling of a Hunter respondent. I made this decision with a degree of regret that only grew stronger as I realized the richness that came from not only talking to the parents but visiting them in their homes.

It was through such home visits that I gained a fascinating look into immigration, class, and culture as experienced by some of the Columbia families. The interviews with the children had given me an impression of their immigrant parents as individuals who spoke Chinese and ate Chinese food, but who only occasionally and very marginally celebrated Chinese holidays, and who, generally speaking, wanted their children to assimilate into the mainstream. Certainly, their socioeconomic means had given them entrée into predominately white, upscale communities. Did it follow that their ethnicity would be absent in the home environment?

What I found during my visits proved quite illuminating. As I mentioned in Chapter 1, in their homes, the Chinese immigrant parents, middle-class or not, kept cultural artifacts which were similar to ones I have seen in my relatives' Chinatown apartments, and which their children generally did not mention at all in the interviews. Interestingly enough, the parents themselves did not mention the artifacts, either: they were merely a part of their lives at home that needed no elaboration. And yet, the artifacts spoke vividly to whom they were—immigrants coming from one world and making their way in another that was quite different from all they had known before.

Categorizing by Family Class Background

As I began to analyze my survey, interview, and field data, I realized there were other complexities related to class that I had not anticipated. For example, I learned that my survey could mask a great deal of variation. On paper at least, most of the parents of Columbia students seemed "middle-class," insofar as they had high levels of education and professional occupations (I was not able to obtain an accurate gauge of income).

It was only during the interviews, however, that I learned about the diversity that is hidden beneath the "middle-class" label. Although most were comfortably settled in their middle-class status, some of the respondents' families had or were encountering financial difficulties. A few respondents told me their parents had taken out loans to put their children through private college since they did not qualify for financial aid. Others told me of at least one parent who was out of a job, or of family businesses that were in a downturn, all of which put a strain on the respective households. Divorce, in a few cases, had led to downward mobility for the single mothers. The opportunity to interview some of these middle-class families at home further highlighted the manifold layers of the suburban, middle-class strata. These middle-class dwellings included a small condominium off a bustling commercial district, a two-story house in a gated community nestled in the hills, and a suburban tract house—in other words, they provided evidence of the wide continuum in "middle-class" homes, both literal and symbolic.

Still, it was relatively easy to categorize the twenty-eight students who I eventually came to describe as *"suburban, middle-class Chinese"*: these households exhibited many similarities in occupation, educational attainment, and neighborhood context. Things were more complex when it came to categorizing the forty enclave-Chinese, nearly 80 percent of them Hunter students. On the one hand, the enclave economy was a crucial identifying characteristic. While this was not a community study, the families proved to be typical, in several respects, of the Chinese living in enclaves or in neighborhoods with substantial Chinese populations that had some link to the enclaves. First, about 74 percent of my Hunter students had parents who were involved with the enclave economy, mainly in the restaurant business or the garment industry. Some of the fathers worked as chefs and waiters in Chinese restaurants hundreds of miles away, in upstate New York, Tennessee, and Pennsylvania, but had found their jobs through Chinatown networks and employment agencies. Second, although the families were part of a social milieu that valued homeownership as an emblem of prestige and as a vehicle for social mobility (Zhou and Logan 1991), only 60 percent of them actually owned their homes (as compared to nearly all the suburban families).

Third, although 43 percent of the Hunter families were from Guangzhou Province, with another 29 percent from Hong Kong, there was also some diversity, with some families hailing from other areas of the People's Republic of China, such as Beijing, Shanghai, Zhongsan, Foochow, and Zhejian. About 12 percent of the families were from Taiwan, and a few were from Vietnam and Burma. They thus reflected some of the ethnic diversity typically found among the enclave immigrant Chinese in New York City. Fourth, the parents typically had low levels of education, certainly when compared to the parents of my suburban respondents. For instance, about 43 percent of the mothers and a bit less than half of the fathers had a high school education, mostly in the home country. About a fifth of both parents had only a grade school or middle school education.

Notwithstanding the similarities I found among these families with respect to the enclave economy, there remained crucial differences that have been less visible in previous educational research accounts. Such differences become clear if we look at the types of activities which engaged the parents within the ethnic economy, and at where and what kinds of homes they lived in. When such factors are included, we see three distinct groups. About 29 percent of the parents whom I describe as belonging to an urban-America ethnic enclave held manual jobs in the ethnic economy, typically as waiters and garment workers, and virtually all lived in rented apartments, mostly in Chinatown or on the Lower East Side. Thus, they were among the working class. Another 40 percent owned or operated restaurants, garment factories, jewelry stores, wholesale goods, or other businesses in the ethnic economy, and these parents often lived in multifamily homes they had purchased outside of Chinatown in Brooklyn and Queens. These families held a middle-class status within the ethnic economy.

An additional 31 percent of families worked outside the ethnic economy. These parents worked for the city or federal government (as city bus drivers, federal postal workers, city engineers) or in the mainstream economy for private firms in teaching, data entry, janitorial services, electrical technician services, and as cashiers. All of them owned their homes, again, mainly multi-unit dwellings in neighborhoods of Brooklyn and Queens that have substantial Chinese populations. Despite their incorporation into the mainstream economy and into more integrated neighborhoods, these families also maintained strong kinship and social ties to a Chinese economic enclave, supporting the claim that living outside of Chinatown has little effect on the depth of one's ties to Chinatown (Zhou and Logan 1991).

INTRODUCTION

1. According to a LexisNexis search, nine *New York Times* articles written in 2003 used the term "immigrant strivers."

2. For example, immigrants from Southern, Central, and Eastern Europe who arrived in the United States during the late nineteenth and early twentieth centuries were vilified as being of inferior races and adherents of foreign religions (largely, Catholicism and Judaism), and unlikely to be assimilated into U.S. culture. Despite such xenophobia, discrimination, and dire predictions, the descendants of these South–Central–Eastern European immigrants were eventually integrated into the Anglo-Saxon mainstream, becoming "white" in the process. For more discussion of how this occurred, see Lieberson 1980, Alba 1990, Waters 1990, Ignatiev 1995, and Brodkin 1998.

3. It should be noted that some Asian ethnic groups, such as the Chinese and the Japanese, have a long history in the United States, dating back to the nineteenth century. Thus, those populations include people who can trace their ancestry in the United States several generations, and who can be classified as "native-born minority groups." Researchers, however, have determined that there is something particular to being *immigrant* Chinese that shapes high educational aspirations and outcomes. As with other groups, the immigrant drive for academic achievement begins to wane as acculturation sets in (Portes and Rumbaut 2001a).

4. I define the 1.5 generation as foreign-born children of immigrants, who arrived in the United States by the age of twelve and thus were largely educated and socialized here.

5. Nearly all my respondents were the children of two Chinese-immigrant parents. The exceptions were three children of mixed unions: a Columbia female student who was the child of a Taiwanese mother and a white, American-born father; and among the Hunter students, one female who was the child of a Chinese father and a Swedish mother, and another male who was the child of a Jap-

anese father who had been raised as Chinese in China and a half-white, half-Chinese mother who had been born and raised in China.

6. I also conducted interviews with the parents of six Columbia students and with two adult siblings, one of a Hunter student and another of a Columbia student. The data from these interviews are included here.

7. Please see Omi and Winant 1986 for a discussion of how this racialization process occurred. Espiritu 1992, Tuan 1998, and Kibria 2002 provide insightful discussions of how some second- and later-generation Asian ethnics have responded to this racialization process by developing a racial consciousness that transcends ethnic boundaries, and in the case of Kibria, of how this pan-ethnic identity exists alongside ethno-national identities.

8. In the years since 1966 press coverage of Asian Americans has increasingly sought to incorporate the findings of social science research to present a more complex image of the group; thus, news coverage has made reference to the demographic diversity among Asian Americans, critiques of the cultural argument, and the stereotype's negative consequences. Such attempts notwithstanding, Osajima (1988) finds that "the core elements of the original model minority thesis" remain—for example, empirical findings of success and culturally based explanations of achievement, with particular emphasis on the family, hard work, and respect for learning. Moreover, the news media failed to address the growing body of research that showed Asian Americans short of parity with whites, despite their high levels of education. Drawing on survey data, Lee (2002) demonstrates the continuing prevalence of Asian Americans as a model minority in American public opinion.

9. The initial aims of the Immigration Act of 1965 were actually ethnocentric, as lawmakers expected the new immigrants to arrive from Europe. However, Alba and Nee (2003) note that the United States continued with and, indeed, expanded immigration even after it became obvious that the new immigrants were coming from Latin America, the Caribbean, and Asia.

10. The Census Bureau reports that 10.24 million Americans described themselves as solely Asian, and this figure represents 3.6 percent of the population.

11. Ironically, Vincent Chin was himself a draftsman, a job that was also dependent on the automobile industry.

12. Another group of Chinese immigrants has settled in ethnic enclaves in upscale suburban communities such as Monterey Park, California. This study, however, does not draw on students from such backgrounds. See Fong 1994, Horton 1995, and Li 1999 for discussion of such suburban enclaves.

13. All names have been changed to protect the identities of the respondents.

14. Goyette and Xie (1999) conducted one of the few quantitative studies that examines ethnic differences among Asian Americans, specifically testing for socioeconomic and background characteristics, tested academic ability, and parental expectations as factors shaping students' educational expectations. They

find, for example, that "socioeconomic and background characteristics explain much of the differences between the educational expectations of the Filipinos, Japanese and South Asians, and those of the Whites, but none of the differences in expectations between the Chinese and Southeast Asians and the Whites" (32–33). A number of ethnic-specific qualitative studies (Kim 1993; Wolf 1997) reveal the multiple pathways through which parental aspirations are formed and transmitted.

15. According to Weinberg (1997), the specific percentages are the following: 17 percent of Chinese immigrants had some college; 20 percent had a bachelor's degree; 13 percent had a master's degree; and 6 percent had a doctorate.

16. The Project on the Second Generation in Metropolitan New York focuses on adults, aged eighteen to thirty-two, who are either native-born (whites, African Americans, and Puerto Ricans) or second-generation (Dominicans, West Indians, Chinese, Russian Jews, Colombians, Ecuadorians, and Peruvians), who were born in the United States to parents who immigrated after 1965, or who were born abroad but who arrived in the U.S by the age of twelve and grew up here. The project draws on three methods: a random-sample telephone survey of respondents; in-person and in-depth interviews with a selected subsample of survey respondents; and targeted ethnographies at various field sites, such as at labor union halls, political community organizations, churches, and a community college.

17. Segmented assimilationists also posit a third trajectory, whereby immigrant children settle in or near poor neighborhoods largely comprised of native-born minority groups and assimilate into the underclass. This trajectory is not generally applied to the experience of the children of Asian immigrants, however.

18. If this debate in its broad outlines seems familiar to some, it is because the cultural and structural frameworks have been pitted against one another in scholarly inquiries of African American outcomes but in very different fashion. In attempts to understand the relatively low levels of African American mobility, in the aggregate, some scholars have argued that African Americans lack the cultural values (hard work, perseverance, a value for education) that lead to success. Other scholars have advanced the idea that it is not culture but systemic structural disadvantages in the form of persistent housing segregation, underfunded and mismanaged inner-city public school systems, and other forms of institutional discrimination that have led to intergenerational poverty.

CHAPTER I

1. Four major groups make up the population of contemporary Taiwan: descendants of the Aborigines, the oldest settlers of the island, who are about 2 percent of the total population; descendants of Hokkien and Hakka migrants from mainland China, who arrived, in waves, from 1500 through the nineteenth century and are the numerical majority; and the Mainlanders, post–World War II

immigrants from the mainland and their children, who make up about 14 percent of the population (Fricke, Chang, and Yang 1994; Tsai, Gates, and Chiu
1994).

2. These figures are based on analyses that I conducted, using Census 2000 Sum-
mary File 3 and the American FactFinder Program. They are based on twenty-one
cases, all Columbia students. In the case of seven other Columbia students, who de-
clined to give their family address, I relied on neighborhood level data.

CHAPTER 2

1. "Paper sons" was one of the extralegal strategies that the Chinese found to
circumvent the Exclusion Acts. When the 1906 San Francisco earthquake de-
stroyed virtually all the city's official birth records, Chinese immigrants discovered they were able to enter the country through falsified birth certificates, identifying themselves as the sons of merchants, or native-born or naturalized
Chinese Americans. Despite this strategy, the number of Chinese immigrants allowed into the United States remained small.

2. The role of the ethnic enclave in the mobility process of post-1965 immigrants has been a central debate in the immigration literature. According to the
ethnic-enclave model, the ethnic enclave provides opportunities for socioeconomic mobility that are not available to immigrants in mainstream society, where
they would work primarily in the secondary sector. Assimilation, then, is not necessarily the ticket to socioeconomic mobility, as has been traditionally argued.
Others have focused on the internal organization of ethnic firms, and on recruitment and training processes, to see whether an apprenticeship system is actually
working. See Portes and Bach 1985 and Waldinger 1993 for more insights into
this debate. In the Chinese American case, the role of the ethnic enclave in the
mobility process has drawn markedly different responses from Zhou (1992) and
Kwong (1987). Zhou argues that New York City's Chinatown is an example of
how immigrants are able to use ethnic resources and ethnic ties to achieve mobility. Kwong, on the other hand, sees Chinatown as a polarized community
comprised of a small, elite class engaged in internal exploitation of working-class
co-ethnics and limiting mobility.

3. The 42 percent figure is based on thirty-three cases, twenty-six from
Hunter and seven from Columbia. In the case of seven Hunter respondents, who
either did not provide family addresses or provided information that could not
elicit the relevant figures through the American Factfinder program, I again relied on neighborhood level data. The guidelines set by the Department of Housing and Urban Development are calculated as a percentage of the local median
family income and are as follows: extremely low income households are those
where earnings represent less than 30 percent of the local median family income;
very low income, less than 50 percent; moderately low income, less than 80 per-

cent; middle income, between 80 percent and 120 percent of the local median family income; and upper income, the equivalent of or more than 120 percent. In the 2000 census, the median household income in New York City was $38,293.

4. Some of these respondents, who grew up in semi-suburban settings in Brooklyn, Queens, and Staten Island with a greater number of whites, were similar to the suburban Chinese in that they thought of themselves as white while growing up. Once they entered racially and ethnically mixed settings in junior high school or high school, however, they started to identify as Chinese and took Chinatown as the focal point of their identity.

CHAPTER 3

1. The parallels between the role of education in the mobility patterns of Asian Americans from the post-1965 period and that of American Jews from the first great wave of immigration to the United States have been much noted (Sowell 1981; Fejgin 1995). Jews supposedly have a high regard for education that has brought them upward mobility (Chiswick 1988; Cowan and Cowan 1989). Indeed, Asian Americans are thought to have inherited the mantle of American Jews as a dramatically successful immigrant group (*New York Magazine*, 10 April 1995), and they have also inherited the same prejudicial stereotypes that have accompanied the success of Jews—for example, a reputation for clannishness and for having too much influence in the United States (American Attitudes towards Chinese Americans and Asian Americans 2001). Some scholars, notably Slater (1969) and Steinberg (1982), have questioned the cultural explanation for the success of American Jews and situate the phenomenon in terms of the structural characteristics associated with each group's immigration. Their argument is that Jewish immigrants who arrived in the United States after the 1880s were indeed laborers, but that they also had a middle-class orientation, high rates of literacy grounded in the tradition of close reading of the Torah, and occupational skills well suited to industrial labor. Thus, in comparing the Jewish and Asian American experiences, Steinberg observed: "It was because education carried with it such compelling social and economic rewards that the traditional value on education was activated, redefined and given new direction" (138).

2. According to a report based on data from the National Educational Longitudinal Study (1988–94), 40 percent of Chinese American high school seniors had a father with a college education or higher, but 90 percent reported their fathers as expecting them to attain a bachelor's degree or higher. About 92 percent of the seniors expected to complete a degree from a four-year college or to go on to a postgraduate education, revealing high levels of agreement with their fathers' aspirations (Kim 1997).

3. According to Siu (1992a), the percentages of admitted students are in fact quite low, ranging from 5 percent in China to 35 percent in Taiwan. In Guang-

dong Province in China, for example, "the number of openings in institutions of higher learning was less than half the number of students taking the entrance examinations" until 1994 (Ikels 1996, 166).

4. Ong (2002) finds that African Americans and Hispanics, for example, remain highly segregated from non-Hispanic whites, both in the neighborhoods they live in and the schools they attend. School segregation has meant that African Americans and Hispanics are overconcentrated in inferior schools. Asian Americans are also segregated, but less so on both dimensions, and they are nevertheless attending better schools.

5. See Waters and Eschbach 1995 and Woo 2000 for a review of this literature.

6. Tang's (1993) study of engineers indicates that this disparity was particularly accentuated for immigrants, as compared to U.S.-born Asian Americans. Immigrant Asians earned 18 percent less than whites and took six to eleven years to reach the same income levels. Other social scientists have depicted Asian Americans as the "middle-man minority," despite their educational attainment. That is, Asian Americans are caught in the middle in the corporate workplace between white supervisors and Hispanic and African American workers (Zweigenhaft and Domhoff 1998, 143), just as some Korean immigrant merchants are caught in the middle between the manufacturers producing the goods they sell and the poor, minority groups they serve (Min 1996).

CHAPTER 4

1. In fact, the numerical majority of female immigrants dates as far back as the 1930s (see Houstoun, Kramer, and Barrett 1984).

2. For discussion of specific immigrant groups, see Hondagneu-Sotelo (1994, 2001), who has done work on the gendered transitions underlying undocumented Mexican immigration and on the domestic work and roles of Mexican and Central American women in affluent Los Angeles households; and Pessar (1984, 1986, 1987), who has studied gender relations in the Dominican immigrant experience.

3. Female infanticide, while not widespread, was also not uncommon, as some families found the cost of raising a daughter to outweigh the benefits (Baker 1979).

4. This could be due, in part, to the fact that more than a third of the suburban Chinese mothers were from Taiwan. As Brinton (2001, 22) notes, there is now gender parity in Taiwanese higher education.

CHAPTER 5

1. This reputation derived from the success of CUNY's working-class immigrant students, many of them from marginalized ethnic groups, notably Ameri-

can Jews. The growing presence of American Jews at elite, private universities during the late nineteenth and early twentieth centuries had become the cause of alarm and the target of restrictive policies, both official and unofficial (Steinberg 1982; Lavin and Hyllegard 1996; Brodkin 1998). No such restrictions existed at CUNY, however, and many of its alumni went on to great success, including Jonas Salk, noted sociologists Nathan Glazer and Daniel Bell, Secretary of State Colin Powell, and a total of eleven Nobel Laureates.

2. The 1960s and 1970s ushered in a period of change for CUNY. A pivotal event came on July 9, 1969, when the Board of Higher Education announced a policy of open admissions, allowing all high school graduates to enter CUNY schools. This policy was designed to provide access to higher education for racial and ethnic minorities and working-class whites, groups who continued to be underrepresented (Rossman et al. 1975). For example, Hunter is open to high school graduates who have at least an 80 percent average, or are in the top third of their class, or scored at least 1020 out of a possible 1600 on the SAT (slightly above the national average SAT score of 1016) (*Chronicle of Higher Education Almanac* 2000). Students who have a GED score of at least 300 are also eligible for admission (*Hunter College Undergraduate Catalog* 1995–1998, 9).

Today, finances and the open admissions policy continue to be the two most pressing issues faced by CUNY. The system has been the subject of both sharp cutbacks in state and city funding, and high-profile disputes over whether students needing remedial work in reading, writing, or mathematics should be allowed to enroll in the senior colleges. CUNY is now criticized in some quarters for allowing a decline in academic standards while others maintain that open admissions has provided crucial opportunities for traditionally underrepresented groups to achieve mobility through education (Rossmann et al. 1975; Lavin and Hyllegard 1996). During the time I conducted my research, media reports regularly depicted faculty and students as "worn down by the constant attacks on the university" (*New York Times*, 24 March 1999, B1).

3. There is a rich literature in social psychology on how stereotypes play out in everyday life. Carol Dweck and her collaborators have argued that group perception and degrees of social stereotyping can be traced to the beliefs people hold about human nature, for example, whether it is fixed or, alternatively, malleable (Levy, Stoessner, and Dweck 1998; Plaks et al. 2004). With respect to the consequences of stereotyping, Claude Steele (1995; 1997) has argued that, for women studying quantitative areas and African Americans, the perceived risk is of confirming a negative group stereotype—in other words, a stereotype threat that can affect academic achievement, even among high achievers. In a similar vein, Nalini Ambady and collaborators have done work with Asian American women on stereotype priming, or how different aspects of an individual's identity can be triggers in test performance (Shih, Pittinsky, and Ambady 1999), as well as work

on how stereotypes shape evaluation of Asian American women's academic performance (Pittinsky, Shih, and Ambady 2000).

4. A pilot comparative study of second-generation immigrants and native-born groups in New York City has suggested that Chinese immigrant parents might indeed be distinctive in that regard. Some of the Chinese parents in the pilot study had little education or English-language facility and worked in low-wage jobs, but nonetheless had more extensive knowledge of the city's high schools compared to other groups of a similar social location, in part from ethnic networks (Kasinitz et al. 1997). The pilot study also points to the lower levels of residential segregation among the Chinese, which facilitated their access to "better schools." This study focused on native-born groups (whites, blacks, and Puerto Ricans) and immigrant groups, (Chinese, West Indians, Dominicans, Colombians, Ecuadorians, Peruvians, Haitians, and Koreans). The authors caution that the results from the study are preliminary and serve more as themes to explore in their larger project on the second generation in New York City, rather than as findings.

CHAPTER 7

1. Given that the core curriculum takes up a significant portion of a student's academic schedule, Columbia College does not mandate that a student graduate with a major—one can graduate with a concentration, for example, a minor. Students who are fulfilling their premedical requirements have additional flexibility. They may take a premedical concentration in a field, such as history, which requires fewer courses than a typical concentration.

CHAPTER 8

1. See Waters 1999, 339–44, for a more detailed discussion.

CONCLUSION

1. The remarks made in 1996 by Julia Harrison, the long-time councilwoman whose district included Flushing, exemplify such neighborhood tensions. She famously remarked that Asian immigrants were "criminal smugglers, robbers, rude merchants and illegal aliens, who depress the wages of American working people." It has been noted that many of the elderly whites living in Flushing shared a similar unease with their numerous Asian neighbors (Dugger 1996).

Abelmann, N., and J. Lie. 1995. *Blue Dreams: Korean Americans and the Los Angeles Riots*. Cambridge, MA: Harvard University Press.

Alba, R. D. 1990. *Ethnicity in America: The Transformation of White America*. New Haven, CT: Yale University Press.

Alba, R. D., and V. Nee. 2003. *Remaking the American Mainstream: Assimilation and Contemporary Immigration*. Cambridge, MA: Harvard University Press.

American Attitudes towards Chinese Americans and Asian Americans: A Committee of 100 Survey. April 2001. http://www.committee100.org/.

Ancheta, A. 1998. *Race, Rights, and the Asian American Experience*. New Brunswick, NJ: Rutgers University Press.

Arenson, K. 1999a. College Board Scores Vary Little from Previous Year's. *New York Times*, 1 September, Education Section, B9.

———. 1999b. Leadership Void Hobbles CUNY as It Faces Severe Problems. *New York Times*, 24 March, Metropolitan Section, B1.

Attewell, P. 2001. The Winner-Take-All High School: Organizational Adaptations to Educational Stratification. *Sociology of Education* 74 (4): 267–95.

Baker, H. 1979. *Chinese Family and Kinship*. New York: Columbia University Press.

Baker, D. P., and D. L. Stevenson. 1986. Mothers' Strategies for Children's School Achievement: Managing the Transition to High School. *Sociology of Education* 59 (3): 156–66.

Bankston, C. L. 1995. Gender Roles and Scholastic Performance among Adolescent Vietnamese Women: The Paradox of Ethnic Patriarchy. *Sociological Focus* 28 (2): 161–76.

Bankston, C. L., and M. Zhou. 2002. Being Well vs. Doing Well: Self-Esteem and School Performance among Immigrant and Nonimmigrant Racial and Ethnic Groups. *International Migration Review* 36 (2): 389–415.

Barringer, H. R., R. W. Gardner, and M. Levin. 1993. *Asians and Pacific Islanders in the United States*. New York: Russell Sage Foundation.

Barringer, H. R., D. Takeuchi, and P. Xenos. 1990. Education, Occupational Prestige, and Income of Asian Americans. *Sociology of Education* 63 (1): 27–43.

Brinton, M. C. 2001. Married Women's Labor in East Asian Economies. In *Women's Working Lives in East Asia*, edited by M. C. Brinton, 1–37. Stanford, CA: Stanford University Press.

Brinton, M. C., Y.-J. Lee, and W. L. Parish. 2001. Married Women's Employment in Rapidly Industrializing Societies: South Korea and Taiwan. In *Women's Working Lives in East Asia*, edited by M. C. Brinton, 38–69. Stanford, CA: Stanford University Press.

Brodkin, K. 1998. *How Jews Became Whites and What That Says about Race in America*. New Brunswick, NJ: Rutgers University Press.

Brubacher, J. S., and R. Willis. 1997. *Higher Education in Transition: A History of American Colleges and Universities*. 4th ed. New Brunswick, NJ: Transaction Publishers.

Busto, R. 1996. The Gospel According to the Model Minority: Hazarding an Interpretation of Asian American Evangelical College Students. *Amerasia Journal* 22 (1): 133–48.

Chai, K. Forthcoming. Chinatown or Uptown? Second-Generation Chinese American Protestants in New York City. In *Becoming New Yorkers: The Second Generation in a Global City*, edited by P. Kasinitz, J. Mollenkopf, and M. Waters. New York: Russell Sage Foundation.

Chan, S., ed. 1994. *Hmong Means Free: Life in Laos and America*. Philadelphia: Temple University Press.

Chan, S., and L. Wang. 1991. Racism and the Model Minority: Asian Americans in Higher Education. In *The Racial Crisis In Higher Education*, edited by P. G. Altbach and K. Lomotey, 43–67. Albany: State University of New York Press.

Chen, H. 1992. *Chinatown No More: Taiwan Immigrants in Contemporary New York*. Ithaca, NY: Cornell University Press.

Chen, H., and W. Lan. 1998. Adolescents' Perceptions of Their Parents' Academic Expectations: Comparison of American, Chinese-American, and Chinese High School Students. *Adolescence* 33 (130): 384–90.

Chen, C., and H. Stevenson. 1995. Motivation and Mathematics Achievement: A Comparative Study of Asian-American, Caucasian-American, and East Asian High School Students. *Child Development* 66 (4): 1215–34.

Chen, X. 1996. *Educational Achievement of Asian American Students: A Generational Perspective*. Ph.D. diss., University of Michigan.

Cheng, K. M. 1998. Can Education Values Be Borrowed: Looking into Cultural Differences. *Peabody Journal of Education* 73 (2): 11–30.

Chiang, L. 2000. Teaching Asian American Students. *Teacher Educator* 36 (1): 58–69.

Chiswick, B. 1988. Labor Supply and Investment in Child Quality: A Study of Jewish and Non-Jewish Women. *Contemporary Jewry* 9 (2): 35–61.

Chronicle of Higher Education. 2000. Vol. 47, no. 1 (Special Almanac Issue).

Clemetson, L. 2002. A Slaying in 1982 Maintains Its Grip on Asian-Americans. *New York Times*, 18 June, A1.

Conley, D. 1999. *Being Black, Living in the Red: Race, Wealth, and Social Policy in America*. Berkeley, CA: University of California Press.

Cowan, N. M., and R. S. Cowan. 1989. *Our Parents' Lives: The Americanization of Eastern European Jews*. New York: Basic Books.

Dasgupta, N., D. E. McGhee, A. G. Greenwald, and M. R. Banaji. 2000. Automatic Preference for White Americans: Eliminating the Familiarity Explanation. *Journal of Experimental Social Psychology* 36 (3): 316–28.

Davis, D., and S. Harrell. 1993. The Impact of Post-Mao Reforms on Family Life. Introduction to *Chinese Families in the Post-Mao Era*, edited by D. Davis and S. Harrell, 1–24. Berkeley: University of California Press.

DeNavas-Walt, C., and R. Cleveland. 2002. *Money Income in the United States: 2001*. Current Population Reports, Series P-60, Consumer Income, no. 218. Washington, DC: U.S. Dept. of Commerce, Economics and Statistics Administration, Bureau of the Census.

Dugger, C. W. 1996. Queens Old-Timers Uneasy as Asian Influence Grows. *New York Times*, 31 March, Metropolitan Desk, sec. 1, p. 1.

Elliot, R., C. Strenta, R. Adair, M. Matier, and J. Scott. 1996. The Role of Ethnicity in Choosing and Leaving Science in Highly Selective Institutions. *Research in Higher Education* 37 (6): 681–709.

Erikson, E. 1968. *Identity: Youth and Crisis*. New York: W. W. Norton.

Erikson, K. T. 1976. *Everything in Its Path: Destruction of Community in the Buffalo Creek Flood*. New York: Simon and Schuster.

Espenshade, T. J., and M. Belanger. 1997. U.S. Public Perceptions and Reactions to Mexican Migration. In *At the Crossroads: Mexican Migration and U.S. Policy*, edited by F. D. Bean, R. O. de la Garza, B. R. Roberts, and S. Weintraub, 227–62. Lanham, MD: Rowman and Littlefield.

Espiritu, Y. L. 1992. *Asian American Panethnicity: Bridging Institutions and Identities*. Philadelphia: Temple University Press.

———. 1994. The Intersection of Race, Ethnicity, and Class: The Multiple Identities of Second-Generation Filipinos. *Identities* 9 (2–3): 249–73.

———. 1997. *Asian American Women and Men*. Thousand Oaks, CA: Sage Publications.

———. 2001. "We Don't Sleep Around Like White Girls Do": Family, Culture, and Gender in Filipina American Lives. *Signs* 26 (2): 414–40.

Farley, R. 1996. *The New American Reality: Who We Are, How We Got Here, Where We Are Going*. New York: Russell Sage Foundation.

Feagin, J., and M. Sikes. 1994. *Living with Racism: The Black Middle Class Experience*. Boston: Beacon Press.

Fejgin, N. 1995. Factors Contributing to the Academic Excellence of American Jewish and Asian Students. *Sociology of Education* 68 (1): 18–30.

Foner, N. 1987. New Immigrants and Changing Patterns in New York City. Introduction to *New Immigrants in New York*, edited by N. Foner. New York: Columbia University Press.

———. 1998. Benefits and Burdens: Immigrant Women and Work in New York City. *Gender Issues* 16 (4): 5–24.

———. 1999. The Immigrant Family: Cultural Legacies and Cultural Changes. In *The Handbook of International Migration: The American Experience*, edited by C. Hirschman, P. Kasinitz, and J. DeWind, 257–64. New York: Russell Sage Foundation.

Fong, T. 1994. *The First Suburban Chinatown: The Re-Making of Monterey Park, California*. Philadelphia: Temple University Press.

Forero, J. 2000. Basketball "Nerds" Get Last Laugh: Boys at Bronx Science Find They're on a Winning Team. *New York Times*, 19 February, B1.

Fricke, T., J. S. Chang, and L. S. Yang. 1994. Historical and Ethnographic Perspectives on the Chinese Family. In *Social Change and the Family in Taiwan*, edited by A. Thorton and H. S. Lin, 22–48. Chicago: University of Chicago Press.

Fukuyama, F. 1994. Immigrants and Family Values. In *Arguing Immigration: Are New Immigrants a Wealth of Diversity or a Crushing Burden?*, edited by N. Mills, 151–68. New York: Touchstone.

Gandara, P. 1995. *Over the Ivy Walls*. Albany: State University of New York Press.

Gans, H. 1979. Symbolic Ethnicity: The Future of Ethnic Groups and Cultures in America. *Ethnic and Racial Studies* 2 (January): 1–20.

———. 1992. Second Generation Decline: Scenarios for the Economic and Ethnic Futures of the Post-1965 America Immigrants. *Ethnic and Racial Studies* 15 (April): 173–92.

Gardner, H. 1989. *To Open Minds: Chinese Clues to the Dilemma of Contemporary Education*. New York: Basic Books.

Geertz, C. 1975. Common Sense as a Cultural System. *Antioch Review* 33 (1): 5–52.

Gibson, M. A. 1988. *Accommodation without Assimilation: Sikh Immigrants in an American High School*. Ithaca, NY: Cornell University Press.

Glenn, E. N., with S. Yap. 1994. Chinese American Families. In *Minority Families in the United States: A Multicultural Perspective*, edited by R. Taylor, 128–58. Englewood Cliffs, NJ: Prentice Hall.

Goldberg, J. 1995. The Overachievers. *New York Magazine*, 10 April, 44–51.

Gordon, M. 1964. *Assimilation in American Life: The Role of Race, Religion, and National Origins.* New York: Oxford University Press.

Goto, S. T. 1997. Nerds, Normal People, and Homeboys. *Anthropology and Education Quarterly* 28 (1): 70–84.

Goyette, K., and Y. Xie. 1999. Educational Expectations of Asian American Youths: Determinants and Ethnic Differences. *Sociology of Education* 72 (1): 22–36.

Hamamoto, D. Y. 1994. *Monitored Peril: Asian Americans and the Politics of TV Representation.* Minneapolis: University of Minnesota Press.

Hing, B. 1993. *Making and Remaking Asian America through Immigration Policy, 1850–1990.* Stanford, CA: Stanford University Press.

Hirschman, C., and M. G. Wong. 1986. The Extraordinary Educational Attainment of Asian Americans: A Search for Historical Evidence and Explanations. *Social Forces* 65 (1): 1–27.

Hochschild, A., with A. Machung. 1989. *The Second Shift: Working Parents and the Revolution at Home.* New York: Viking Press.

Hochschild, J. 1995. *Facing Up to the American Dream: Race, Class, and the Soul of the Nation.* Princeton, NJ: Princeton University Press.

Hondagneu-Sotelo, P. 1994. *Gendered Transitions: Mexican Experiences of Immigration.* Berkeley, CA: University of California Press.

———. 1999. Gender and Contemporary U.S. Immigration. *American Behavioral Scientist* 42 (4): 565–76.

———. 2001. *Domestica: Immigrant Workers Cleaning and Caring in the Shadows of Affluence.* Berkeley: University of California Press.

Horton, J. 1995. *The Politics of Diversity: Immigration, Resistance, and Change in Monterey Park, California.* Philadelphia: Temple University Press.

Houstoun, M. F., R. G. Kramer, and J. M. Barrett. 1984. Female Predominance of Immigration to the United States Since 1930: A First Look. *International Migration Review* 18 (4): 908–63.

Hsia, A. 2001. Chinatown in Limbo. *Village Voice,* May 30–June 5, Citystate Section.

Hsia, J. 1988. *Asian Americans in Higher Education and at Work.* Mahwah, NJ: Lawrence Erlbaum Associates.

Hsia, J., and M. Hirano-Nakanishi. 1989. The Demographics of Diversity: Asian Americans and Higher Education. *Change* 21 (November/December): 20–36.

Hsu, F. 1971. *Under the Ancestors' Shadow: Kinship, Personality, and Social Mobility in China.* Stanford, CA: Stanford University Press.

Hsu, M. 2000. *Dreaming of Gold, Dreaming of Home: Transnationalism and Migration between the United States and South China, 1882–1943.* Stanford, CA: Stanford University Press.

Hune, S. 1998. *Asian Pacific American Women in Higher Education: Claiming*

Visibility and Voice. Washington, DC: Association of American Colleges and Universities Program on the Status and Education of Women.

Hune, S., and K. S. Chan. 1997. Special Focus: Asian Pacific American Demographic and Educational Trends. In *Minorities in Higher Education,* vol. 15, edited by D. Carter and R. Wilson. Washington, DC: American Council on Education.

Hunter College Undergraduate Catalogue, 1995–1998. 1995. New York: Office of the Provost, Hunter College.

Hurh, W. M., and K. C. Kim. 1989. The "Success" Image of Asian Americans: Its Validity and Its Practical and Theoretical Implications. *Ethnic and Racial Studies* 12 (4): 512–38.

Ignatiev, N. 1995. *How the Irish Became White.* New York: Routledge.

Ikels, C. 1996. *The Return of the God of Wealth: The Transition to a Market Economy in Urban China.* Stanford, CA: Stanford University Press.

Jacobs, J. A. 1996. *Gender, Race, and Ethnic Segregation between and within Colleges.* Paper presented at the 1996 American Sociological Association Meeting, New York, August.

James, C. 2003. Upward Mobility and Downright Lies. *New York Times,* 12 January, Arts and Leisure Section, p. 1.

Johnson, K. 2001. A City Changed Forever? Maybe Not. *New York Times,* 7 October, Section 1A, p. 39.

Kao, G. 1995. Asian Americans as Model Minorities? A Look at Their Academic Performance. *American Journal of Education* 103 (2): 121–59.

———. 2000. Group Images and Possible Selves Among Adolescents: Linking Stereotypes to Expectations by Race and Ethnicity. *Sociological Forum* 15 (3): 407–30.

Kao, G., and M. Tienda. 1995. Optimism and Achievement: The Educational Performance of Immigrant Youth. *Social Science Quarterly* 76 (1): 1–19.

———. 1998. Educational Aspirations of Minority Youth. *American Journal of Education* 106 (3): 349–84.

Kasinitz, P., J. Mollenkopf, M. Waters, N. Lopez, and D. Y. Kim. 1997. The School to Work Transition of Second Generation Immigrants in Metropolitan New York: Some Preliminary Findings. Paper presented at the Levy Institute Conference on the Second Generation, Bard College, Annandale-on-the-Hudson, NY, 25 October.

Kibria, N. 1993. *Family Tightrope.* Princeton: Princeton University Press.

———. 1999. College and Notions of "Asian American": Second-Generation Chinese and Korean Americans Negotiate Race and Identity. *Amerasia Journal* 25 (1): 29–51.

———. 2000. Race, Ethnic Options, and Ethnic Binds: Identity Negotiations of Second-Generation Chinese and Korean Americans. *Sociological Perspectives* 43 (1): 77–95.

————. 2002. *Becoming Asian American*. Baltimore: Johns Hopkins University Press.

Kim, C. J. 2000. *Bitter Fruit: The Politics of Black–Korean Conflict in New York City*. New Haven, CT: Yale University Press.

Kim, E. Y. 1993. Career Choice among Second-Generation Korean Americans: Reflections of a Cultural Model of Success. *Anthropology and Education Quarterly* 24 (3): 224–48.

Kim, H. 1997. *Diversity among Asian American High School Students*. Princeton, NJ: Educational Testing Service.

Kim, U., and M. Chun. 1994. Educational "Success" of Asian Americans: An Indigenous Perspective. *Journal of Applied Developmental Psychology* 15 (3): 329–43.

Kwong, P. 1987. *The New Chinatown*. New York: Noonday Press.

————. 1997. Manufacturing Ethnicity. *Critique of Anthropology* 17 (4): 365–87.

————. 2001. *Chinatown, N.Y.: Labor and Politics, 1930–1950*. Rev. ed. New York: New Press.

Lareau, A. 1987. Social Class Differences in Family–School Relationships: The Importance of Cultural Capital. *Sociology of Education* 60 (2): 73–85.

Lavin, D. E., and D. Hyllegard. 1996. *Changing the Odds: Open Admissions and the Life Chances of the Disadvantaged*. New Haven, CT: Yale University Press.

Lawrence Lightfoot, S. 1978. *Worlds Apart: Relationships between Families and Schools*. New York: Basic Books.

————. 1994. *I've Known Rivers: Lives of Loss and Liberation*. Reading, MA: Addison-Wesley.

Lee, S. 1996. *Unraveling the "Model Minority" Stereotype: Listening to Asian American Youth*. New York: Teacher's College Press.

Lee, S., and M. Fernandez. 1998. Trends in Asian American Racial/Ethnic Intermarriage: A Comparison of 1980 and 1990 Census Data. *Sociological Perspectives* 41 (2): 323–42.

Lee, T. 2002. From Myth to Mobilization: Public Opinion Among and About Asian Americans. Briefing paper commissioned for roundtable discussion at Emerging Civil Rights Issues in the Asian American Community, sponsored by the Harvard Civil Rights Project and the UCLA Asian American Studies Center, 4 October.

Leong, F. T. L., and T. J. Hayes. 1990. Occupational Stereotyping of Asian Americans. *Career Development Quarterly* 39 (2): 143–54.

LeVine, R. A. 1984. Properties of Culture: An Ethnographic View. In *Culture Theory: Essays on Mind, Self, and Emotion*, edited by R. A. Shweder and R. A. LeVine, 67–87. Cambridge: Cambridge University Press.

Levy, S. R., S. J. Stroessner, and C. S. Dweck. 1998. Stereotype Formation and Endorsement: The Role of Implicit Theories. *Journal of Personality and Social Psychology* 74 (6): 1421–36.

Li, J. 2003. U.S. and Chinese Cultural Beliefs about Learning. *Journal of Educational Psychology* 95 (2): 258–67.

———. 2001. Chinese Conceptualization of Learning. *Ethos* 29 (2): 111–37.

Li, W. 1999. Building Ethnoburbia: The Emergence and Manifestation of the Chinese Ethnoburb in Los Angeles' San Gabriel Valley. *Journal of Asian American Studies* 2 (1): 1–28.

Lieberson, S. 1980. *A Piece of the Pie: Black and White Immigrants Since 1880.* Berkeley: University of California Press.

Lien, P., C. Collet, and J. Wong. 2001. Asian Pacific-American Public Opinion and Political Participation. *PS: Political Science and Politics* 34 (3): 625–30.

Lin, C., and V. R. Fu. 1990. A Comparison of Child-Rearing Practices among Chinese, Immigrant Chinese, and Caucasian-American Parents. *Child Development* 61 (2): 429–33.

Ling, H. 1997. A History of Chinese Female Students in the United States, 1880s–1990s. *Journal of American Ethnic History* 16 (3): 81–109.

Lopez, N. 2001. *Hopeful Girls, Troubled Boys: Race and Gender Disparity in Urban Education.* New York: Routledge.

Louie, V. 2003. "Becoming" and "Being" Chinese American in College: A Look at Ethnicity, Social Class, and Neighborhood in Identity Development. In *Immigrant Life in the U.S.: Multi-disciplinary Perspectives*, edited by D. Gabaccia and C. W. Leach, 113–29. New York: Routledge.

———. Forthcoming. Being Practical or Doing What I Want: The Role of Parents in the Academic Choices of Chinese Americans. In *Becoming New Yorkers: The Second Generation in a Global City*, edited by P. Kasinitz, J. Mollenkopf, and M. Waters. New York: Russell Sage Foundation.

Lowe, L. *Immigrant Acts: On Asian American Cultural Politics.* Durham, NC: Duke University Press, 1996.

Lucas, C. J. 1994. *American Higher Education: A History.* New York: St. Martin's Press.

Luttrell, W. 1997. *School-Smart and Mother-Wise: Working-Class Women's Identity and Schooling.* London: Routledge.

Lyman, S. 1974. *Chinese Americans.* New York: Random House.

Massey, D., and N. Denton. 1993. *American Apartheid: Segregation and the Making of the Underclass.* Cambridge, MA: Harvard University Press.

Mau, R. 1995. Barriers to Higher Education for Asian/Pacific-American Females. In *The Asian American Educational Experience: A Sourcebook for Teachers and Students*, edited by D. T. Nakanishi and T. Yamano Nishida, 235–48. New York: Routledge.

McCoy-Patillo, M. 1999. *Black Picket Fences: Privilege and Peril among the Black Middle Class.* Chicago: University of Chicago Press.

Min, P. G. 1996. *Caught in the Middle: Korean Communities in New York and Los Angeles.* Berkeley: University of California Press.

Min, P. G., and R. Kim. 1999. *Struggle for Ethnic Identity: Narratives by Asian American Professionals*. Walnut Creek, CA: Altamira Press.

Mollenkopf, J., M. Waters, J. Holdaway, and P. Kasinitz. 2004. The Ever-Winding Path: Ethnic and Racial Diversity in the Transition to Adulthood. In *On the Frontier of Adulthood: Theory, Research, and Public Policy,* edited by R. A. Settersten, Jr., F. F. Furstenberg, Jr., and R. G. Rumbaut. Chicago: University of Chicago Press.

Murnane, R. J. 1994. Education and the Well-Being of the Next Generation. In *Confronting Poverty: Prescriptions for Change,* edited by S. H. Danziger, G. D. Sandefur, and D. H. Weinberg, 289–307. New York: Russell Sage Foundation; Cambridge, MA: Harvard University Press.

Nakayama, T. K. 1988. Model Minority and the Media: Discourse on Asian America. *Journal of Communication Inquiry* 12 (1): 65–73.

National Asian Pacific American Legal Consortium. 2002. *Backlash, Final Report: 2001 Audit of Violence Against Asian Pacific Americans, Ninth Annual Report.* Washington, DC: NAPALC. http://www.napalc.org/literature/annual_report/2001_Audit.pdf.

Nee, V., and B. Nee. 1973. *Longtime Californ': A Documentary Study of an American Chinatown.* New York: Pantheon Press.

Nee, V., and H. Wong. 1985. Asian American Socioeconomic Achievement: The Strength of the Family Bond. *Sociological Perspectives* 28 (3): 281–306.

Newman, K. 1999. *No Shame in My Game: The Working Poor in the Inner City.* New York: Alfred A. Knopf and the Russell Sage Foundation.

Nossiter, A. 1995. Anxiety 101: Taking Test to Attend Stuyvesant. *New York Times,* 3 December, Metropolitan Desk, sec. 1, p. 51.

Ogbu, J. U. 1995. Cultural Problems in Minority Education: Their Interpretations and Consequences—Part Two: Case Studies. *Urban Review* 27 (4): 189–205.

Okihiro, G. 1994. *Margins and Mainstreams: Asians in American History and Culture.* Seattle: University of Washington Press.

Oliver, M. L., and T. M. Shapiro. 1995. *Black Wealth / White Wealth: A New Perspective on Racial Inequality.* New York: Routledge.

Omi, M., and H. Winant. 1986. *Racial Formation in the United States: From the 1960s to the 1980s.* New York: Routledge and Kegan Paul.

Ong, P. 2002. *Asian American Demographics and Civil Rights.* Briefing paper commissioned for roundtable discussion at Emerging Civil Rights Issues in the Asian American Community, sponsored by the Harvard Civil Rights Project and the UCLA Asian American Studies Center, 4 October.

Ong, P., and K. Umemoto. 2000. Life and Work in the Inner City. In *Contemporary Asian America: A Multidisciplinary Reader,* edited by M. Zhou and J. V. Gatewood, 233–53. New York: New York University Press.

Osajima, K. 1988. Asian Americans as the Model Minority: An Analysis of the

Popular Press Image in the 1960s and 1980s. In *Reflections on Shattered Windows: Promises and Prospects for Asian American Studies*, edited by G. Okihiro, J. Liu, and A. Hansen, 165–74. Pullman: Washington State University Press.

Pan, L. 1990. *Sons of the Yellow Emperor: A History of the Chinese Diaspora.* Boston: Little, Brown.

Park, R. E. 1950. *Race and Culture.* New York: Free Press.

Pedraza, S. 1991. Woman and Migration: The Social Consequences of Gender. *Annual Review of Sociology* 17: 303–25.

Pessar, P. 1984. The Linkage between the Household and Workplace in the Experiences of Dominican Women in the U.S. *International Migration Review* 18: 1188–1212.

———. 1986. The Role of Gender in Dominican Settlement in the United States. In *Women and Change in Latin America*, edited by J. Nash and H. Safa, 273–94. South Hadley, MA: Bergin and Garvey.

———. 1987. The Dominicans: Women in the Household and the Garment Industry. In *New Immigrants in New York*, edited by N. Foner, 103–29. New York: Columbia University Press.

Phinney, J. S., I. Romero, M. Nava, and D. Huang. 2001. The Role of Language, Parents, and Peers in Ethnic Identity among Adolescents in Immigrant Families. *Journal of Youth and Adolescence* 30 (2): 135–53.

Pittinsky, T. L., M. Shih, and N. Ambady. 2000. Will a Category Cue Affect You? Category Cues, Positive Stereotypes, and Reviewer Recall for Applicants. *Social Psychology of Education* 4 (1): 53–65.

Plaks, J. E., S. R. Levy, C. S. Dweck, and S. J. Stroessner. 2004. In the Eye of the Beholder: Lay Theories and the Perception of Group Entitativity, Variability, and Essence. In *The Psychology of Group Perception,* edited by V. Yzerbyt, C. M. Judd, and O. Corneille, 127–46. New York: Psychology Press.

Portes, A., and R. Bach. 1985. *Latin Journey: Cuban and Mexican Immigrants in the United States.* Berkeley: University of California Press.

Portes, A., and R. Rumbaut. 1980. *Immigrant America.* Berkeley: University of California Press.

———. 2001a. *Legacies.* Berkeley: University of California Press; New York: Russell Sage Foundation.

———. 2001b. Conclusion. In *Ethnicities*, edited by R. Rumbaut and A. Portes, 301–18. Berkeley: University of California Press; New York: Russell Sage Foundation.

Portes, A., and M. Zhou. 1993. The New Second Generation: Segmented Assimilation and Its Variants. *Annals of the American Academy* 520: 74–96.

Ramirez, A. 1999. News of Quake in Taiwan Prompts Worries in Flushing. *New York Times*, 21 September, B3.

Rawski, E. S. 1979. *Education and Popular Literacy in Ch'ing China*. Ann Arbor: University of Michigan Press.

Richardson, L. 2001. Developer Looks Beyond the Buildings of Harlem. *New York Times*, 2 August, B2.

Rosenthal, D. A., and S. S. Feldman. 1991. The Influence of Perceived Family and Personal Factors on Self-Reported School Performance of Chinese and Western High School Students. *Journal of Research on Adolescence* 1 (2): 135–54.

Rossmann, J. E., H. S. Astin, A. W. Astin, and E. H. El-Khawas. 1975. *Open Admissions at City University of New York: An Analysis of the First Year*. Englewood Cliffs, NJ: Prentice-Hall.

Rumbaut, R. 1997. Ties That Bind: Immigration and Immigrant Families in the United States. In *Immigration and the Family: Research and Policy on U.S. Immigrants*, edited by A. Booth, A. C. Crouter, and N. Landale, 3–46. Mahwah, NJ: Lawrence Erlbaum Associates.

Rumbaut, R., and A. Portes. 2001. Introduction to *Ethnicities*, edited by R. Rumbaut and A. Portes, 1–20. Berkeley: University of California Press; New York: Russell Sage Foundation.

Sachs, S. 1999. Advocates for Immigrant Students Protest New English Exam. *New York Times*, 18 June, Metropolitan Section, B1.

Sanchirico, A. 1991. The Importance of Small-Business Ownership in Chinese American Educational Achievement. *Sociology of Education* 64 (4): 293–304.

Schneider, B., and L. Yongsook. 1990. A Model for Academic Success: The School and Home Environment of East Asian Students. *Anthropology and Education Quarterly* 21 (4): 358–77.

Schuck, P. H. 2003. *Diversity in America*. Cambridge, MA: The Belknap Press of Harvard University Press.

Schuman, H., C. Steeh, L. Bobo, and M. Krysan. 1997. *Racial Attitudes in America: Trends and Interpretations*. Cambridge, MA: Harvard University Press.

Settersten, R. A., Jr., F. F. Furstenberg, Jr., and R. G. Rumbaut, eds. 2004. *On the Frontier of Adulthood: Theory, Research, and Public Policy*. Chicago: University of Chicago Press.

Shih, M., T. Pittinsky, and N. Ambady. 1999. Stereotype Susceptibility: Identity Salience and Shifts in Quantitative Performance. *Psychological Science* 10 (1): 80–83.

Siu, S. F. 1992a. *Toward an Understanding of Chinese American Educational Achievement*. Report no. 2. Baltimore: John Hopkins University, Center on Families, Communities, Schools, and Children's Learning.

———. 1992b. How Do Family and Community Characteristics Affect Children's Educational Achievement? The Chinese American Experience. *Equity and Choice* 8 (2): 46–49.

————. 1996. *Asian American Students at Risk: A Literature Review*. Report no. 8. Baltimore: Johns Hopkins University and Howard University Center for Research on the Education of Students Placed at Risk.

Siu, S. F., and J. Feldman. 1995. *Success in School: The Journey of Two Chinese American Families*. Report no. 31. Baltimore: Johns Hopkins University, Center on Families, Communities, Schools, and Children's Learning.

Slater, M. 1969. My Son the Doctor: Aspects of Mobility Among American Jews. *American Sociological Review* 34 (3): 359–73.

Slaughter-Defoe, D. T., K. Nakagawa, R. Takanishi, and D. J. Johnson. 1990. Toward Cultural/Ecological Perspectives on Schooling and Achievement in African- and Asian-American Children. *Child Development* 61 (2): 363–83.

Song, M. 1999. *Helping Out: Children's Labor in Ethnic Businesses*. Philadelphia: Temple University Press.

Sowell, T. 1981. *Ethnic America*. New York: Basic Books.

Stacey, J. 1983. *Patriarchy and Socialist Revolution in China*. Berkeley: University of California Press.

Stanton-Salazar, R. D. 1997. A Social Capital Framework for Understanding the Socialization of Racial Minority Children and Youths. *Harvard Educational Review* 67 (1): 1–40.

————. 2001. *Manufacturing Hope and Despair: The School and Kin Support Networks of U.S–Mexican Youth*. New York: Teacher's College Press.

Steele, C. 1997. A Threat in the Air: How Stereotypes Shape Intellectual Identity and Performance. *American Psychologist* 52 (6): 613–29.

————. 1999. Thin Ice: Stereotype Threat and Black College Students. *Atlantic Monthly Online Edition*, August. http://www.theatlantic.com/.

Steele, C. M., and J. Aronson. 1995. Stereotype Threat and the Intellectual Test Performance of African Americans. *Journal of Personality and Social Psychology* 69 (5): 797–811.

Steinberg, L., S. Dornbusch, and B. B. Brown. 1992. Ethnic Differences in Adolescent Achievement: An Ecological Perspective. *American Psychologist* 47 (6): 723–29.

Steinberg, S. 1982. *The Ethnic Myth: Race, Ethnicity, and Class in America*. New York: Atheneum.

Stevenson, H. W., and J. W. Stigler. 1992. *The Learning Gap: Why Our Schools Are Failing and What We Can Learn from Japanese and Chinese Education*. New York: Simon and Schuster.

Suarez-Orozco, C. 2001. Understanding and Serving the Children of Immigrants. *Harvard Educational Review* 71 (3): 579–89.

Suarez-Orozco, C., and M. Suarez-Orozco. 2001. *Children of Immigration*. Cambridge, MA: Harvard University Press.

————. Forthcoming. *Moving Stories: The Interpersonal Worlds of Immigrant Youth*. Cambridge, MA: Harvard University Press.

Sue, D. W. 1973. Ethnic Identity: The Impact of Two Cultures on the Psychological Development of Asians in America. In *Asian-Americans: Psychological Perspectives*, edited by S. Sue, 140–48. Ben Lomond, CA: Science and Behavior Books.

Sue, D. W., and C. A. Frank. 1973. A Typological Approach to the Psychological Study of Chinese and Japanese American College Males. *Journal of Social Issues* 29 (2): 129–48.

Sue, S., and S. Okazaki. 1990. Asian-American Educational Achievements: A Phenomenon in Search of An Explanation. *American Psychologist* 45 (8): 913–20.

Sue, D. W., and D. Sue. 1999. *Counseling the Culturally Different: Theory and Practice*. New York: John Wiley.

Sun, Y. 1998. The Academic Success of East-Asian-American Students—An Investment Model. *Social Science Research* 27 (4): 432–56.

Sung, B. L. 1987. *The Adjustment Experience of Chinese Immigrant Children in New York City*. New York: Center for Migration Studies.

Suzuki, B. H. 1989. Asian Americans as the Model Minority: Outdoing Whites? Or Media Hype? *Change* 21 (November/December): 13–19.

Swartz, T. T. Forthcoming. *Growing Up But Not Apart: Intergenerational Relations and the Transition to Adulthood Among Diverse Families*.

Takagi, D. Y. 1998. *The Retreat from Race: Asian American Admissions and Racial Politics*. New Brunswick, NJ: Rutgers University Press.

Takaki, R. 1989. *Strangers from a Different Shore: A History of Asian Americans*. New York: Penguin Books.

Tang, J. 1993. The Career Attainment of Caucasian and Asian Engineers. *Sociological Quarterly* 34 (3): 467–96.

Tang, J., and E. Smith, eds. 1996. *Women and Minorities in American Professions*. Albany: State University of New York Press.

Tchen, J. 1999. *New York before Chinatown: Orientalism and the Shaping of American Culture, 1776–1882*. Baltimore: Johns Hopkins University Press.

Thorton, A., and H. S. Lin. 1994. Introduction to *Social Change and the Family in Taiwan*, edited by A. Thorton and H. S. Lin, 1–21. Chicago: University of Chicago Press.

Tienda, M., and K. Booth. 1991. Gender, Migration, and Social Change. *International Sociology* 6 (1): 51–72.

Toupin, E., and L. Son. 1993. Preliminary Findings on Asian Americans: "The Model Minority" in a Small Private East Coast College. *Journal of Cross-Cultural Psychology* 22 (3): 403–17.

Trudeau, G. B. 1989. *Read My Lips, Make My Day, Eat Quiche and Die! A Doonesbury Book*. Kansas City, MO: Andrews and McMeel.

Tsai, S.-L., H. Gates, and H. Y. Chiu. 1994. Schooling Taiwan's Women: Educational Attainment in the Mid-20th Century. *Sociology of Education* 67 (4): 243–63.

Tuan, M. 1998. *Forever Foreigners or Honorary Whites: The Asian Ethnic Experience Today*. New Brunswick, NJ: Rutgers University Press.

U.S. Bureau of the Census. 1999. *Educational Attainment in the United States: Current Population Reports* (Series P-20, no. 528). Washington DC: U.S. Government Printing Office.

———. 2002a. Table A-2: Percent of People 25 Years Old and Over Who Have Completed High School or College, by Race, Hispanic Origin and Sex: Selected Years 1940 to 2002. Washington, DC: U.S. Bureau of the Census. http://www.census.gov/population/socdemo/education/tabA-2.pdf.

———. 2002b. Table 1.1: Population by Sex, Age and Citizenship Status, March 2002. In *Foreign-Born Population of the United States: Current Population Survey—March 2002*, Detailed Tables (PPL-162). Washington, DC: U.S. Bureau of the Census. http://www.census.gov/population/www/socdemo/foreign/ppl-162.html.

U.S. Commission on Civil Rights. 1988. *The Economic Status of Americans of Asian Descent: An Exploratory Investigation*. Washington, DC: U.S. Commission on Civil Rights.

Useem, E. L. 1992. Middle Schools and Math Groups: Parents' Involvement in Children's Placement. *Sociology of Education* 65 (4): 263–79.

Waldinger, R. 1993. The Ethnic Enclave Debate Revisited. *International Journal of Urban and Regional Research* 17 (3): 444–52.

Wallin, D., M. H. Schill, and G. Daniels. 2002. *State of New York City's Housing and Neighborhoods 2002*. Report of the Furman Center for Real Estate and Urban Policy. New York: New York University School of Law.

Wang, G. 1988. The Study of Chinese Identities in Southeast Asia. In *Changing Identities of the Southeast Asian Chinese since World War II*, edited by J. W. Cushman and G. Wang, 1–21. Hong Kong: Hong Kong University Press.

Waters, M. C. 1990. *Ethnic Options: Choosing Identities in America*. Berkeley: University of California Press.

———. 1999. *Black Identities: West Indian Immigrant Dreams and American Realities*. Cambridge, MA: Harvard University Press.

Waters, M. C., and K. Eschbach. 1995. Immigration and Ethnic and Racial Inequality in the United States. *Annual Review of Sociology* 21: 419–46.

Weinberg, M. 1997. *Asian-American Education: Historical Background and Current Realities*. Mahwah, NJ: Lawrence Erlbaum Associates.

Whyte, M. 1991. Introduction to Part 3: Society. In *The Chinese: Adapting the Past, Facing the Future*, edited by R. F. Dernberger, K. J. Dewoskin, and S. M. Goldstein, 295–316. Ann Arbor: Center for Chinese Studies, University of Michigan.

Wilson, W. J. 1980. *The Declining Significance of Race: Blacks and Changing American Institutions*. Chicago: University of Chicago Press.

————. 1987. *The Truly Disadvantaged: The Inner City, The Underclass, and Public Policy*. Chicago: University of Chicago Press.

————. 1997. *When Work Disappears*. New York: Vintage.

————. 1999. *The Bridge Over the Racial Divide: Rising Inequality and Coalition Politics*. Berkeley: University of California Press; New York: Russell Sage Foundation.

Wolf, D. L. 1997. Family Secrets: Transnational Struggles among Children of Filipino Immigrants. *Sociological Perspectives* 40 (3): 457–82.

Wong, B. P. 1982. *Chinatown: Economic Adaptation and Ethnic Identity of the Chinese*. Fort Worth, TX: Holt, Rinehart and Winston.

Wong, M. 1995a. Chinese Americans. In *Asian Americans: Contemporary Issues and Trends*, edited by P. G. Min, 58–94. Thousand Oaks, CA: Sage Publications.

————. 1995b. The Education of White, Chinese, Filipino and Japanese Students: A Look at High School and Beyond. In *The Asian American Educational Experience: A Sourcebook for Teachers and Students*, edited by D. T. Nakanishi and T. Yamano Nishida, 221–34. New York: Routledge.

Wong, S. L. 1988. The Language Situation of Chinese Americans. In *Language Diversity: Problem or Resource?* edited by S. L. McKay and S. L. C. Wong, 191–228. New York: Newbury House.

Woo, D. 1994. *The Glass Ceiling and Asian Americans*. Research monograph for the Federal Glass Ceiling Commission, Washington, DC. http://www.ilr.cornell.edu/.

Woo, D. 2000. *Glass Ceilings and Asian Americans: The New Face of Workplace Barriers*. Walnut Creek, CA: Altamira Press.

Yang, F. 1999. *Chinese Christians in America: Conversion, Assimilation, and Adhesive Identities*. University Park: Pennsylvania State University Press.

Yu, W. H. 2001. Family Demands, Gender Attitudes, and Married Women's Labor Force Participation: Comparing Japan and Taiwan. In *Women's Working Lives in East Asia*, edited by M. C. Brinton, 70–95. Stanford, CA: Stanford University Press.

Zeltzer-Zubida, A. Forthcoming. Identity Construction among Young Russian-Jewish-Americans in New York. In *Becoming New Yorkers: The Second Generation in a Global City*, edited by M. Waters, J. Mollenkopf, and P. Kasinitz. New York: Russell Sage Foundation.

Zhao, Y. 2001. Preparing Early for the First of the All-Important Tests. *New York Times*, 10 October, Education Page, D9.

Zhou, M. 1992. *Chinatown: The Socioeconomic Potential of an Urban Enclave*. Philadelphia: Temple University Press.

————. 1997. Segmented Assimilation: Issues, Controversies, and Recent Research on the New Second Generation. *International Migration Review* 31 (4): 975–1008.

———. 2001. Chinese: Divergent Destinies in New York. In *New Immigrants in New York*, edited by N. Foner, 141–72. 2nd ed. New York: Columbia University Press.

———. 2002. How Neighborhoods Matter for Immigrant Adolescents. *CPRC Brief* (California Policy Research Center, University of California), vol. 14, no. 8.

Zhou, M., and C. L. Bankston III. 2000. *Straddling Two Worlds: The Experience of Vietnamese Refugee Children in the United States.* New York: ERIC Clearinghouse on Urban Education.

Zhou, M., and G. Cai. 2002. Chinese Language Media in the United States: Immigration and Assimilation in American Life. *Qualitative Sociology* 25 (3): 419–41.

Zhou, M., and J. R. Logan. 1991. In and Out of Chinatown: Residential Mobility and Segregation of New York City's Chinese. *Social Forces* 70 (2): 387–407.

Zhou, M., and R. Nordquist. 1994. Work and Its Place in the Lives of Immigrant Women: Garment Workers in New York City's Chinatown. *Applied Behavioral Science Review* 2 (2): 187–211.

Zweigenhaft, R. L., and G. W. Domhoff. 1991. *Blacks in the White Establishment? A Study of Race and Class in America.* New Haven, CT: Yale University Press.

———. 1998. *Diversity in the Power Elite: Have Women and Minorities Reached the Top?* New Haven, CT: Yale University Press.

Academic struggles, 84, 91
Affirmative action, 162–63, 180–82, 184
Alaska, 106
American dream, 183, 185
American identity: v. imposed ethnic identity,
    xx, 8, 61, 165–67, 172–74, 177, 179; defined
    as white, 169–70; defined as African
    American, 171; tensions between parents and
    children, 138–39
ancestor worship, 29, 67, 161
Ancheta, A., 180
anti-Chinese movement, 19–21
Asian Americans: definition of, xvii passim; class
    and, xxi; comparison to other groups,
    xvii–xviii, xx, 166, 180, 186, 205n; ethnic
    diversity of, xix, 185; racialization of, xvii, 41,
    170, 202n; marital trends of, 147; political
    participation of, 162–63
Asian American educational performance:
    career choices, 130; effort v. ability, xxviii,
    47–48; ethnic culture v. structural
    explanations of, xv, xxviii–xxx; patterns of,
    xvi, xix, xxvii; racial discrimination as
    influencing, 55–56
Assimilation theories, 164–65

Baker, D. P., 98
Baker, H., 67
Bargaining with patriarchy, 66
Beijing, 24, 198
Blacks (African Americans): socioeconomic
    gains, xiii; attitudes toward education, 56, 86;
    compared to immigrant groups, 166, 171f,
    180–81, 185, 187, 206n, 208n; discrimination
    against, xiv; 187. See also affirmative action.
bragging rights, 89 passim, 92. See also ethnic
    networks.
brain drain, 116, 130
Brooklyn (New York City), 18, 23–24, 38–39,
    168
Burma, 22ff, 198

California, 7, 11, 19, 202n. See also Anti-
    Chinese Movement.

Cantonese, 16, 22, 24, 28, 32
Chan, J., 31
Cheng, K. M., 49
Cheung, L., 31
Chiang Kai Shek, 1
Chin, Vincent, 202n
China: Civil War, 1 passim; gender, 67, 75, 80;
    immigration from, xxii, 18–24, 198, 203;
    relationship with Hong Kong, 127;
    relationship with Taiwan, 4
Chinatown (New York City), 18 passim, 22–25.
    See also ethnic enclave.
Chinese Americans, xviii, xxii–xxiii, 203n, 205n
Chinese Exclusion Act, 20
Chinese Family, 48, 67–68
Chinese New Year, 9f
Chores, 30, 76–77, 80–82, 110
Chow, S., 31
Civil Rights Movement, xiv passim, xix, 41, 187
Co-ethnic/panethnic associations, 11–12, 115
College application process, 101–3, 111–13
Communist Party, 1 passim, 71
Community college, 84
Competition between parents, 91–92
Cram schools, xv, 17

Dalton, 106
Dating and intermarriage: attitudes of parents,
    42, 44, 148ff, 153f; with blacks and Latinos,
    148ff; with Chinese, 151–52, 155–57; with
    whites, 150, 153–55; and social boundaries,
    149, 208n
Discipline, 45, 50, 78–79
Discrimination: children's attitudes toward,
    174–85, 187–88; from police, 168; influencing
    parental views on education, 56–63, 133; in
    neighborhoods, 167–69. See also affirmative
    action, under Asian American educational
    performance, racial discrimination as
    influencing, blacks, Jewish Americans, white
    ethnics
Divorce, 26, 55, 74, 79, 96–97, 108, 125–26, 158,
    197
Domhoff, G. W., 178